PATERNOSTER BIBLICAL AND THEOLOGICAL MONOGRAPHS

Thou Traveller Unknown

The Presence and Absence of God
in the Jacob Narrative

PATERNOSTER BIBLICAL AND THEOLOGICAL MONOGRAPHS

A complete listing of all titles in this series
will be found at the close of this book.

PATERNOSTER BIBLICAL AND THEOLOGICAL MONOGRAPHS

Thou Traveller Unknown

The Presence and Absence of God
in the Jacob Narrative

Kevin Walton

Foreword by
R. W. L. Moberly

PATERNOSTER PRESS

Series Preface

At the present time we are experiencing a veritable explosion in the field of biblical and theological research with more and more academic theses of high quality being produced by younger scholars from all over the world. One of the considerations taken into account by the examiners of doctoral theses is that, if they are to be worthy of the award of a degree, then they should contain material that needs to be read by other scholars; if so, it follows that the facilities must exist for them to be made accessible. In some cases (perhaps more often than is always realised) it will be most appropriate for the distinctive contribution of the thesis to be harvested in journal articles; in others there may be the possibility of a revision that will produce a book of wider appeal than simply to professional scholars. But many theses of outstanding quality can and should be published more or less as they stand for the benefit of other scholars and interested persons.

Hitherto it has not been easy for authors to find publishers willing to publish works, that while highly significant as works of scholarship, cannot be expected to become 'best-sellers' with a large circulation. Fortunately the development of printing technology now makes it relatively easy for publishers to produce specialist works without the commercial risks that would have prevented them from doing so in the past.

The Paternoster Press is one of the first publishers to make use of this new technology. Its aim is quite simply to assist biblical and theological scholarship by the publication of theses and other monographs of high quality at affordable prices.

Different publishers serve different constituencies. The Paternoster Press stands in the tradition of evangelical Christianity and exists to serve that constituency, though not in any narrow way. What is offered, therefore, in this series, is the best of scholarship by evangelical Christians.

Since the inception of this series in 1997 the scope of the works published has broadened considerably. The opportunity is now being taken to initiate parallel series which will cater in a more focussed way for the history and theology of the evangelical movement and other interests. Alongside this series we now have *Studies in Evangelical History and Thought* and *Studies in Baptist History and Thought*. This development will leave the present series with a sufficiently wide field in biblical studies and theology.

Contents

Foreword

As the study of the Gospels and Jesus has always been at the heart of modern New Testament criticism, so the study of the Pentateuch has always been at the heart of modern Old Testament criticism. The intensity of scholarly research is a kind of reflection of the foundational religious importance that these specific portions of the Bible have had, and continue to have, for Christians and Jews.

In recent years numerous substantial monographs have continued the tradition of Wellhausen in offering proposals for the origins and composition of the Pentateuch as a whole. Yet while such studies have their place, there is a great need for work of a different kind - more specific, more exegetical, more concerned to understand the meaning and significance of the biblical text in the kind of way that relates to the actual questions and concerns of most of those for whom the biblical text is holy Scripture - that is a book which, in one way or other, offers truth, guidance and wisdom from God and so makes life richer and more mysterious.

Kevin Walton's study of Genesis 25-35, the Jacob narrative, is a fine example of biblical exegesis and interpretation, which is philologically, historically, and theologically alert. Walton is fully conversant with the larger debates of contemporary pentateuchal criticism, and draws on their insights as appropriate (while recognizing the unsettled nature of the debates). He acknowledges that an understanding of the Genesis narrative may require various different kinds of approach to the text. At a time when many scholars focus *either* on the formation and composition of the biblical text *or* on a reading of the text as a literary work, Walton attends consistently to both concerns; for his overall purpose - to understand the text in its received form - requires him to attend to those ways in which the possible formation of the text may impact upon its interpretation.

Walton sees the theological issues posed by the text as integral to its interpretation. At the heart of his study he addresses one of the enduring issues of Christian and Jewish faith in, and understanding of, God - the relationship between those moments when God speaks and acts and those times when God appears silent and absent, and the correlative issue of divine initiative and grace in relation to human responsibility. For Walton takes with full seriousness the tensions posed by those famous passages where Jacob encounters God at Bethel and Penuel in relation to the mundane (and regularly manipulative) human action within most of the story. He shows how these tensions are not incidental to, but rather constitutive of, the portrayal of Jacob and he suggestively relates these to the continuing significance of the text for Christians and Jews.

Walton's work has helped me to read the Jacob narrative with fresh eyes and to see things that I previously had missed. I am confident that it will do the same for others too.

Walter Moberly
University of Durham
April 2002

Acknowledgements

At times, working on this book has seemed like a gigantic, solitary struggle, but I am also aware of the support that I have received from so many quarters.

This book started as a thesis, and I am extremely grateful to the Revd Dr Walter Moberly at the University of Durham, for his consistent encouragement in supervising my work, and in helping me to form my own thinking about the Jacob narrative.

In terms of financial and moral support, I am also indebted to the Diocese of Durham for enabling me to carry out this work. A generous ecumenical scholarship from the Evangelische Kirche in Germany also enabled me to spend an invaluable year studying at Heidelberg before starting this work.

This book has been written in the context of three parishes in the North-East of England where I have served as priest. I would like to express my thanks to colleagues and people of these parishes, who have allowed me the time to undertake this work, and whose own lives so often bear witness to the struggles of faith.

Finally, I am grateful to my family, and especially to Linda, for supporting me through this long process.

Kevin Walton
Sunderland S. Mary & S. Peter
Holy Week, 2002

Abbreviations

1. Periodicals, serials and reference works

BA	*Biblical Archeologist*
BDB	Brown, F., et al. *The New Brown-Driver-Briggs-Genesius Hebrew and English Lexicon* (see bibliography)
Bib	*Biblica*
BO	*Bibliotheca orientalis*
BZ	*Biblische Zeitschrift*
BZAW	Beihefte zur Zeitschrift für die alttestamentliche Wissenschaft
CBQ	*Catholic Biblical Quarterly*
ExpTim	*Expository Times*
FRLANT	Forschungen zur Religion und Literatur des Alten und Neuen Testaments
HSM	*Harvard Semitic Monographs*
HTR	*Harvard Theological Review*
HUCA	*Hebrew Union College Annual*
Int	*Interpretation*
JAAR	*Journal of American Academy of Religion*
JBL	*Journal of Biblical Literature*
JSOT	*Journal for the Study of the Old Testament*
JSOT Supp	JSOT Supplement series
JTS	*Journal of Theological Studies*
PIBA	*Proceedings of the Irish Biblical Association*
RB	*Revue Biblique*
SJOT	*Scandinavian Journal of the Old Testament*
ST	*Studia theologica*
TZ	*Theologische Zeitschrift*
VT	*Vetus Testamentum*
WMANT	Wissenschaftliche Monographien zum Alten und Neuen Testament
ZAW	*Zeitschrift für die alttestamentliche Wissenschaft*
ZTK	*Zeitschrift für Theologie und Kirche*

2. Translations, texts, miscellaneous

ANE	Ancient Near East
ET	English Translation
JPS	Jewish Publication Society
LXX	Septuagint
MT	Masoretic Text
NEB	New English Bible
NRSV	New Revised Standard Version
REB	Revised English Bible
RSV	Revised Standard Version
TEV	Today's English Version (= Good News Bible)

Introduction

The Theme: Presence and Absence of God; The Divine-Human Contrast

The story of Jacob is theologically complex. On the one hand are clear indications of divine revelation and purpose for Jacob. On the other hand are events surrounding Jacob, as well as his own character and actions, which show little evidence of divine presence or faithful response.

This contrast permeates the whole of the Jacob story, and although widely acknowledged, it is hardly taken much further by most commentators. This work attempts to look at this paradox and see how it can be used as an interpretive key for the Jacob story.

The paradox can be seen in various ways. It centres around the presence and absence of the divine. It can also be expressed in terms of the divine and the human. In many places, God is explicitly present as a character in the plot: God chooses, blesses, addresses, guides and protects Jacob, whether directly or through human agents. Absence refers to the lack of any mention of the divine in much of the narrative, the way that Jacob often seems to take his fate into his own hands, and the lack of much explicit moral or theological comment. There is interest in the character and motivation of Jacob: in terms of moral behaviour (often articulated in terms of the 'guilt' or 'innocence' of Jacob) and religious acts (often seen as part of the wider question of the 'patriarchal religion'). On the one hand, Jacob is singled out by divine oracle as the one to receive the patriarchal blessing even before his birth, it is he who receives the name of Israel and is father of the twelve sons who become the twelve tribes, and he has the remarkable experience with God at Penuel. On the other hand, he cheats his father and brother, endures a long inglorious stay with his uncle Laban, and even his experience at Penuel is far from a straightforward giving and receiving of a blessing.

Structure

The Jacob story finds a structural unity around the motif of flight and return. It begins in a setting of family conflict between the two brothers. As a result of Jacob's deception of Esau and his father Isaac, he is forced to leave and stay with his uncle Laban. This journey sets up a tension that is resolved at his return.

It is however noticeable that at key points in the narrative, there is an encounter with the divine. These encounters stand out because of the high concentration of explicitly theological content and, it will be argued, they offer an interpretive key for the whole of the narrative. The most significant episodes are the nocturnal encounters at Bethel and Penuel, both coming unexpectedly at points of transition for Jacob, and the oracle given to Rebekah before the birth of Jacob and Esau. This latter episode is less distinctive from the surrounding narrative but is nevertheless significant for its theological content and for creating a certain expectation.

For this reason we shall consider these three passages individually in some detail before looking at the wider plot. This will enable us to look at the passages in their own right, doing justice to their peculiar nature, to ask related questions of prehistory, and to begin to ask how these passages might anticipate the development of the wider story. It might be argued that by treating these episodes separately we are not doing justice to how they fit into the wider story, and also that we might be prejudging the historical relation of these passages to the wider narrative, inasmuch as this is an issue. Nevertheless, reference will be made to these passages later on regarding how they relate to their wider context, and regarding historical questions, we shall see that the same solutions will not be offered for each passage. It might also be argued that these are not the only episodes containing divine appearances or communication. However, these are the most developed. The one exception is the return of Jacob to Bethel in chapter 35. This will be considered at the end to allow us to see how various strands in the Jacob story are brought to a conclusion or a redefinition.

After studying the three episodes, we shall look at the larger blocks of narrative: the first part of the Jacob and Esau plot, in particular chapter 27, the Jacob-Laban plot, the conclusion of the Jacob and Esau plot, and chapters 34 and 35. Throughout this, we shall still be exploring the contrast between the human and the divine, the extent to which God seems present or absent.

Justification should also be given for locating the end of the Jacob story at Gen. 35:29. This is especially in the light of the argument put forward by

Westermann regarding chapters 37 and 46-50, where a distinction is made between the Joseph story in its strictest sense and material which has been added in the framing chapters which in reality concludes the Jacob story.[1] In this way, argues Westermann, the Joseph story has been made part of the Jacob story. However, there is some unclarity on this, since Westermann also makes the point that chapter 37, in its present form and context, is the introduction to the Joseph story, and a distinction is made between the nature of the family conflict in chapters 25-36 and that in the Joseph story.[2]

From the point of view of the final form of the narrative, a distinction can be made between the Joseph story and the Jacob story. It is of course true that there is an overlap, and that the distinction is not complete, but there is a transition at the end of chapter 35 and the beginning of chapter 37, with chapter 36 marking the division. This also does justice to the structure of the final text, where the story of Jacob (and Esau) is dealt with as the 'descendants (תולדת -toledot) of Isaac' (25:19), and the story of Joseph (and his brothers) is under the 'descendants of Jacob'. Furthermore, just as the latter section may contain material originally distinct from the Joseph story but more in common with the Jacob story, so chapter 26 within the 'descendants of Isaac' has little to do with the story of Jacob and Esau, and the material of chapter 34 has a great affinity to the Joseph material. Thus, the restriction of consideration to chapters 25-35 is justified on the basis of a marked shift in the plot once Isaac is buried and on the final structuring of the patriarchal narrative around the toledot formulae. This does not deny an underlying unity across different sections nor a varied traditio-historical development.

Major Works Consulted

In the course of this work, it will become evident that some names appear more often than others. Below are those scholars that have been of greatest help in shaping my own views on the text. It is of course recognized that the list is not comprehensive, and other works will also be mentioned where appropriate.

Gunkel's commentary on Genesis remains a classic text that must be

---

1 Westermann, C., *Genesis 37-50*, London: SPCK, 1987 (ET of 1982), 22ff.

2 Westermann, *Genesis 37-50*, 34. Rendtorff, R., *The Old Testament: an Introduction*, London: SCM, 1985 (ET of *Das Alte Testament: Eine Einführung*, 1983, 136) sees ch. 48 as an insertion at the end of the Joseph story, uniting what he calls the Jacob narrative with the Joseph story into a wider 'Jacob story'. Nevertheless, he is still able to see the two as discrete stories.

taken into consideration in any study.[3] In dialogue with Gunkel we will be able to draw in considerations of the classic source critical approach which Gunkel takes as a starting point, but also of course the form critical approach which Gunkel championed: the study of the individual unit, literary genre, elements of folk tradition. Gunkel is also valuable for a sense of the aesthetic and for an instinctiveness in his approach, which often survives particular form critical judgements.

Von Rad's commentary is also a great monument to the study of Genesis.[4] Like Gunkel, von Rad shares much of the accepted critical view of his day, including the principle of source criticism and Gunkel's form critical approach. However, unlike earlier or contemporary commentaries, von Rad is much less rigorous in finding sources to the extent that for large parts of the text the source critical approach plays no part. His particular contribution is, like Gunkel, an instinctive approach to passages, but unlike Gunkel, von Rad also shows a concern for the dynamics of the text in its present form as well as for its theology, albeit combined with a consistent historical-critical approach.

Westermann's commentary is also included for its comprehensiveness, rigour and detail.[5] In many ways, this commentary in its wider approach has not found the acceptance which Gunkel and von Rad have, perhaps partly because of the independence of view that Westermann takes, making it difficult to categorize with any trend or school of thought. On the other hand, this independence is also its strength together with the weight of scholarship, and one feels that the contribution of this commentary is by no means exhausted.

Among most recent treatments of the patriarchal narratives is Blum's *Komposition der Vätergeschichte*.[6] This is distinct from the above commentaries in that it is more consciously part of the move in Pentateuchal studies away from the documentary hypothesis associated with Wellhausen. This is done by what Blum sees as a more thorough and consistent outworking of Gunkel's form critical work, building also on the work of

3 Gunkel, H., *Genesis*, Macon, Georgia: Mercer University Press, 1997 (ET of *Genesis*, Göttingen: Vandenhoeck & Ruprecht, 3rd ed., 1901).
4 von Rad, G., *Genesis*, London: SCM, 1972 (ET of *Das erste Buch Mose: Genesis*, 9th ed., 1972).
5 Westermann, C., *Genesis 12-36*, London: SPCK, 1986 (ET of 1981).
6 Blum, E., *Die Komposition der Vätergeschichte*, WMANT 57, Neukirchen-Vluyn: Neukirchener Verlag, 1984.

Rendtorff.[7] Blum also claims to give equal consideration to both the diachronic and synchronic dimensions of the text,[8] although one suspects that the first sentence of the conclusion better betrays his interest, where Blum states that his goal has been to trace the development of the narrative from the smallest unit to the final result.[9] It is too early to judge the long term impact of Blum's work, but it is certainly a significant attempt to strike out in a different direction.

The works mentioned so far have all operated within historical-critical frameworks, even if with greatly differing methods and results. One work which stands in stark contrast is Fokkelman's *Narrative Art in Genesis* which refuses to take any consideration of historical questions and looks at the text from a purely modern literary perspective.[10] As shall be seen this brings to light many aspects of the text otherwise neglected, and this book is an important witness to the integrity of the text itself and a challenge to more conventional approaches.

Presuppositions

Before starting the investigation, comment should be made about our own starting-point and some of the presuppositions behind the approach offered in this study.

One of the main issues in reading a text in the present climate is the conflict between diachronic and synchronic interests. The purpose of this work is to understand the Jacob story as it is rather than to trace for their own sake historical traditions which may lie hidden in the text. However, it is also part of the purpose to show how historical-critical approaches, when used with caution, can indeed highlight features within the text and so enrich our reading. Thus our dialogue with different commentaries and view-points will also be an exercise in method, testing which approaches bear exegetical fruit. In addition, it is not inappropriate to try to draw conclusions about tradition and development, but this is not the main purpose of this work. It is also acknowledged that finding a balance

---

7 In particular, Rendtorff, R., *The Problem of the Process of Transmission in the Pentateuch*, JSOTSup, 89, Sheffield: JSOT Press, 1990 - (ET *Das überlieferungsgeschichtliche Problem des Pentateuch*, Berlin: BZAW 147, Berlin: de Gruyter, 1977).

8 Blum, *Die Komposition der Vätergeschichte*, 2.

9 'Unsere Analyse hatte das Ziel, das Werden der Vätergeschichte von den kleinsten Einheiten...bis zu dem uns vorliegenden Überlieferungsganzen nachzuziehen.' (Blum, *Die Komposition der Vätergeschichte*, 461.)

10 Fokkelman, J. P., *Narrative Art in Genesis*, Assen: van Gorcum, 1975.

between synchronic and diachronic methods is very difficult, although this work is one such attempt with regard to the Jacob story.

In terms of applying any particular hypothesis or historical method the approach will be inductive, not starting with any overall model and then applying it to individual passages, but seeking to treat each passage on its own before seeing what overall conclusions may be drawn. This seems particularly necessary given the lack of any consensus concerning the development of the patriarchal narratives. Certainly, the documentary hypothesis is widely challenged, although there is little prospect of any alternative finding a similar consensus and the hypothesis still finds its proponents.[11] Perhaps less challenged is the idea of the narrative being the result of a growing together of smaller units once told independently,[12] although there is a move to date material later than previously thought and to link it to the exile and/or to a Deuteronomic ('Dtr.') school.[13]

A challenge from a different perspective which perhaps has not been given enough attention is that of de Pury, who questions the assumption that the smaller unit must necessarily be older than the wider cycle and puts forward the idea of an early Jacob cycle where the different elements would always have found a part.[14] These questions all justify a certain caution in

---

11   Among recent text books: Schmidt W. H., *Introduction to the Old Testament*, London: SCM, 1984 (ET of *Einführung in das Alte Testament*, 2nd ed., 1982). Surprisingly, Schmidt hardly mentions recent criticisms of the old consensus: 'Despite all doubts the number and sequence of the documentary sources seems firmly established since Wellhausen's day,' (p. 50). Contrast Rendtorff, R., *The Old Testament: an Introduction*, London: SCM, 1985 (ET of *Das Alte Testament: Eine Einführung*, 1983). Part of the reason for the persistence of the documentary hypothesis is the recognition given to the work of redactors - so Blum, E., *Studien zur Komposition des Pentateuch*, BZAW 189, Berlin: de Gruyter, 1990, 2.

12   As stated most famously by Gunkel, for whom the simplicity or smallness of a unit is a mark of its antiquity. See especially the introductory paragraphs to his commentary, and the famous opening statement: 'Genesis is a Collection of Legends' (*Genesis*, vii). This is still assumed to be self-evident by Blum (*Die Komposition der Vätergeschichte*), whose method is to identify the smallest units and then trace their development to larger units.

13   e.g. Van Seters, J., *Prologue to History: The Yahwist as Historian in Genesis*, Westminster: John Knox Press, 1992; Schmid, H. H., *Der sogennante Jahwist: Beobachtungen und Fragen zur Pentateuchforschung*, Zürich: Theologischer Verlag, 1976; tentatively: Blenkinsopp, J., *The Pentateuch: An Introduction to the First Five Books of the Bible*, London: SCM, 1992, 123ff; Blum, *Die Komposition der Vätergeschichte* and *Studien zur Komposition des Pentateuch*. Also, Levin, C., *Der Jahwist*, FRLANT 157, Göttingen: Vandenhoeck & Ruprecht, 1993.

14   de Pury, A., *Promesse Divine et Légende Culturelle dans le Cycle de Jacob: Genèse 28 et les traditions patriarchales*, vols 1 and 2, Paris: J. Galbalda & Cie, 1975. Also Hendel, R. S., *The Epic of the Patriarch: The Jacob Cycle and the Narrative Traditions of Canaan and Israel*, HSM 42, Atlanta: Scholars Press, 1987; and in a wider context: Cross,

starting with assumptions or in jumping too readily to conclusions.

Finally, the overt nature of this study is theological rather than purely literary, historical or sociological. This means acknowledging the overall religious dimension of the scriptures, seeing them as reflecting and addressing the faith of Israel. It is also natural and legitimate to take into account their privileged position within contemporary communities of faith, including from my own perspective, the Christian Church.

From these comments a certain affinity with the broadly 'canonical' approach may be observed.[15] The aim is to bring together theological, literary and historical tools. The starting and end point is the final text which is also seen as having a religious significance. Furthermore, this study will aim to show that the concept of canon in a general sense is not one imposed at a later date on what were once untheological texts but was inherent in the whole process of transmission. In terms of the Jacob story, the 'divine' coexisted with the 'human' from the earliest levels of tradition, as far as we can tell.

Nevertheless this work does not seek to identify itself with any particular method or approach in such a way that it rejects others out of hand. Whereas diversity is to be welcomed, one regrettable aspect of the present diversity among scholars is a sense of fragmentation of approaches and a frequent inability to find common ground or interest. Certainly my own reading of the Jacob story has been enriched by all sorts of insights: from the historical, from the purely literary, from theological, and from Jewish writers whose questions and insights can seem startling and refreshing.

In short, this work aims to lead to a richer appreciation of the theological complexity of the Jacob narrative, around the polarity of divine presence and absence, the divine and the human, and it offers a model for reading Genesis and the Pentateuch in the present climate of methodological uncertainty and diversity.

F. M., *Canaanite Myth and Hebrew Epic: Essays in the History of the Religion of Israel*, Cambridge: Massachusetts: Harvard University Press, 1973 (e.g. ch. 6).

15   See especially Childs, B. S., *Introduction to the Old Testament as Scripture*, London: SCM, 1979.

PART 1

POINTS OF DIVINE DISCLOSURE

Chapter 1

The Opening Oracle
(25:19-26)

Introduction

The formula 'These are the descendants (תלדת) of *x*' gives a clear indication of a new section. Our main consideration will be vv. 19-26, since from v. 27 the focus shifts from the divine oracle and also because the final phrase giving Isaac's age at the birth of the twins forms an inclusio with the opening notice of his age on marrying Rebekah.

Nevertheless, we shall also consider how vv. 27-34 are linked with this opening, enabling us to see how at this early stage of the narrative there is already a contrast of the divine and the human.

Historical-Critical Issues

There is widespread agreement that vv. 19-20, together with v. 26b, are part of the Priestly source. This is due to the distinctive opening phrase ('these are the descendants of'), used by P to structure the whole of the book of Genesis. Whether the source should be seen as independent or redactional from the outset depends on wider arguments, though in this section such a distinction between the source and the final redaction is unclear. Certainly v. 26b ('when she bore *them*') presupposes the birth of the twins.[1] Regarding the rest of the passage, there is little scope for division along source critical lines, with few of the traditional source critical criteria appearing within the passage.[2]

---

1 So Westermann, *Genesis 12-36*, 411.
2 Gunkel finds traces of E, for instance with the reference to the hairiness of Esau which anticipates 27:11 (which he sees as an E text). However, he can only base his argument on assumptions: 'Both sources must have recounted the birth,' (*Genesis*, 288). Certainly, more recent commentators have been reluctant to divide the text into J and E sources, though Levin sees the reference to the Lord answering Isaac's prayer as part of a later 'Yahwistic' redaction of the basic narrative. This is part of his outworking of a supplementary view of the growth of the Pentateuch, where a later theological Yahwistic redaction is worked into

Besides source critical considerations, an indication of traditio-historical development may be the relationship of the oracle (vv. 22-23) to the rest of the passage. In this regard, Westermann argues that v. 24 flows better from v. 21, with the result that the oracle can be seen as an independent unit inserted at this point.[3] The original setting of the oracle, argues Westermann, would be the Davidic period, giving grounds in the patriarchal period for Israel's later defeat of Edom.

As part of his argument he claims that v. 24b ('behold there were twins in the womb') contradicts the oracle itself, since it seems to suppose that the discovery of twins was not expected. However, this does not do justice to the text as it is, where the force of 'behold' (והנה) is the discovery that the oracle was correct.[4] Furthermore, v. 24a draws a line at the end of the pregnancy, reinforcing the idea that an ordeal is over. More significantly, the oracle itself presupposes the situation of the pregnancy and so is more difficult to disentangle from its present context than might appear to be the case. Finally, although Westermann sees the political relationship of Israel and Edom as key to the original setting of the oracle, this relationship can only be positively identified in the light of v. 30, itself seen as a gloss by Westermann.

Regarding the setting for the passage, most scholars suggest that vv. 21ff were themselves written as an introduction to the Jacob story, anticipating many of the motifs of the story.[5] The Priestly frame enhances this introductory character, whilst drawing the whole of the Jacob story into the 'descendants of Isaac'.

Finally the passage contains the tradition of the long awaited child, born of the barren mother, and seen as a gift from God. Most obvious parallels are the stories of the barrenness of Sarai/Sarah and the eventual birth of

---

the text (Levin, *Der Jahwist*, 197).

3   Westermann, *Genesis 12-36*, 411.

4   Oddly, this is reflected in the translation in the Westermann's commentary: 'When the time came for her to give birth there were *indeed* twins in her womb,' *Genesis 12-36*, 411 (own italics).

The word והנה ('behold') is not reflected in translation - e.g. NRSV.

5   e.g. von Rad, *Genesis*: 'an expository preface to the whole' (265). Van Seters disagrees (*Prologue to History*, 280-1), calling the section (including vv. 27-34, though excluding the P additions) 'a very common and widespread folk-tradition at the pre-Yahwistic level of composition.' This however does not relate to the clear function of the passage in introducing the Jacob story. The most that can be said in Van Seters' support is that this section may well contain elements which have now been formed into this 'expository preface' - see below, p. 24.

Isaac, the birth of Samson (Judg. 13) and of Samuel (1 Sam. 1).[6] However these passages all have their distinctiveness and are too widely distributed to draw any traditio-historical link. It seems therefore that the narrator is drawing on a well-known motif.[7] Likewise the oracle has similarities to other predictions in Genesis about later Israel (e.g. Gen. 9:25-27, Gen. 27:27-29, 39-40, Gen. 49, also Num. 23-24), although these other examples are all blessings rather than oracles.

A Reading of 25:19-26

The passage can be structured as follows:
vv. 19-21 setting the scene, introducing the necessary elements for the familiar story of a long awaited child;
vv. 22-23 describing the further complication, prompting Rebekah to seek an oracle;
vv. 24-26 recounting the births and namings, complicated because of the presence of twins. The note on Isaac's age provides a formal conclusion.

Exegesis

vv. 19-20: The heading of the 'descendants of Isaac' places the story within the wider toledot framework stretching back through the book of Genesis. It also reminds us that this is not the story exclusively of Jacob, but also involves his brother Esau. In terms of the wider context, v. 19 recapitulates details already known: that Isaac is born of Abraham and married to Rebekah. What is new is the age of Isaac (40 years) on marrying Rebekah.

v. 21 introduces the action proper. The description is very stereo-typical with one half of the verse paralleling the other.[8] There is as yet no hint that all this will have taken twenty years (v. 26b), and any tension arising from Rebekah's barrenness is passed over. This contrasts with the Abraham story

---

6 Hauge, M. R., ('The Struggles of the Blessed in Estrangement', *ST* 29, 1975, 1-30), adding the birth of Joseph to the list, sees the tradition of the long awaited child as a key motif to the patriarchal narratives in particular, although in each occurrence of the motif a different aspect is emphasized. In this case, there is the unique focus on struggle.

7 Alter, R. (*Genesis: translation and commentary*, WW Norton & Co: New York, 1996, 126) calls it an 'annunciation type scene'. Also, within a wider Canaanite context, Hendel, *The Epic of the Patriarch*, 37ff.

8 The Hebrew verb עתר is at the root of both the terms 'pray to' and 'granted his prayer'. More specifically, the two parts share the same syntactical structure: waw + verb (עתר√) + ליהוה/יהוה + לו/יצחק + (clause concerning) Rebekah.

where the desire for a son for Sarah stretches over several episodes. Here, the same problem, lasting twenty years, is dealt with in one verse.[9] Thus, what is not of interest to the writer is passed over and the focus on the circumstances of the birth is all the stronger. The formality of this verse also belies the pain and upset that the answer to this prayer will bring about in the lives of the protagonists. As it is, the verse lulls the reader into a sense that all is to be well: there is relief that the anguishings of Sarah and Abraham (not to mention Hagar and Ishmael) are not to be repeated (though anguish there must have been!), and there is the added expectation that this child (there is as yet no expectation of twins) will have a special place in God's plan since he is a gift from God.

So far, Isaac is the central subject with Rebekah as the almost passive object. At first she is simply mentioned as 'his wife' and 'she' (הוא) , and when she is named as the subject of a clause, she is still 'Rebekah *his wife*'. This reflects the formal side of the patriarchal narratives, the story of the promise given to the patriarchs who then pass it to the next generation. In this way, it corresponds closely in style and form to the previous verse (P).

Before moving on, comment should be made about the use of the divine name YHWH in this passage, since it is found four times whereas the general term for God (Elohim) is not found at all. Although some sort of source critical explanation should not be dismissed, it is perhaps significant that the writer should want to emphasize the identity of the divine as YHWH at the beginning of the Jacob story, making it clear that wherever God is mentioned, it is YHWH who is meant.[10] Furthermore, the use of the divine name might be expected in these verses given the stereo-typical language -terms 'prayed' (עתר) and 'inquire' (דרש) both evoke a picture of Israel's settled cultic religious practice.[11] Finally the use of the divine

---

9 Ehrlich, A. B., (*Randglossen zur Hebräischen Bibel*, vol. 1, Hildesheim: Olms, 1968, 117) notes a further factor in this contrast, where ten years of childlessness ends in a child for Abraham (16:3), double the time ends with a double miracle in the birth of twins. However, the contrast does not quite work since in the former case it is Ishmael who is born, and there is a further wait for a son to be born of Sarah.

10 Wenham, G. J. ('The Religion of the Patriarchs.' in Millard, A. R., and Wiseman, D. J., eds, *Essays on the Patriarchal Narratives*, Leicester: IVP, 1980, 180ff) makes the observation that there is a tendency in the patriarchal narratives to mention YHWH at the beginning and end of scenes, as indeed in the opening and closing episodes of the Abraham cycle (chs 12 and 24). This would seem to indicate an editorial hand. See below, pp. 60-1 on the use of the divine name.

11 The root עתר (pray) is found in a wide variety of passages in different forms (Qal, Hiphil and Niphal), although almost always in an Israelite context - exceptions being the book of Job (22:27, 33:26), and Is. 19:22. However, the latter, concerning Egypt, is a clear reference to the plague traditions of Exodus, where the strongest concentration of the term

name is consistent with the idea that this episode is the work of writers who have the wider narrative and later religious perspective in view.

vv. 22-23 introduce the complication. Now Isaac retreats to the background, and Rebekah becomes the focus of attention. The struggle of the twins graphically illustrates how the relationship between the two will develop, and it is clear that this is the interest of the passage. Unlike with Isaac, Rebekah's speech is reported directly and graphically, drawing the reader into a greater sympathy, and we sense that Rebekah feels the situation much more directly and profoundly.[12] The unclear syntax of v. 22b reflects that this is an outcry, perhaps in pain.[13] Whether Isaac knows any of this, we are not told. Certainly this picture of Isaac being more passive and less in control is consistent with chapter 27 as well as chapter 24. The words 'to her' (לה -v. 23aα) again emphasize the chief role of Rebekah.[14]

---

is found. In this case, the term describes Moses' action in asking YHWH to lift a plague from the Egyptians. Other instances of the term include a prayer to end famine (2 Sam. 21:14), to stop a plague (2 Sam. 24:25), for help in battle (1 Chron. 5:20), safety on a perilous journey (Ezr. 8:23) and release from imprisonment in exile (2 Chron. 33:13, 19).

It is evident that in all these cases the term denotes a supplication for rescue from a particular distress. Isaac is seen as following this pattern as the lack of a child is itself a cause for distress, and indeed threatens the whole patriarchal story of promise. One divergence from this use is Judg. 13:8, where Manoah asks for guidance about how to bring up his promised son (Samson).

It should however be noted that the term is not used exclusively with YHWH - occasionally the prayer is answered by Elohim (e.g. Judg. 13:8, 2 Sam. 21:14); in Ezr. the object is 'our God' (אלהינו), though this term should not be considered synonymous with YHWH; in Job, the lack of the divine name is consistent with the bulk of that book. Given this, it would be rash to claim that the term could ever have only been understood in an exclusively Yahwistic sense. Nevertheless the term does have strong associations with the Israelite turning to YHWH in case of need.

For דרש ('inquire'), see below.

12 In this way, the passage anticipates her offer to Jacob later on (27:13).

13 Alter, *Genesis*, 127 suggests that Rebekah's speech is broken off mid-sentence; Westermann, *Genesis 12-36*, 413: 'It is the primeval cry of 'Why?' about the meaning of life.' Certainly, von Rad is dismissive in his judgement: 'Judged as a narrative, however, this report is remarkably without vividness. The prayers to Yahweh...are simply asserted, but not related' (*Genesis*, 265): on the contrary, in these few words of Rebekah are packed a great deal of emotion and anguish which anticipates much that will come for the twins and their mother.

14 Allen, C. G. ('On Me be the Curse, My Son!', in M. J. Buss ed., *Encounter with the Text*, Philadelphia: Fortress Press, 1979, 167-8) wonders whether we should in fact see Rebekah as the necessary link between Abraham and Jacob. For a more detailed consideration of her approach see below, pp. 107-10. It is certainly significant that Rebekah and not Isaac should receive this crucial information about the twins, and this contributes

It is surprising that we are told simply that Rebekah went to inquire of YHWH. What this means in practical terms is clearly assumed or regarded as unimportant. The idea of going to 'inquire of YHWH' (דרש) is one well attested in the Hebrew Bible, particularly in relation to the monarchic period. The picture seems to be of a prophet whose chief funtion is to provide inquirers with a message from God - see especially 1 Sam. 9:9. Passages such as 1 Sam. 28:7, where Saul goes to a medium, 1 Ki. 22:5ff, which distinguishes between 'the prophets' and 'a prophet of the Lord', and 2 Ki. 1:2ff, where Ahaziah sends messengers to consult Baal-Zebub, hint at a sense of competition between Yahwistic prophets and other prophets.[15] Those who have given these traditions their canonical form are unanimous in wanting to make clear a distinction between these different sets of prophets, and so it is not at all surprising that this oracle, given at the beginning of the story of Israel's ancestor, should explicitly come from YHWH, even if in the wider Pentateuchal picture, the idea of a prophet of YHWH seems anachronistic.[16]

The vocabulary and parallelistic structure of the oracle give it a distinctive poetic tone. In itself, the oracle gives no clear indication of which two nations are meant. There would be no doubt that Jacob/Israel would be one, and in the context of v. 25, Edom is meant by the other. No doubt some reference to the subjugation of Edom in the time of David can be understood, though this does not exhaust the scope of the oracle.[17] The

---

to the wider picture of Rebekah and Isaac. One of the motifs in the patriarchal narratives is that of the matriarchs who, each in their own way, form a contrast to the respective patriarch. In terms of the interest in the divine-human encounter, this contrast adds a further perspective to that understanding, as shall be seen in relation to ch. 27, where the relationship between the matriarch's acts and the divine plan is very unclear.

15 At 1 Ki. 22:5ff four hundred prophets prophesy (albeit falsely) about YHWH (v. 6b). This may suggest some overlap between prophecies concerning YHWH and other gods.

16 Westermann (*Genesis 12-36*, 413) makes the point that the setting for 'enquiring of Yahweh' is consistent with the monarchic setting of the oracle which follows. This is also true, but does not recognize the similarity with the motif of praying to YHWH in distress. Regarding this motif, Westermann suggests that it survives from a 'narrative from the patriarchal period' since 'it is in accord with the patriarchal period in that the father is the intercessor'.

However, this in turn fails to do justice to the strong Yahwistic overtones of the description which suggests a later setting than any pre-Yahwistic patriarchal age.

17 2 Sam. 8:12-14. This is widely agreed among commentators. What is less clear is how far we should go in translating the individual traits of each twin and their relationship with each other (Esau being older than Jacob) into national-historical terms. Even Blum, who sees the national dimension as foundational to the story, accepts that the twins are depicted as characters in their own right, rather than as allegorical ciphers (*Die Komposition der Vätergeschichte*, 79).

effect of such an oracle placed at the beginning of the Jacob story is to make clear from the outset that as well as dealing with two brothers, the story has in its view two neighbouring peoples. However, it also makes the theological point that what is to happen is within the foreknowledge of God.

vv. 24-26 return to the patriarchal era and Rebekah's pregnancy, and also from the divine perspective back to the human, graphically depicting the fraternal rivalry which is a consequence of what is predicted in the oracle. The opening phrase of v. 24 ('When the time...') emphasizes the duration of the pregnancy but also takes the reader to the moment of birth.[18] The narrated perspective is still that of Rebekah (*'her* days', twins in *'her* womb'). The force of 'behold' (והנה) is to confirm the oracle: now that the birth is about to take place, we discover that there are indeed twins.[19] For Rebekah, of course, this has a special significance since she alone, we might assume, is party to the divine perspective.

The description of Esau has a comic touch as the reader is invited to imagine a baby covered in red hair popping out of the mother.[20] There may also be cultural overtones of an uncultured, 'wild' way of life.[21] However the description also introduces into the Jacob-Esau story elements which will have a later significance: the colour red anticipates Esau's craving for

---

18   The translation of the word וימלאו to 'were at hand' (NRSV) does not really do justice to the sense of 'fulfil' or 'complete' conveyed in the original word.

19   The word והנה is not translated in NRSV or NIV.

20   The only other use of the word אדמוני (red) is a reference to David (1 Sam. 6:12, also 17:42). In this case it describes the hero's ruddy appearance. Could it be that we have in this less complimentary description of Esau a very subtle ironic allusion to David, the subjugator of the Edomites, since the oracle spoken to Sarah will be fulfilled through another ruddy (אדמוני) character? Note also:

> Even at birth and before, he [Esau] had all the symptoms of a violent, sinful person. As an embryo he fought to approach the temple of the idols, he was born with the redness that is symbolic of bloodshed. As a youngster he was drawn to the excitement of the hunt ... King David, too had the redness of bloodshed, but he surmounted all obstacles to become the Sweet Singer of Israel. (Scherman, N. and Zlotowitz, M., *Bereishis/Genesis: A New Translation with a Commentary anthologized from Talmudic, Midrashic and Rabbinic Sources*, Artscroll Tanach Series, New York: Mesorah, 1980, vol. 3, 1013.)

21   '[A] sign in this instance of excessive sensual vigour and wildness': Keil, C. F. and Delitzsch, F., *The Pentateuch: Volume 1 (Biblical Commentary on the Old Testament)*, Edinburgh: T & T Clark, 1864, (ET), 268.

For Ancient Near Eastern parallels: Speiser, E. A., *Genesis*, Garden City: Doubleday & Company, Inc., 1964, 196; Hendel, *The Epic of the Patriarch*, 111ff. This description of Esau as a type for the uncultured man is also relevant to the next episode (v. 27ff).

the red soup in v. 30, and more importantly, his hairy mantle will be a crucial factor in Jacob's deception (27:11). Furthermore there are gentle allusions to both Edom and Seir, Edom's dwelling place (33:16). The word 'hair' (שער) also anticipates the naming of Esau (עשו), and is the nearest to any etymology for Esau in Genesis.[22] This cluster of allusions establishes the link between the individual Esau and the people of Edom, though Esau also remains an individual in his own right.

The fact that Jacob is second to be born is emphasized by the adverbial phrase 'afterwards'. This is of course of vital importance in the whole question of the right of the first-born.[23] The passage also anticipates chapter 27 where Jacob steals the natural right of the first-born, the father's blessing, by reversing the order of their birth: he is the first to see his father and so secures the advantages of the first-born. Furthermore, the first reference to Jacob is as the brother of Esau, thereby indicating that the fate of the two will be tied up in each other.

Whereas interest in Esau centres on appearance, in Jacob the interest is in his action. The picture of grasping the heel gives the 'human' side to the divine oracle: if it is true that the older will serve the younger, it is not least because of the blatant efforts of the younger to secure the advantage.[24] For the time being he has failed, but we know he will bide his time. That this action of Jacob is not a fleeting grasp but an accurate indication of his personality is confirmed in the etymology, where this episode is to be permanently remembered through his name.[25]

---

22   In Hebrew there is a similarity between Esau (עשו), hair (שער) and Seir (שעיר).

23   See following excursus, p. 21ff.

24   For an interpretation of 'heel' as a euphemism for genitalia, see Smith, S. H., '"Heel" and "Thigh": The Concept of Sexuality in the Jacob-Esau narratives.' *VT* 40 (1990), 465. In this case, the image is of Jacob attempting to appropriate for himself the procreative powers of Esau.

25   Apart from the Piel form found at Job 37:4, the verb עקב (supplant) is only used at Gen. 27:36, Jer. 9:3, Hos. 12:4 - in two cases, with a clear link to Jacob, and in Jer. with a probable allusion to this tradition. However, Hamilton, V. P. (*The Book of Genesis: chapters 18-50*, Grand Rapids: Eerdmans, 1995, 227) refers to examples of the verb in Ugaritic texts where the root is used in a metaphorical way.

What any original etymology for the name יעקב (Jacob) might have meant is unclear. None other is offered in the Bible, although the scholarly view is that the name is a shortened form of the name 'Jacob-El' which does not occur in the Biblical text but widely in other Ancient Near Eastern literature.

See 'יעקב' - Zobel, H.-J., *Theological Dictionary of the Old Testament*, vol. 6, Grand Rapids: Eerdmans, 1977-1990 (ET of *Theologisches Wörterbuch zum Alten Testament*, Stuttgart, 1970ff), 188-90.

Regarding the change in the form of the verb קרא (call/name) between the naming of

The final clause brings this episode to a close with a formal tone and by moving back to the perspective of Isaac. That twenty years have elapsed before the birth is only now revealed.

vv. 27-34: their Thematic Relationship to the Preceding Verses

It has already been argued that these verses form a further scene within the introduction to the Jacob story. Our interest here is how the verses contrast with the oracle.

v. 27, connecting the birth to the following scene begins to clarify the differentiation between the twins as predicted in the oracle (v. 23). Unlike Isaac's preference for Esau, we are not told why the mother should prefer Jacob: perhaps because he was more domesticated or because of the oracle. In any case, Isaac's preference is based on self-interest and his love of game, whereas no motive of self-interest is indicated for Rebekah.[26] This may play a part in determining how we should judge Rebekah's action in chapter 27.

The incident concerning the stew centres around the key concept of the right of the first-born (בכרה). From this passage alone, it is not clear exactly how this term corresponds to the idea of the patriarchal promise or blessing (ברכה), and this probably requires some traditio-historical consideration:[27] on the one hand, the two are not exactly the same; on the other hand, within the wider narrative context, the promise motif provides

---

Esau (3rd person plural - cf. v. 30) and Jacob (3rd person singular), the MT reading seems secure despite textual variants (LXX, Syriac and the Vulgate, which also have a singular verb in v. 25). The variants are probably to be explained as a harmonization with v. 26. On other hand, the Targum and the Samaritan text make the verb in v. 26 plural - again, probably to bring the two verses in harmony.

As to why there should be two different verb forms, it is probably simply a stylistic variation, although the suggestion has been made that a more definite 'He called' could refer to God or Isaac as subject (Rashi in Rosenbaum, M. and Silbermann, A. M. eds, *Pentateuch with Targum Onkelos, Haphtorah and Rashi's Commentary*, New York: Hebrew Publishing Company, 115).

26   An interesting parallel is made by Kunin, S. D. (*The Logic of Incest: A Structuralist Analysis of Hebrew Mythology*, Sheffield: JSOT Supp 185, 1995, 113) between the words used by Rebekah during her period of pregnancy (25:22) and Esau on his declaration that he is dying of famine (25:32). He uses this to show that in this sense Esau and his mother share the common factor of being 'outside' in terms of the divine blessing in contrast to Isaac and Jacob.

27   See below, pp. 110-1.

an overall uniting key.[28] More importantly for our concern at the moment, the term picks up the contrast of the older and younger in the oracle, and sharpens the irony set in the oracle of the older (the real first-born) serving the younger. The irony is particularly sharp because the term 'first-born' carries with it connotations of divine favour, here reversed (e.g. Dt. 21:17).

The contrast between this scene and the oracle is that in this later scene, the status rightly given to the first-born is not given to Jacob by God (as might be expected from the oracle) but is extorted from Esau through cold calculation: whereas divine favour might be hinted at in the oracle, now, the only factor is human craftiness. Thus these verses add to the impression already given of a real struggle by one brother to get on top of the other, a struggle no less real despite the wider divine perspective given by the oracle before their birth.

Nevertheless, this scene also introduces the motif of Esau's unworthiness to receive the birthright, an aspect which helps to make the sordid tale of human deception and struggle more palatable to religious sensibilities. This motif is nowhere clearer in the story of Jacob and Esau than in the matter of fact but outright statement that Esau despised his birthright (v. 34b). In interpreting this motif commentators vary from Gunkel, who sees this simply as a humorous tale of the clever Jacob deceiving his clumsy brother,[29] to commentators giving a much more moral interpretation, emphasizing Esau's shortsightedness and lack of interest in the birthright on the one hand, and Jacob's intense desire for it, on the other.[30]

---

28   Von Rad (*Genesis*, 268): 'The divine promise is like a sign before and over all these individual narratives, and within this bracket, so to speak, there is much good and evil.' The value of von Rad's approach here is that he is able to treat each discrete episode with its own historical particularity and distinctiveness, whilst also seeing each as contributing to the wider narrative context.

29   Gunkel, *Genesis*, 297-99.

30   e.g. Keil-Delitzsch, (*The Pentateuch*), 269; Delitzsch, F., (*A New Commentary of Genesis*, Edinburgh: T & T Clark, 1889 ET), 137: Esau forfeits the blessing of the first-born because he is 'minded κατα σαρκα. The brotherly artifice of Jacob is indeed sinful, and we see this one sin produce the first sin of deceiving his ageing father...By reason however of the fundamental tendency of his mind towards the promised blessing, Jacob is the more pleasing to God of the two brothers.'

   Better grounded in the narrative itself is the observation that Esau is depicted as 'uncouth' or a 'glutton', especially in the way he exaggerates his hunger, in the bluntness of his speech and the quick succession of verbs in v. 34aβ - see Alter, R., *Art of Biblical Narrative*, London: George Allen & Unwin, 1981, 44; Bar-Efrat, S., *Narrative Art in the Bible*, Sheffield: JSOT Supp. 70, 1989, 79. 216-7; Hamilton, *The Book of Genesis: chapters 18-50*, 182.

   By contrast, Bar-Efrat sees the description of Jacob as 'a quiet man' (איש תם -v. 27)

This final clause, a very rare judgement by the narrator, certainly adds to the complex depiction of Jacob and Esau and the varying forces at play in their destinies. There is some condemnation and especially mockery of Esau, and we might agree that at least Jacob could see beyond his immediate needs. Nevertheless, the passage remains open-ended and refuses any black and white judgements in favour of one or the other of the brothers. Instead, we are left with the impression of the very human story of rivalry between two brothers, neither of whom emerges in an exemplary way.[31]

Excursus: the Motif of בכרה (First-Born)

Besides vv. 31ff, the term birthright or first-born is used in chapter 27 (v. 19 and 32), and ironically, in blessing the sons of Joseph, Jacob deliberately treats the younger Ephraim as the first-born (Gen. 48:17ff). More broadly, the contrast of the older and the younger, and the idea of the supremacy of one over the other lies at the heart of the whole of the Jacob-Esau narrative.

The idea of the first-born, expressed in the root *bkr* (בכר), is widespread in the Old Testament, as more generally in the Ancient Near East.[32] In the Pentateuch it concerns the first-fruits of the field (e.g. Ex. 23:16) or of beasts and indeed of sons (Ex. 13:2). With human beings, in some cases the first-born is defined by the father, the first-born being the first of the father's strength (Dt. 21:17bα); elsewhere the first-born of the mother is the defining principle, where the first-born is the one to open the womb (Ex. 13:2). In the case of Jacob's sons, it is Reuben who is recognized as the first-born, defined as the first strength of his father Jacob (Gen. 49:3).

Dt. 21:15-17 deals with the 'right of the first-born' (משפט הבכרה), where it is made clear that in a state of polygamy, the first-born of the father has a right over any other son, even of a more favourite mother. How this

---

as a positive evaluation of Jacob (*Narrative Art in the Bible*, 33).

31 'Jacob has a sharp mind and no conscience, but Esau is all belly and no brain,' Mann, T. W., *The Book of the Torah: The Narrative Integrity of the Pentateuch*, Atlanta: John Knox Press, 1988, 52. In this light, it is probably inappropriate to give too much weight to the term תם, used to describe Jacob in v. 27. It can certainly mean 'innocent', but may also denote simplicity; furthermore, far from being a straightforward description of Jacob, there may be a degree of irony in the use of the term (see Alter, *Genesis*, 128). By contrast, Ibn Ezra sees the word as denoting integrity, being antithetical to the deceit used by Esau, the trapper of animals - though we may wonder how this sits alongside Jacob's behaviour in this episode and elsewhere (Strickman, N. and Silver, M. eds, *Ibn Ezra's Commentary on the Pentateuch: Genesis*, New York: Menorah Publishing Company, 1988, 251).

32 For much of the following, see Tsevat, *Theological Dictionary of the Old Testament*, vol. 2, 121-27. Also Speiser, *Genesis*, 194-5, on Mesopotamian legal practice.

passage might be related to the state of Jacob and Esau is not clear.[33] Tsevat argues that in narrative, the status of the first-born is less fixed, although he also states that the several exceptions to the rule in narrative emphasize the choice of God as disrupting the natural order. His suggestion that the patriarchal narratives want to describe a time in which the first-born did not enjoy a privileged position does not really do justice to the tension within the narratives where the status of the first-born son does matter. In the light of this principle, Tsevat also argues that what Esau sells to Jacob is simply the special portion due to the first-born: 'Esau's rank and position are not affected by this transaction, as chapter 27 shows quite clearly.'[34] However, in chapter 27, it is questionable whether such a clear distinction can be made, and the repeated use of the term by Jacob seems to indicate that the status of the first-born is tied up with the theme of the blessing.

The other concentration of the term of the first-born is in the exodus tradition where Israel is described as YHWH's first-born, and where all the first-born Egyptians are slain because of Pharaoh's refusal to allow Israel to leave Egypt (see especially Ex. 4:22-23). This tradition provides a historical basis for the idea of the first-born, particularly in relation to the law of redemption for the first-born son (Ex. 13:15).

Regarding the particular privileges of the first-born, it is important to bear in mind the spiritual or even priestly aspect brought out by some Jewish commentators. Because he is set apart, the first-born son is deemed quasi-holy,[35] and, before the institution of the Levitical priesthood, the first-born is seen as acting as priest.[36] This aspect is important in highlighting the divine responsibility of the first-born.

Two recent treatments are worth special mention. Syrén's recent monograph on the theme of the first-born who loses his status is restricted

---

33 Carmichael, C. M., *Women, Law, and the Genesis Traditions*, Edinburgh: Edinburgh University Press, 1979, 31 sees the Deuteronomic law as written in the light of the ill-treatment of Leah and her son Reuben.

34 Tsevat, *Theological Dictionary of the Old Testament*, vol. 2, 126.

35 Plaut, W. G., ed., *The Torah: A Modern Commentary*, New York: Union of American Hebrew Congregations, 1981, 175.

36 So Hertz, J. H., *The Pentateuch and Haftorahs: Genesis*, London: Oxford University Press, 1929, 220, also Calvin, J., *A Commentary on Genesis*, vol. 2, London: Banner of Truth Trust (ET of 1554) 53, and Delitzsch (*A New Commentary on Genesis*, 136) who cites the Mishna tradition that the first-born had the Abodah (priestly office). Based on this understanding, Rashi finds an extra meaning to Esau's remark that he is about to die (v. 32): 'Esau said, 'What is the nature of this Service [of the first-born]? Jacob replied, 'Many prohibitions and punishments and many acts involving even the punishment of death are associated with it...He [Esau] said: If I am going to die through it, why should I desire it' Rosenbaum and Silbermann eds, *Pentateuch*, 117.

to Genesis and especially the Abraham-Ishmael and Jacob-Esau stories.[37] His interest is on understanding the idea of the first-born in its narratological context, and his contribution is in showing how the idea fits the national and theological interests of Israel (in particular, he argues, of the post-exilic community), since the repeated favouring of the younger over the first-born, and their consequent peaceful separation, relate to Israel's self-understanding against its neighbours, as a nation elected by God.

Whereas Syrén's interest is in the developed narrative concept of the first-born, Levenson bases the concept in what he sees as the ancient cultic tradition of Israel.[38] Starting with the practice of child sacrifice, he controversially argues that this practice was once much more acceptable in Israelite religion than later prophetic critiques and most Jewish and Christian commentators would allow. Furthermore, Levenson argues that this idea provides a key motif to narratives in Genesis, not to mention in New Testament christological understanding.

Levenson points to the striking paradox underlying the idea of the first-born: like the first-fruits of a crop, the first-born son represents the best, and as such belongs to God. Hence, if not literal sacrifice, then at least redemption 'is necessary because the first-born son belongs to YHWH...The underlying theology of the redemption of the first-born son is that...the life of the son in question is his not by right, but by gift.'[39] As a result, 'Justice is not done to the complicated role of the first-born son if we fail to note both his exalted status and the precariousness of his very life. The beloved son is marked for both exaltation and for humiliation. In his life the two are seldom far apart.'[40] This also applies to the idea of 'chosenness' which overlaps greatly with the concept of first-born.

This idea is played out in the story of those who are exalted to the status of first-born in Genesis, and for Jacob it means that since he is the one chosen over Esau and thereby attains the status of first-born, he must undergo a state of humiliation, a symbolic death, before enjoying his exalted status. This is what Jacob's exile from the Promised Land and his

---

37 Syrén, R., *The Forsaken First Born: A Study of a Recurrent Motif in the Patriarchal Narratives*, Sheffield: JSOT Supp 133, 1993.
38 Levenson, J. D., *The Death and Resurrection of the Beloved Son*, New Haven and London: Yale University Press, 1993.
39 Levenson, *The Death and Resurrection of the Beloved Son*, 59.
40 This idea relates to the above-mentioned priestly understanding of the status of the first-born as both a privilege and a responsibility, although Levenson does not really give explicit consideration to this tradition.

human father represent.

To sum up, the idea of the first-born, whether human, animal or of crops, is widespread not just in Israel but in the Ancient Near East in general. A law such as Dt. 21:15ff may be regarded as a tightening up of the more varied application of the idea, just as the tying of it to the exodus tradition gives it a salvation-historical basis. Theologically, the idea proves fruitful to Israel's religious traditions, especially in giving a concrete expression to the idea of Israel being elected or chosen, bringing with it both privilege and responsibility.

A frequent twist to this motif which contradicts the Deuteronomic law, but which proves to be particularly fruitful is that of the younger son gaining the status of the first-born. This emphasizes even more the free choice of YHWH, and sets his choosing of Israel in a certain dialectic: his choice is not natural, but stems from his sovereign will. It is also played out in the lives of human beings where one man's exaltation means another's humiliation. This gives Israel a means of understanding its own special status among other nations which depends not upon its own power or historical primacy, but on its relationship with YHWH. Finally, as Levenson has shown, the idea of the first-born touches on the theologically suggestive paradox of exaltation and humiliation stemming from the resilient idea of sacrifice. It is within this understanding of the first-born, as much inferred as spelt out, that the Jacob narrative operates as the very human events around the life of this individual and his family are part of the wider workings of the divine scheme.

Conclusion

Historical-Critical Summary

As already mentioned, vv. 19-26 - with vv. 27-34 - have been constructed as an introduction to the Jacob story, though probably using older traditions. This introduction emphasizes the link of the Jacob story with the Yahwistic faith of Israel. In addition, the Priestly framework emphasizes that this scene marks a new stage in the patriarchal story, and draws the story of Jacob into its own understanding of the story of the 'descendants of Isaac', one effect of which is to make this the story of both sons of Isaac.

In both theme and the wider structuring of the book of Genesis, this opening scene stands in close relationship to the following verses. These verses themselves seem to draw on the motif of the contrasting lifestyles and on the story of the selling of the birthright - itself probably already a tradition about Jacob and Esau. Together, vv. 19-34 provide a series of scenes of the early life of the twins which anticipate what is to follow and introduce the link with the neighbouring peoples of Israel and Edom.

God

Most obviously, this scene brings a divine perspective to the life of Jacob. Even before his birth, it is clear that all that will follow is set within the wider providential scheme. This is particularly emphasized by formal, stereo-typical elements: the opening toledoth formula placing the life of Jacob within the wider unfolding of history from creation, the initial emphasis on Isaac reminding us of the patriarchal promise, the motif of the long-awaited child as a divine gift arousing great expectations, the words of the oracle.

Nevertheless God's providential scheme creates its own paradoxes. The first of these relates to the initial barrenness of Rebekah. As Hamilton points out, Rebekah's barren state might put into question the certainty with which she is depicted as the chosen wife for Isaac in chapter 24.[41] In the end, of course, the motif of barrenness serves to emphasize the providential nature of the birth of the twins, whereas the narrative passes over the waiting and the doubts.

The other striking paradox is the notion of one - and especially the younger - twin favoured over the other. The oracle given to Rebekah carries all the solemnity of a declaration of divine will, raising the idea of election with related questions of fairness.[42] For Calvin, this is a clear example of God's election acting contrary to human nature, of the divine working counter to the human: 'The sum of the whole, then, is that the preference which God gave to Jacob...was not granted as a reward for his merits, neither was obtained by his own industry, but proceeded from the mere grace of God himself.'[43]

Nevertheless, in the following episode, the harshness of this aspect of election is softened by hints of Esau's unworthiness, most notably in the

---

41 Hamilton, *Genesis 18-50*, 175. Calvin sees the issue in more dogmatic terms: 'This small and contemptible origin, these slow and feeble advances, render more illustrious that increase, which afterwards follows, beyond all hope and expectation, to teach us that the Church was produced and increased by divine power and grace, and not by merely natural means' (Calvin, *A Commentary on Genesis*, vol. 2, 42). Also Brueggemann, W., *Genesis: a Bible Commentary for teaching and preaching*, Atlanta: John Knox, 1982, 212.
42 The idea of election is much clearer in Mal. 1:2-3, and theological questions around it are raised in Rom. 9:10-13.
43 Calvin, *A Commentary on Genesis*, vol. 2, 45.

rare unequivocal judgement of the narrator that Esau despised his birthright (v. 34). In contrast to the above approach, this motif of the relative worthiness and unworthiness of Jacob and Esau respectively tends to be maximized in traditional Jewish interpretation. Thus, for instance, the struggling in the mother's womb shows the twins each trying to run, but in different directions: Jacob to the Torah schools and Esau to the pagan temple;[44] the colour red depicts bloodshed; Esau's tendency to hunting symbolizes how he ensnares his father, whereas Jacob's attachment to the tents refers to the tent of Shem and Eber (where Torah is studied);[45] Esau is not really deceived but chooses the material lentils over the spiritual birthright.[46] This particular hermeneutic tends to see the human and divine as less of a paradox, since the divine plan is consistent with the natural tendencies and actions of Jacob and Esau.

Interestingly, Calvin in treating the episode of the birthright agrees that Esau's behaviour is unworthy.[47] He draws the theological distinction between Esau as natural man, left to his own disposition, and Jacob, renewed by the Holy Spirit through God's election and therefore now demonstrating the grace of adoption by even denying himself food in favour of 'heavenly things'. In other words, Jacob's disposition to God results from divine election rather than causes it.[48] To a reader, working outside the doctrinal framework of Calvin, this may seem just as convoluted as some of the more ingenious rabbinic readings.

Our own approach has been to see both ideas held together in the text, but the focus of interest is less on the paradox of nature and grace (as for Calvin) as on human and divine. There is an interest in the divine, how God's will is worked out, and how the divine plan works through human agents, with a strong sense of paradox and mystery; but there is also an interest in Jacob and Esau - and indeed Rebekah - as human agents, responsible for their own action, with strong emotions.

In terms of the more general depiction of God, unlike in many episodes in the patriarchal narratives, the depiction of the divine is impersonal and mediated. Twice, God is the subject of a clause, though in one case this is in a stereo-typical context (v. 21a), and the other instance (v. 23a) brings

---

44   Cited by Rashi in Rosenbaum and Silbermann eds, *Pentateuch*, 115.
45   Rashi in Rosenbaum and Silbermann eds, *Pentateuch*, 116.
46   Scherman and Zlotowitz, *Bereishis*, vol. 3, 1025.
47   Calvin, *A Commentary on Genesis*, vol. 2, 52.
48   However, on commenting on Jacob's deceit in ch. 27 (*A Commentary on Genesis*, vol. 2, 93) Calvin abandons and contradicts this approach by arguing that Jacob gains the blessing in spite of his unworthy behaviour (in contrast to Esau who obeys his father).

with it suggestions that the divine speech is not given directly to Rebekah but through a cultic prophet. Thus God is not depicted as a character in the plot but as the mysterious mover behind the scenes.

Regarding the use of the divine name, we have suggested that this may be part of the redactorial hand, making it clear at the beginning of Jacob's life, that it is YHWH, the God of Israel, who is meant. Furthermore the notions of inquiring at a prophet and of answering in distress are anachronistic links with the religious life of Israel.

The Human

As just indicated, interest in the human is far from being subsumed in this opening scene. Indeed, in the wider patriarchal story, it is through a family story that the divine is manifest. This is now made clear as we are introduced to the 'descendants of Isaac', but especially as the focus shifts to Rebekah and the twins in her womb. It is the mother who feels the struggle, indeed her very body is the location of that struggle. She it is who seeks and finds the divine perspective. Nevertheless, although she is told what the struggle means, there is no hint as to how the oracle is to be fulfilled. We can probably assume that the oracle is not just a prediction but also an indication of the divine plan, but it is left to Jacob (and his mother) to bring the plan about.

The struggling in the womb provides the human side to the divine word. Likewise, Jacob's grasping at the heel of his brother offers a view on how the divine plan will be fulfilled, borne out in the etymology for Jacob itself, that the founder of Israel is to be characterized by his grasping nature. His status is as much something he grasps as he receives.

An indication of the writer's interest in the human side of this story is also to be found in the subtle characterization. As Vawter writes: 'The character of Jacob is by far the most carefully and subtly delineated of all the patriarchal figures, and from these legends he emerges as the most clearly defined human with a personality that develops and matures.'[49] As we proceed through the Jacob story we shall see how this proves to be the case, though not simply in the characterization of Jacob but in other members of his family and in their interrelationship as well.

One additional perspective is that of Israel: just as the language used in relation to the divine draws the reader into Yahwistic beliefs, so the contents of the oracle and allusions to the nation of Edom make the reader aware that this is the story not just of two brothers but of two neighbouring

---

49 Vawter, B., *On Genesis: A New Reading*, London: Geoffrey Chapman, 1977, 289-90.

peoples. This identification furthermore makes the point that YHWH is as much involved in the relative status of these peoples as he is in the individuals depicted.

Thus within the opening scene, although there is a clear indication of the divine perspective, this perspective is ambiguous leaving many open questions, and we see that the graspings of Jacob will be just as much a factor in the story ahead as any providential guiding of events. The two aspects will be two sides of the one coin. Finally, as we move to the second scene from v. 27 the plot moves fully to the human side leaving the divine behind for the time being - or so it seems. Thus the scene of Jacob buying the birthright is a very crude contrast to the opening scene of the oracle. The next clear indication of the divine perspective will not be until some years later, when Jacob seems to have achieved his mastery over his brother but is left vulnerable: seeming to have gained all, he seems to lose all in consequence.

Chapter 2

Bethel
(28:10-22)

Introduction

Although, as we have seen, the divine has already been present in the story of Jacob, this is Jacob's first direct encounter with God. This is particularly striking because the experience, with its unsolicited and unambiguous self-revelation of YHWH and its accompanying promises, follows the morally questionable behaviour of Jacob in cheating his father and elder brother, and the consequential escape. A further significance in its placement is that it bridges the Esau and Laban sub-plots. Thus in the very placement of this passage between two sets of family entanglements, the contrast of human and divine is thrown into sharp relief.

A further note of interest picked up by scholars is the variety of divine themes in the passage: elements in the vision, the words of YHWH concerning both Jacob's life and beyond, the reactions of Jacob both immediately and in the next morning. Added to this is strong interest in the place of Bethel.

Given this concentration of differing themes it is no surprise that this passage is generally considered to have a complex pre-history, being a favourite passage for demonstrating the existence of the written sources of the Pentateuch and for investigating questions of tradition history behind written sources.

Source Criticism

Given the presence of the traditional criteria, it is often seen as self-evident that the sources J and E can be found in this passage. Indeed it is to be noted that in two popular student handbooks on exegesis in the German language this is the passage chosen for an exemplary approach, with source criticism playing a main role.[1] In addition, the reoccurrence of Bethel in chapter 35, brings in the question of doublets, although this wider aspect shall be considered later.

Aspects of the passage judged to be criteria for source division are as follows:

- variations in the divine name.[2]
- v. 16 and 17 as doublets.[3]
- in v. 17, the place *is* the house of God, in v. 22 it is to be so *after* Jacob's return.[4] (See also v. 19a.)
- is it appropriate for Jacob to be afraid *after* the divine speech?[5]
- it is argued that a conditional oath is inappropriate after a promise from God.[6]

The clearest division of the passage is as follows:[7]

J -vv. 13-16, 19
E -vv. 10-12, 17-22 (excluding v. 19).

What is unusual about this is that the basic frame is provided by E (generally seen as the later source) with J texts seeming to elaborate within this frame, in particular by giving content to the dream.

Variations within Source Critical Approaches

There is basic agreement among source critical approaches regarding the above division. Most differences are minor, such as the place of v. 10, or the reference to Luz (v. 19b).

v. 21b (E) also causes a problem because of the name YHWH, thus Gunkel ascribes this part to the redactor.[8]

One issue faced in some studies is the relationship between J and E. Barth-Steck notices that the verses ascribed to J appear to be secondary. To investigate their relationship a comparison is made of the two sets of verses

---

1   Fohrer, G., *Exegese des Alten Testaments*, 5th ed., Heidelberg. Wiesbaden: UTB Theologie 1989, and H. Barth and O. H. Steck, *Exegese des Alten Testaments: Leitfaden der Methodik*, 12th ed., Neukirchener Verlag, 1989.
2   Gunkel, *Genesis*, 308; von Rad, *Genesis*, 283.
3   Gunkel, *Genesis*, 308; von Rad, *Genesis*, 283.
4   Barth-Steck, *Exegese des Alten Testaments*, 123.
5   Barth-Steck, *Exegese des Alten Testaments*, 122.
6   ' It would be inconceivable for the pious to combine the two. God's promise would only be called into question by a human vow,' (Gunkel, *Genesis*, 308; also von Rad, *Genesis*, 283).
7   von Rad, *Genesis*, 283.
8   Gunkel, *Genesis*, 313.

in Genesis 28, drawing in the reference in Hosea 12:5-7 (MT) as a third set. By treating these three hypothetical accounts as independent variations of the same form, thereby assuming that Hosea is not dependent on Genesis 28 or on either of its main sources, it is noted that Hosea and J have most in common, with an appearance by God, followed by speech from God to Jacob.[9] Since these agree, Barth-Steck argue that they better preserve the older form, and that E is a later form which has transformed the divine promise into a vow by Jacob.[10] The two sources were woven together by a 'yahwistic redaction' using E as the framework.[11] Thus Barth-Steck end by affirming the traditional view of two independent sources, now woven together.

Fohrer carries out a similar exercise to Barth-Steck but ends with a very different picture. In a preliminary examination he points out parts of the passage which do not really 'belong together'. These fragments are sorted into groups, resulting in a 'basic unit' to which other strands have been added. This basic unit is fairly much the same as the parts ascribed to E above, and Fohrer indeed agrees with this ascription because of the use of the term Elohim.

However, Fohrer does not treat the other verses as a parallel account, since he sees the promises in vv. 13-16 as dependent on the E version, in particular on Jacob's vow, their purpose being to shift the emphasis from the localized place to the land in more general terms. He calls these 'yahwistic', but they are not the source J but a redactional layer.

Form and Tradition Criticism

For the studies considered above, source criticism is but the first step to tracing signs of development behind the written sources.

As expected Gunkel sees much evidence of pre-literary development. He identifies several motifs which contain 'an extremely ancient, originally mythological conception', including the symbol of the ladder which points to the idea of God sending messengers from heaven where he lives.[12] He also points to many parallels in other literature. Furthermore, the phrase 'House of God' reveals an ancient conception where the heavenly house inhabited by the deity would have been thought to be sited above the earthly

---

9   Barth-Steck make this assumption without seeking to justify it. Also E. Otto, 'Jakob in Bethel. Ein Beitrag zur Geschichte der Jakobüberlieferung.' *ZAW* 88 (1976), 177.
10   Barth-Steck qualify this with the view that the promises in their present form show evidence of strong reformulation by J.
11   Barth-Steck, *Exegese des Alten Testaments*, 135.
12   Gunkel, *Genesis*, 309.

shrine. Added to this is the tradition of venerating stones.

In a separate conclusion, Gunkel argues that the story as it is predates the prophetic period, because of the positive view of Bethel as YHWH's shrine.[13] In its earliest form the stone would have been considered to be 'God's house', with the appearing divinity being the local numen, the 'El' of Bethel. Later development makes this connection weaker.

Thus Gunkel sees a long prehistory, going back to 'pre-Israelite' times, although he does not enter into detailed analysis of this development. Implicit in his approach is the religious-historical idea of religion developing from the 'primitive' concrete conception of a localized god to the developed belief in God who does not literally dwell in one place.

Likewise, Barth-Steck think there may be traces of a Palestinian pre-Canaanite culture, which considered the divinity to be dwelling in the stone. The first tangible tradition is a narrative dating from the time when Bethel became a Canaanite cultic shrine with the worship of El.[14] A 'proto-Israelite Jacob' group adopted the shrine, identifying El with the patriarchal god, and introducing Jacob. Then the independent story becomes incorporated into the Jacob-Esau-Laban cycle, with the emphasis shifting from the place Bethel to the journey motif and to the character of Jacob. From this developed the two sources, each adapting the episode.

Fohrer also sees pre-Israelite origins because of non-Israelite religious elements, the name Bethel containing the name El, and archaeological excavations uncovering a pre-Israelite settlement.[15]

Of course, not all critics employing historical-critical methods accept the use of source criticism as the correct starting-point. Among such approaches are Westermann and Blum.

Westermann starts by noting two aspects of the narrative: etiological interest in Bethel and interest in Jacob.[16] He sees this dual interest as an indicator of development, with an original pre-Israelite cult etiology reshaped by the Israelite writer(s) who introduced the character of Jacob and the promise of v. 15. To this were added vv. 13b, 14 and 20-22, which expand the promise and add the vow, and which introduce aspects relevant

---

13   Gunkel, *Genesis*, 313.
14   Barth-Steck, *Exegese des Alten Testaments*, 132.
15   Fohrer points to Gen. 35:7, and 31:13 and Jer. 48:13 for other possible traces of the El-Bethel. Otto ('Jakob in Bethel') carries out a more extensive attempt to root the tradition of Jacob in Bethel to the pre-monarchic tribal period. This approach assumes the existence of a pre-monarchic tribal system in Israel, where each tribe had its own shrine with its own particular traditions, some of which were promoted, some suppressed, depending on the influence of the particular tribe which bore the tradition.
16   Westermann, *Genesis 12-36*, 452.

to later Israel. He also sees some incongruity between the divine promise and the vow: 'The same thing cannot simultaneously be a divine promise and the condition of a vow.' He therefore sees a simple three-stage reconstruction, running parallel to the formation of the people of Israel. Regarding the differing designations for God, he argues that each has to be considered in its own context - something we shall consider in the exegesis.

The Bethel episode is the important starting-point for the whole of Blum's study of the patriarchal narratives, as he sees it as the key building block in the Jacob story, itself the oldest part of the patriarchal narrative. Apart from those verses which contain the divine promise and the vow, the passage contains nothing to indicate that it belonged to a wider narrative context, forming instead an independent, self-contained narrative unit (vv. 11-13a, 16-19) which cuts across traditional source division but which looks to be skilfully formed.[17] This original unit belonged to the genre of the 'cult foundation', though Blum does not offer any consideration of a specific setting.

Later Blum considers the place of vv. 20-22 concerning Jacob's oath.[18] Besides v. 21b, which contains a Deuteronomic covenant formula, the oath

---

17 Blum, *Die Komposition der Vätergeschichte*, 8ff. In his work Blum seems to use two criteria for distinguishing an original unity: the first, articulated at the start (p. 7), is the extent to which the passage or elements within it are dependent upon the wider context. The second criterion that he seems to use is to look for an inner coherence between the different elements. For this he uses what he calls 'synchronic' methods (e.g. p. 19). However these concepts are nowhere analysed in any detail, and in the former case, it is difficult to distinguish between a literary dependency and a more general affinity or influence which different stories can have on each other.

In the case of the Bethel passage, having eliminated elements presupposing the wider context (i.e. v. 10, the divine promises and the oath) - essentially a diachronic judgement, a 'synchronic' investigation of the remaining verses reveals a 'künstvoll gestaltete und thematisch in sich ruhende Erzählung' (p. 34).

In particular he finds an inner and outer narrative framework around the description of the dream: v. 12a (ויחלם - 'and he dreamed') corresponding to v. 16a (וייקץ - 'and he woke'); and v. 11* to v. 18*, which contain similar expressions and syntax but which also stand in an antithetical relationship. Thus the text divides naturally into four sections (beginning ויפגע - 'and he came to' (v. 11), והנה - 'and behold' (v. 12a), וייקץ - 'and he woke' (v. 16), וישכם - 'and he rose' (v. 18)). Within each section, and between each one, are thematic and linguistic links. Hence Blum finds no room for division along source critical or any other lines.

For a criticism of the method and conclusions of Blum, see McEvenue, S., 'A Return to Sources in Genesis 28:10-22?' *ZAW* 106 (1994), 375-89; also Wynn-Williams, D. J., *The State of the Pentateuch: A comparison of the approaches of M. Noth and E. Blum*, BZAW 249, Berlin: de Gruyter, 1997, 118-24.

18 Blum, *Die Komposition der Vätergeschichte*, 88-89.

itself should be seen in the historical context of the temple at Bethel in the Northern Kingdom some time between its institution by Jeroboam and its destruction by Josiah. The verses thus transform the story into an etiological justification for the setting up of the Bethel cult by the Northern monarchy.

Finally, within the promise made by YHWH (vv. 13ab-15), v. 15 belongs to the same redactorial layer as Gen. 31:3 and 32:10-13 where Jacob recalls the promise.[19] He sees them as part of a wider Deuteronomic redaction which goes beyond the patriarchal narratives and which shifts the emphasis from the particular place of Bethel to the promised land in general. Regarding v. 13aβ-14, Blum considers these to be presupposed by v. 15 (hence the summary phrase 'what I have promised you'), and to be part of a pre-Deuteronomic story of the patriarchs.[20]

Overall Blum's approach is a clear attack on the documentary hypothesis. In particular he has rejected the criterion of which divine term is used. He is also cautious in his treatment of the earliest stages of the passage even though he sees this as one of the oldest passages in the Jacob narrative.

Significantly, however, he never really considers the theological dimension of the passage, not even in the religio-historical sense of Gunkel, preferring instead a national-political model.

Although Van Seters' work is often considered to be a logical development of the source critical approach, his treatment of the Bethel passage leans heavily on Blum.[21] In general terms, he agrees with Blum in finding a basic unit to which additions were made. The content of this early cult etiology is different for Van Seters only because he excludes two references to YHWH: v. 13aα - because of the unclear meaning of the preposition and because he regards it as doubtful that YHWH would appear without speaking (something unique within the Old Testament, he claims)[22] - and v. 16a, since Jacob would not have been able to identify the numinous without the deity making his identity quite clear.[23]

Unlike Blum, Van Seters considers all additions to have come from the

---

19 Blum, *Die Komposition der Vätergeschichte*, 152-64

20 Blum, *Die Komposition der Vätergeschichte*, 163.

21 Van Seters, *Prologue to History*.

22 Van Seters, *Prologue to History*, 291. Of course, in the final form, YHWH does speak, but not in the basic form identified by Blum and adapted by Van Seters. This, of course, begs the question as to whether an original unit might have contained some message.

23 Van Seters draws on Ex. 3 as an example of the deity making clear his identity after a numinous experience. One could also draw on the Peniel experience (32:10ff) as an instance where Jacob cannot know the identity of the entity he has encountered without it disclosing its name. If Van Seters is correct here, he has merely shown that Blum's reconstruction of the earliest form does not quite work.

same source - the Yahwist who incorporates the Bethel story into a much wider narrative. Thus unlike all critics discussed above, he does not consider the promise and the vow to be incongruous, arguing instead that the vow is closely related to the divine appearance and promise. He also rejects the traditio-historical model of Blum which attempts to see different layers within promise texts.

When it comes to determining a setting for this Yahwistic work, Van Seters agrees with Blum in seeing evidence of a Deuteronomistic hand, and also sees the work as fitting into an exilic context. Thus for instance, he sees the vow as 'the paradigm of the individual Israelite faced with the crisis of exile'.[24] The tithe and promised house of God correspond to the exilic community's commitment to rebuild the Jerusalem temple - the fact that the tithe has no relevance within the story itself means that its inclusion is due to some external historical reference. Finally, the motif of divine presence until the return from Mesopotamia fits into the context of anticipating return from Babylonian exile, and is also a 'democratisation' of the assurance of assistance ('Beistandsformel'), whose original setting was the assurance given to a king going to war and being promised success.[25]

This will be considered in due course, although it needs to be noted that Van Seters does not really deal with the obvious objection that Bethel with its associations with the Northern Kingdom and the cult of Jeroboam, would be problematic to any Deuteronomic writer.

In a more recent study Wahl goes further than Van Seters in arguing for a later origin of the Bethel story.[26] In his quest for a historical basis for the traditions of Jacob, he examines the religious motifs found in this passage and rejects the common view that they show pre-Israelite origins. Instead, he argues that in the spectrum of the development of religious thought in the Hebrew Bible, they have greatest affinity with exilic or post-exilic traditions. In particular, the idea of God being in heaven, with angels going

---

24 Van Seters, *Prologue to History*, 300. Likewise, Wyatt, N., 'Where did Jacob dream his dream?', *SJOT* 2 (1990), 55: 'This is the vow of every exiled Jew'. Wyatt goes further than Van Seters in seeing the whole story composed in exile. Where Van Seter's and Wyatt's conclusions are weak is that they fail to see how the vow relates above all else to the situation (and perhaps character) of Jacob. Instead they give a methodological priority to finding a historical setting ('Sitz im Leben') over and against the more obvious and secure literary setting ('Sitz im Text'). This is also pertinent to the supposed context for the motif of divine presence.

25 Thus Van Seters compares Jacob's flight from Esau with David's flight from Saul, the former being a more developed form of the motif found in the latter.

26 Wahl, H. M., *Die Jakobserzählungen: Studien zu ihrer mündlichen Überlieferung, Verschriftung und Historizität*, Berlin; New York: de Gruyter, 1997, 267-78.

between heaven and earth, points to a transcendent view of God, where 'bridges' and 'mediators' are needed between the two worlds.[27] This presupposes the view stated in Ecclesiastes that 'God is in heaven, and you upon earth'.[28] The reference to Jacob calling the place 'Bethel' (v. 19a) is in itself no hint of an older tradition but is part of the creation of a writer wishing to link the patriarch Jacob with the place of Bethel, thus rehabilitating the status of this shrine.

One further study from the traditio-historical perspective that stands out is that of de Pury.[29] Like Blum (and indeed before Blum), de Pury considers the Bethel incident to be a key building block to the Jacob story. However, unlike Blum, de Pury defends a division of sources, but more importantly, he is almost alone in arguing for the primacy of the whole story, or 'geste' of Jacob, over against individual units.[30] This attack on the consensus, stemming from Gunkel, regarding the primacy of the small unit needs taking more seriously than it has been, and is based on a questioning of many of the presuppositions behind how Old Testament scholars have imagined oral tradition to have operated.

With regard to the elements of the Bethel episode, de Pury makes the point that, from the outset, any storyteller would only have been able to evoke interest in such a story if the hero - and indeed the place - were already known to the audience - thus both motifs of place and person are needed for the story to have any dynamic (contra Westermann and Fohrer).[31] Likewise such a context would also have required some concrete outcome, such as the promises and vow which we now find. To take such elements away in the hope of finding an original form is to leave a story hardly worth telling![32]

Regarding the promise and the vow themselves, de Pury thus starts from the presupposition that if neither of these were present in the original episode, then some other consequence would need to have existed for

---

27   Wahl, *Die Jakobserzählungen*, 276.
28   Ecc. 5:2.
29   de Pury, *Promesse Divine*.
30   de Pury, *Promesse Divine*, vol. 2, 501. Here he is relying on the work carried out, for instance, by Lord, A. B., *The Singer of Tales*, Cambridge, Massachusetts: Harvard University Press, 1960. De Pury also finds support from Couffignal, R. ('Le songe de Jacob: Approches nouvelles de Genèse 28, 10-22', *Bib* 58 1977, 342-60) who uses Propp's framework of the folktale to find an essential integrity to the Jacob story as a whole.
31   'L'on observera notamment que le récit ne prend un sens que dans la mesure où il se rattache à un héros connu par ailleurs. Aucun *hieros logos* ne met en scène un personnage inconnu ou anonyme,' de Pury, *Promesse Divine*, vol. 2, 367.
32   Similarly, Wynn-Williams, *The State of the Pentateuch*, 118.

Jacob. Furthermore, de Pury dismisses the commonly held assumption that a passage cannot have originally contained both an interest in a special place and a promise. When he comes to look at the promises themselves, whilst admitting that they show signs of development, de Pury nevertheless claims to find elements which would correspond to an original story. In particular, given Jacob's expulsion from his homeland, both the promise of land for grazing his flocks and the promise of protection on the journey would be pertinent. Likewise, such concerns would be of relevance to listeners and narrators in a semi-nomadic context.[33]

Thus, for de Pury, the Bethel incident is part of an original, wider story of Jacob, itself an oral hero cycle ('geste patriarchale') reaching back to the semi-nomadic grouping which claimed to be the descendants of Jacob, and for whom Bethel was an important pilgrimage centre before starting their precarious journey into the steppes.

Literary Approach

Because Fokkelman sets himself so consistently against the historical-critical approach, and interprets the text as he goes along, one cannot really do him justice by treating him in an introduction.[34] However a few points can be distilled from his approach.

One is a methodological point he makes part way through: 'Historical research that starts from a literary text is not possible and thus not adequate until it has been determined to what degree the elements signified have been integrated into the structure.'[35] In other words, the meaning or significance of a word or object is determined first and foremost by its role in the structure. Thus Fokkelman implicitly rejects the approach of Gunkel and others who try to understand the meaning of symbols such as the ladder or the stone pillar by drawing on external material. It can be seen how this literary approach works out:
- *the structure of the dream* - the repetition of the particle הנה ('behold') takes us from the perspective of the narrator to that of Jacob.[36] The order of the three parts of his dream reflects the order in which he experiences things. Thus the possibility of different sources or of doublets does not come into the reckoning. Likewise the transition from amazement to fear

---

33 de Pury, *Promesse Divine*, vol. 1, 173-185.
34 'I shall arrange my results...by working unilinearly, parallel to the reading-process proper: accompanied by the reader I intend to follow the text from front to back, listening to its words and style patiently and closely,' *Narrative Art in Genesis*, 46.
35 Fokkelman, *Narrative Art*, 70.
36 See below, p. 45.

corresponds to the psychological experience of gradually coming aware
as one wakes up.

• *the 'place'* - Fokkelman plays down any sense of the place having an
inherently numinous quality, since, for him, the narrative context makes
it clear that this anonymous place only becomes significant after the
action of God. In this case, one might question how much the form really
conveys this idea, and how much he reflects an Enlightenment Protestant
perspective.

• *the ladder* - instead of drawing on Ancient Near Eastern material,
Fokkelman makes a contrast with the tower of Babel:

> Opposed to the various human initiatives of primeval history in general
> comes, from Gen. 12 onwards, God's initiative...The patriarch of Israel
> now beholds how God himself provides a connection: heaven and earth are
> now really connected, but not from below! For this ladder has been let
> down from heaven.[37]

• *the stone* - again, meaning is determined not by religio-historical
comparison but from the context. As the place, the stone itself is
indefinite, insignificant, with 'minimum personality'. Through the
anointing, and more importantly through God's revelation, it is given 'a
maximum individuality and personality as a milestone in the history of
salvation'.[38] Thus there is no consideration of Canaanite ideas influencing
the thought of the passage.[39]

As well as exploring these motifs in their context, Fokkelman considers the
structure of the passage. In several places he finds chiasms, but most
significantly in the overall structure.

Conclusion

It is only in looking at the passage that some of the ideas expressed above
can really be tested. Nevertheless a few comments can be made at this stage.

Fokkelman has reminded us of the primary unit of the final text. He is
right in starting with the text as it is, and in seeking to understand the
elements of the text in their literary context before setting up other

---

37   Fokkelman, *Narrative Art*, 53 (footnote).
38   Fokkelman, *Narrative Art*, 67.
39   Similarly, de Pury (*Promesse Divine*, vol. 2, 422ff) plays down the idea of the stone
having any sort of numinous quality. He argues that the stone is anointed by Jacob to
function as a witness to the divine promise and to his vow.

hypothetical contexts. Thus for instance, we should not start from the assumption that there are certain doublets which lead us automatically to divide the text into sources. This for instance is a problem with Fohrer and Blum, who first identify what they see as the basic unity, and then look at the literary structure of this.

In response to the source critical treatment of the passage, the main problem is that the E texts are fundamental to the passage, so much so that the promise texts - which by all standard criteria are seen as J texts - would seem to be more secondary. Thus 'E' constitutes the framework, and it is difficult to see the other verses coming from an independent, older source. Whereas Gunkel does not consider this problem, Barth-Steck have to resort to the reconstruction of a hypothetical original form of the Bethel story to reach a conclusion that best fits the documentary hypothesis.

With Fohrer also, fundamental questions need to be asked about the alleged criteria for source division. Even if these criteria point to unevenness in the text, we cannot assume that this unevenness did not exist at an oral level. Especially in the light of the work of Fokkelman and Blum in finding substantial unity in the text, each criterion will have evaluated in its context, as part of a careful reading of the passage. But already, a few notes of caution can be voiced: the criterion of the divine name has rightly come under criticism,[40] and in a passage where divine revelation is central, we must consider how each term for God might contribute to the theme, and so whether there is some deliberate variation, or at least whether the variation reflects something more than source. The question of how Bethel is conceived to be 'God's house', or how the place or stone is thought to have some special quality again are central to the passage, and if we decide that the passage as a whole gives a less than straightforward conception of these issues we should not jump to the conclusion that there must be different sources. In particular there is a tendency to underestimate the capacity of ancient writers to deal with complex ideas or paradox. This comment also appertains to the somewhat arrogant assumption of Gunkel (expressed less forthrightly by others) that for the 'pious' to make an oath on the condition of the fulfilment of a promise given by God would be unthinkable - how can we know what is unthinkable if not from the text itself? Furthermore, how can we assume that the narrator intends the reader to consider Jacob as a paradigm for religious faith, without considering

---

40   See Rendtorff, R., 'Jakob in Bethel: Beobachtungen zum Aufbau und zur Quellenfrage in Gen 28, 10-22.' *ZAW* 94, 1982, 515-6.

other more subtle intentions?[41]

On the other hand, we should be prepared to consider the possibility that in order to express the complexity of the above theological ideas, the writer(s) drew on traditional material - whether stories, characters or motifs. In particular, Fokkelman does no justice to the seeming archaic elements of the text identified by Gunkel and others. The passage does seem to contain motifs that would not fit easily into Israelite religion as depicted elsewhere, and surely this is an invitation to consider the relation of Israel's faith to the religious practice of Jacob here. Motifs - whether religious or not - should be understood from their literary context, but surely also from a wider context. This obviously touches on the complex debate about meaning and text, but it would seem to be appropriate to the passage itself, with its archaic features, to seek to penetrate behind the text to understand the dynamics of the text as it is. In particular, Fokkelman's interpretation of how the place and objects are considered to be significant seems to rely heavily on a view of matter which would deny an inherent quality of certain places or objects, until they have been invested with some specific meaning or memorial. We need to question how he comes to this view.

Thus some consideration of historical development need not be ruled inappropriate. Among form critics, there seems to be some consensus that the text contains pre- or non-Israelite motifs. In particular, this interest seems to be clustered around the place of Bethel. First of all, we should give some consideration to the name Bethel itself, containing the Canaanite epithet El - whether the head of the Canaanite pantheon or a local 'el', numen. Linked to this are the various motifs - the vision of the ladder, the idea of a place as the house of God, the anointing of a stone - which seem to sit a little uneasily with Israelite religion. Further, we should take into account the 'official' view of the cult of Bethel in the divided monarchy. By itself, this does not point definitively to a specific Canaanite Sitz im Leben since much depends upon wider reconstructions and assumptions, but pre- or non-Israelite provenance seems likely.[42]

We should also recognize that Jacob is clearly identified with Bethel, not just here but in chapter 35 and Hosea 12, and that in all probability the link goes deeper than the final narrative (so, de Pury). De Pury is correct in

---

41 So Cartledge, T. W., *Vows in the Hebrew Bible and the Ancient Near East*, Sheffield: JSOT Supp. 147 1992, 166-75, who argues that the vow adds to the picture of Jacob as conniving and distrustful, turning divine promises into obligations.

42 See also Vawter, *On Genesis*, 311-7, who tries to relate elements in the passage to a wider reconstruction of the development of patriarchal religion and to the standing of Bethel in Israelite religion.

pointing out that the dynamic of the passage comes from this combination of person and place. It is certainly difficult to imagine how this story, stripped of any reference to a known hero such as Jacob, or of any context for his arrival at this place, or of any consequences following this appearance, could really have much to say. Here we run into a question which often seems to be ignored of what constitutes a self-standing narrative. But in response to de Pury, it could be argued that a narrative could presuppose a wider context whilst having a certain independence, with the main character of the story and aspects of his life commonly understood from a body of tradition.

Regarding the presence of the divine name in this passage, this would have been introduced at some stage of the development of the story, and contents of the promise and the journey motif would have been developed as the passage became part of a wider narrative, involving Jacob's life, and the wider patriarchal story with its specific patriarchal promises.

Regarding views about the late date of the passage, it seems highly unnecessary and unlikely to ascribe so much of the narrative to the exilic period. Evidence drawn up by Van Seters, and to a lesser extent Blum, for Deuteronomic influence is not only scarce, but even contradicted by the positive stance towards Bethel and to cultic practices carried out there. It could be that some phrases show some Deuteronomic influence, but this depends on the wider issue of Deuteronomic influence in Genesis, especially in the promise texts, and on the distinction between immediate dependency and a general affinity to be expected in a common canon of literature.

By contrast, Wahl does not point to Deuteronomic influence, but bases his argument on an evolutionary view of the development of religious ideas. Thus, this passage shows evidence of a 'developed' view of the transcendence of God. Nevertheless, criticisms made regarding Van Seters also relate to Wahl, in that no reason is offered as to why an exilic or post-exilic writer should wish to promote the religious centre of Bethel by associating it with Jacob.[43] More widely, there seems to be no other trend within the later writings of the Hebrew Bible towards a positive view of Bethel, but rather a centralization towards the Temple at Jerusalem.

Thus there is some justification for the view that this passage shows evidence of a long prehistory, possibly reaching back to Canaanite

---

43 Wahl makes no mention of the identification of Jacob with Bethel in Hosea. Instead, he seems to argue that this identification is invented by the later author: 'The author...writing after the destruction of Bethel, now allows Jacob to discover this place "renown, since the time of Abraham" ' (own translation), *Die Jakobserzählungen*, 277.

influences, but also showing evidence of a 'Yahwistic' reworking, though with little attempt to 'reform' practices which might be frowned upon by later 'orthodoxy'. However it is difficult to be specific, especially as so much depends upon how one sees the early history of Israel. Some link with Northern Israel must be considered possible, though not necessarily with the period of the divided monarchy, and there is certainly no concrete evidence to link the passage with the cult instituted by Jeroboam (contra Blum).[44] However caution is also needed in how the terms 'Canaanite' and 'patriarchal' are used, especially regarding the vexing question of how 'patriarchal religion' ever existed as a distinct entity, and what its relationship to 'Canaanite' religion or Yahwistic religion might have been.

Likewise, as already stated, caution is needed in identifying specific theological concepts with different stages of religious development. It might be possible to comment on the likely setting of certain religious practices, but regarding concepts behind such practices more caution is needed, especially against a tendency to regard some views as 'primitive' and others as more 'developed'. To make such judgements is to underestimate the place of metaphor or the capacity of other cultures for complex theological thought.

A Reading of 28:10-22

The passage can be divided into five sections.

A: vv. 10-11 - This introduces the episode.
B: vv. 12-13aα - The vision of Jacob.
C: vv. 13aβ-15 - The words of YHWH to Jacob.
A further division can be made at the beginning of v. 15, since before that, the promises made go beyond the life of Jacob, whereas the promise of v. 15 is more immediate.

---

44 Despite the importance of the place of Bethel and the link with the important personage of Jacob, there is nothing in the passage to relate to the particulars of the cult instituted by Jeroboam, nor any sense of anticipating in the promise or oath anything outside of a general 'Israelite' perspective. There is not even any specific mention of sacrifice - either by Jacob or later generations. The promise to tithe could relate to any period or circumstance.

Regarding any links between the tradition of Jacob at Bethel and the Jeroboam cult, it could just as easily be argued that Jeroboam gave backing to the Bethel cult (whether it had fallen into disuse or not) because it already had the prestige of being connected with the figure of Jacob.

D: vv. 16-17 - Jacob's immediate reaction.

E: vv. 18-22 - Jacob's reaction in the light of day.

Each section is introduced by a verb indicating the new stage (literally: 'and he left' - ויצא, 'and he dreamed' - ויחלם, 'and he said' - ויאמר, 'and he woke' - וייקץ, 'and he rose' - וישכם).

If we consider sections B-E to be the main substance of the passage, we can see a certain correspondence between different sections: C and E, with C containing the promise of God, giving rise to E with the promise of Jacob; also B and D, with the experience of and reaction to the numinous.

Exegesis

A: vv. 10-11: (ויצא - 'he left') - Journey and Arrival

The first part (v. 10) places what is to come into the wider context of Jacob's journey, reminding the reader of what has provoked the journey. The name Haran refers the reader back to Rebekah's urging to flee there (27:43), underlining the fact that Jacob is on the run from his brother.[45] Beersheba is a name with strong patriarchal associations, as the place where Abraham and Isaac often stayed (22:19, 26:23, 33). It is also associated with security (twice being the scene of a treaty with Abimelech - 21:31, 26:26ff), divine assurance (26:24), and patriarchal worship (21:33, 26:25, also 46:1, completing the pattern of the three patriarchs). Clearly this place is as near to anywhere that Jacob might call 'home' (particularly with the ownership of the well - 26:33), and is also associated with the presence and worship of God. Thus the reminder that Jacob is leaving this place, emphasizes the sense of absence he is to feel - from place, from family and from God.

The opening v. 11 is highly suggestive. The verb 'came to' (פגע) suggests the chance arrival at the place.[46] The noun 'place' (מקום) likewise suggests the anonymity and chance arrival at this place. However the definite article suggests that this is not just any place:[47] as Westermann notes, the definite article draws attention to the word and hints at a

---

45 Thus bypassing the intervening verses.

46 See also below, p. 182, relating to 32:2 (MT).

47 Translated in NRSV as 'a certain place'. More literally: 'he came to *the* place.' A similar use of the definite article is found at Ex 3:2 (הסנה - '*the* burning bush'). In both cases, the article marks the object or place as significant because of some divine presence. In that passage, the noun is repeated in a similar way to the repetition of מקום here.

Gunkel (*Genesis*, 309) also points to Gen 12:6 as a similar use of the definite article with מקום.

secondary meaning of the word as 'holy place'.[48] This seems a better
account for the combination of anonymity and definiteness here, than does
Fokkelman's claim that the place has no inherent significance until God's
appearance. The emphasis on the place is also drawn out by the repetition
of the word (v. 11b). Likewise the stones which Jacob chooses may seem
random, but they are stones 'of the place'. Again the impression is not so
much that these stones are 'nothings' but that they are suggestive of
something to come.

Another element contributing to the sense of coincidence is that Jacob has
only stopped here because this happens to be where the sun was falling.
Now, as noted ominously by Fokkelman, the sun will not rise again for
Jacob until after the Peniel experience (32:32 ET).[49]

Thus on his way from a place of familiarity and assurance to a place of
uncertainty, Jacob stumbles upon this place. But the use of the definite
article and repetition hint that this will not be just any place.

v. 10 both links this episode to the wider narrative (and so may be
editorial) but also provides a suggestive contrast and preparation to v. 11
and the new place Jacob discovers.

B: vv. 12-13aα: (ויחלם) - the Dream

From the perspective of Jacob, there is no expectation of any extraordinary
dream.[50]

The *structure* of the dream is clear - the verb 'dream' is followed by three
clauses with the different elements introduced by the same word (...והנה -
literally 'and behold'). Fokkelman also notes how this pattern moves the
reader from the perspective of a detached, omniscient narrator to the
perspective of Jacob.[51]

Furthermore the *content* of the dream is progressive: at first, Jacob sees
the ladder, an inanimate object; then, angels of God; and as the culmination,

---

48   Westermann, *Genesis: 12-36*, 454.

49   Fokkelman, *Narrative Art*, 49.

50   Thus it is different from the usual form of incubation (see Ottoson - *Theological
Dictionary of the Old Testament*, vol. 4, 421-32; also Sarna, N. M., *Genesis*, JPS Torah
Commentary, Philadelphia: Jewish Publication Society, 1989). T. H. McAlpine (*Sleep,
Divine and Human, in the Old Testament*, Sheffield: JSOT Supp 38, 1987, 158-61) refers
to similarities with the Ancient Near Eastern idea of incubation, but points out that it is very
rare in the Old Testament, perhaps because of a concern to avoid the idea of God being
manipulated.

51   Fokkelman, *Narrative Art*, 51: 'There is no longer a narrator who looks back to a past;
there is only the present as Jacob experiences it - there, a ladder! oh, angels! and look, the
Lord himself!'

YHWH himself. The clear structure supporting the progressive content seems to indicate anything but the presence of doublets and, rather than contradicting each other, the three elements take the reader (as well as Jacob) further towards his direct and awesome experience with God.[52]

The imagery of the first part is highly suggestive of Ancient Near Eastern ideas, as most commentators acknowledge. This may reflect the origins of this passage and is also an implicit acknowledgement of the 'non-Israelite' aspects of the religion of the patriarchs.[53] The picture of the ladder or ramp stretching from heaven to earth is highly suggestive, giving rise to various interpretations, but in the text it is best seen as a multivalent sign, whose function is to suggest and cause to stop and wonder, rather than to be decoded precisely, since Jacob's attention is quickly drawn onwards.[54]

---

52   For an extended interpretation of this progression, see Scherman and Zlotowitz, *Bereishis*, vol 4, 1182ff. The ladder indicates the ability to rise to an understanding of God by studying creation and through philosophical enquiry. Jacob was not satisfied with such a limited knowledge of God and so God tested him with a second level of revelation, that of the angels representing a deeper spirituality. This still failed to satisfy Jacob and so he reached a true vision of God himself.

53   A comparative approach is thus appropriate here. By contrast, Fokkelman's note (*Narrative Art*, 53) which sees Jacob's ladder against the background of all of Genesis, with a specific parallel to the tower of Babel, whilst not totally inappropriate in a wider canonical perspective, probably goes further than the passage allows, especially as he cannot identify any explicit links in vocabulary.

54   The image of a ladder would seem to suggest a link between heaven and earth -e.g. Delitzsch: 'The ladder is an image of the invisible, but actual and unceasing connection in which God, by the ministry of His angels, stands with the earth,' (*A New Commentary on Genesis*, 163).

Griffiths, J. G. ('The Celestial Ladder and the Gate of Heaven (Genesis xxviii 12 and 17), *ExpTim* 76 (1964-5), 229-30) sees influence from the Egyptian pyramid texts -see also Westermann (*Genesis 12-36*, 454). Millard, A. R., ('The Celestial Ladder and the Gate of Heaven' (Genesis xxviii 12, 17), *ExpTim* 78 (1966-7), 86-7) prefers Babylonian influence - also von Rad (*Genesis*, 284), seeing the word סלם (itself a hapax legomenon) as derived from Akkadian for stairway, and so the image conveyed is of a stone ramp. The particular parallel is the Babylonian Temple where a ramp connected the uppermost chamber (symbolic of the deity's heavenly dwelling place) with the temple, the place where the deity appears, particularly in the cult.

However, the link need not be taken too far (Millard), but can be seen as reflecting a more general conception of communication between heaven and earth, which would have been quite conceivable in Canaanite culture. Certainly, Wyatt ('Where did Jacob dream his dream?') seems to take the parallel with the Babylonian stairway too literally in seeing the vision of Jacob composed during the exile, where the dreamer is confusing Babylon and Jerusalem.

In his study Houtman, C. ('What Did Jacob see in His Dream at Bethel? Some Remarks on Genesis xxviii 10-22', *VT* 27 (1977), 337-51) sees the word סלם referring to the slope of the mountain of Bethel, where Jacob was asleep. He also comments on the fact that the

Above all, it points beyond itself to the appearance of YHWH and to his words. In this way, it has a similar function to the burning bush described in Exodus 3.

Nevertheless, the imagery adds to the impression that this place is significant, especially that it is conceived in some sense as a meeting of heaven and earth, a place where the divine communicates with the human. This is in spite of outer appearances in the light of day.

The second image of the angels leads naturally from the first. There is not really any suggestion that these angels are meant to be some accompanying presence with Jacob, rather their presence is more associated with this specific place.[55]

The final clause mentions YHWH explicitly. This occurrence of the divine name after the general term for God (Elohim) has led to a division along source critical lines. However this misses the point, since the use of the divine name here creates a climactic effect which the more general term would not, since a contrast with the angels 'of God' is now formed: now Jacob sees not merely a divine messenger, but YHWH himself! This daring depiction takes the reader by surprise, especially as YHWH is seen standing. It could be further argued that if this story originally told of the appearance not of YHWH but of El, then the use of the divine name here is a bold move to claim this story for the God of Israel with no room for ambiguity.[56] Given the non-Israelite imagery noted above, this need would have been strongly felt.

---

ladder stretches from heaven to earth, showing that the initiative in this communication rests with the divine.

On another level of interpretation, Couffignal, R. ('Le songe de Jacob: Approches nouvelles de Genèse 28, 10-22.' *Bib* 58 (1977), 342-60), sees Jacob's dream as a variant of Freud's interpretation of the Oedipal myth, where the ladder is a phallic symbol, and Jacob is dreaming of the union of his parents. The consequent erection of a stone and pouring of oil represents his symbolic incest, and the vow marks a reconciliation with the Father figure. For Couffignal, this is an example of how religion sublimates primal desire.

55   For a different view: Jacob, B. (*Das erste Buch der Tora*, New York: Katz Publishing House (reprinted from 1934), 579-80), who sees the ascending angels as those angels of Jacob's home country and the descending angels coming to accompany Jacob on his journey. (Also Rashi, in Rosenbaum and Silbermann eds, *Pentateuch*, 132.) They thus symbolize God's continued protection of Jacob. This is part of a wider denial of a comparative approach to this passage, preferring to draw its meaning solely from the Torah.

56   So Wenham, 'The Religion of the Patriarchs', in Millard, A. R. and Wiseman, D. J. eds, *Essays on Patriarchal Narratives*, Leicester: IVP, 1980, 181, supported by Moberly, R.W.L., *The Old Testament of the Old Testament*, Philadelphia: Augsburg-Fortress, 1992, 72-3.

Critical commentators are generally so keen to note the 'discrepancy' in the use of the divine name, that they overlook what would be striking to any later Israelite: Jacob has seen God, admittedly in a dream, but nevertheless clearly, and...he has lived.[57] In addition, the fact that Jacob is granted a vision of YHWH, highlights how privileged he is, especially after his deception of his father and brother.[58]

Regarding the ambiguity of the preposition עליו - whether before/above/beside it/him - there is little to add to the range of opinion, although given the sense of progression already mentioned, to now state that YHWH was standing by Jacob rather than at the top of the ladder would be something of an anticlimax and make the ladder superfluous.[59]

C: vv. 13aβ-15: (ויאמר) - the Divine Speech

In terms of content, the speech can be divided at the end of v. 14. Formally, this is confirmed again by the particle והנה ('and behold').

vv. 13aβ-14: The first part contains stereo-typical elements common to the patriarchal story: the self-introduction, and the promise of land, posterity, and blessing.

The promise begins with a self-introductory formula. The significance is not just in what is said, but also that here, for the first time, God speaks to Jacob. So far, Jacob's experience with God has been through his parents, but now God speaks to him directly.[60] It is surprising that there is no hint of reproach for what has happened, but neither is there any mention or hint of the blessing (or birthright).[61] Nevertheless, we can assume that this dream is meant as an assurance to Jacob (as the words will show) and as a confirmation of the blessing he has received, with all that this means in terms of the patriarchal blessing first given to Abraham. Any doubts about whether Jacob has really inherited the Abrahamic promises are now dispelled.

The divine name is this time contained in the speech. Apart from any historical-critical suggestions, its use here again affirms the identity of the

---

57 This theme is more explicit in the Peniel incident - see below, pp. 86-7. In both cases, a parallel and a contrast can be drawn to Ex. 3 where Moses is told to cover his face because he is standing on holy ground.

58 cf. Ps. 24:4-6, Matt. 5:8!

59 So Jacob, *Das erste Buch der Tora*, 580.

60 Wenham, *Genesis 16-50*, 226.

61 The lack of any explicit reference to what has happened prior to this episode is a possible hint of tension between the function of this passage in the wider story and its more independent traditio-historical origins.

God of the patriarchs with YHWH. The nearest parallel in the patriarchal narratives is the self-introduction to Abram (15:7); elsewhere the phrase El Shaddai is used (17:1, 35:11), or the phrase 'God of...' (26:24, also Ex. 3:6 completing the patriarchal line). Outside of Genesis, the most usual phrase is 'I am YHWH' (see especially the Holiness laws).

It is striking that Abraham and not Isaac is described as 'your father', though this probably reflects the importance of Abraham in the family line. (Note, for instance, the phrase 'the blessing of Abraham' - 28:4).

The promise of land is itself a common aspect of the patriarchal promises. Often the reference is specific to the location of the patriarch (12:7 - 'this land'; 13:15 - 'all the land which you see'); elsewhere it is more general (15:18; 17:8, 26:3, 35:12). Here, the land is specified as the land on which Jacob is lying, although we can take this place to be representative of the promised land as a whole.

What is implied at the end of this first part of the promise ('and your seed') is brought out with the promise of innumerable descendants. The particular image used (dust) is also found at 13:15. Elsewhere similes of stars or grains of sand convey the same idea (15:4, 22:16, 26:3). The directional terms combine the impression of numbers of descendants with geographical space.

The next clause is also found elsewhere. The meaning of the reflexive verb form seems literally to be that families 'will bless themselves by means of' Jacob and his family.[62] The same form is found at Gen. 12:3 and 18:8.[63] Fundamentally, as much in the patriarchal stories illustrates, the idea seems to be that other nations fare either well or badly depending on how they relate to the patriarchs.[64] Although finding outworkings in the lives of the patriarchs, these stories are probably best seen as illustrations of how it will be with Israel and her neighbours - see Ps. 72:17, also the story of Balaam and Balak (Nu. 24:9). Interestingly, this is the only part of the promise which relates back to the blessing of Isaac (27:29b), though there is

---

62   The Niphal verbal form. A precise definition of the meaning of this verbal form is difficult - see Waltke, B. K. and O'Connor, M., *An Introduction to Biblical Hebrew Syntax*, Wincona Lake, Indiana: Eisenbrauns, 1990, 378-391.

63   The Hithpael form is used at Gen. 22:18, 26:4 (preceding the story of Isaac and Abimelech), though there seems to be no significance in the difference of form.

64   For instance the story of Abraham in Egypt (coming soon after 12:3); Sodom and Gomorrah - both in Abraham's intercessory role and in the respective fates of Lot and the inhabitants (again this comes soon after 18:18); Abraham and Abimelech; Isaac and Abimelech (which contains the relevant promise - 26:4). As we shall note, the same motif is present in the Laban plot. Finally, the same idea may be reflected in the narrative of Joseph in Egypt.

probably no special significance in this. There, the image is linked to the idea of national strength (as in Nu. 24) and is easier to conceive against a national military or political background.

Although these promises look beyond the Jacob narrative, they are partially fulfilled in the life of Jacob: in the following episode with Laban, the number of Jacob's sons hints at the promise of many descendants, especially when set in the context of the fertility of his animal stock; also Laban himself admits to being blessed through Jacob's presence (30:27). Furthermore, the itinerary notes about Jacob after his return to the land of promise (ch. 35) give the impression of him making the land his own.

Even so, the scope of the promises here, and their similarity to the promises running through the patriarchal narrative into the book of Exodus, move from the immediate context to the wider. No doubt this promise for the distant future implies safety and blessing for the immediate future, but Jacob needs more immediate, tangible promises, and this is where the second part of the divine speech goes.

v. 15: The particle 'and behold' (והנה - v. 15) reconcentrates the attention of Jacob and the reader: if the previous promises seemed a bit distant, Jacob is now assured of YHWH's immediate presence with him. The language used to express God's presence and protection ('I am with you', 'I will keep you', 'I will not leave you') is common to the faith of Israel,[65] and so, no doubt, God's assurance to Jacob can be read as a paradigm for his protection of the believer/Israel, although it is not possible to trace the imagery of this verse to any particular setting or tradition, since the language is so widespread.[66] Within the Jacob narrative, the promise corresponds to 31:3.5 where God reaffirms his presence with Jacob once Jacob has to set out on a journey again, and where Jacob is able to confess to his wives that God has been with him during the difficult years with Laban.

Thus Jacob is assured that God's presence goes beyond the confines of the family home (Beersheba) or of the promised land (including Bethel) - God's presence might be specially tangible in some places, but for Jacob, as for Abraham and Isaac, God is identified chiefly by relationship rather than place. Nevertheless, God will bring Jacob back to this land. Thus in this promise relating more immediately to Jacob are the twin ideas of

---

65 e.g. Ex. 23:20, Nu. 6:24, Josh. 1:5, Is. 8:10, Ex. 3:12, Ps. 23:4, Ps. 121.
66 Contra Van Seters who sees it as reflecting the individual piety of the exilic community (*Prologue to History*, 302-6).

relationship and place - the relationship between God and Jacob involves place, but that relationship goes beyond place. No doubt this is something Israel was to learn in the exile but it is also part of the theological tension that sees the presence of God focused in a particular place (whether Temple, cult, people, Sinai, Zion) but not being limited there.

Regarding the relationship of the two parts of the speech to each other, they are clearly complementary, with one reaching more beyond Jacob's life (though there are also some signs of fulfilment in it), and the other more immediate to Jacob's concerns and being worked out in his life (although wider parallels can be seen in the story of Israel).

It is quite conceivable that the two parts reflect different stages of growth. Certainly the patriarchal promises stand out, and would only really relate to an already well established and wider plot involving the patriarchal story as a whole. It could of course be argued that any story can have elements pointing outside of itself, without having to conclude that they are secondary. However, the vocabulary of these promises is particularly distinctive within the passage and they bear a strong likeness to other promises in the patriarchal narratives. They would thus be added to any earlier form of the Bethel story, and as promise texts elsewhere, serve to unite the whole of the patriarchal narrative, as well as the early chapters of Exodus.[67]

The second part of the speech links the Bethel incident more specifically to the Jacob story as a whole, and so would stem from an earlier stage in the development of this passage in particular, and of the Jacob story more generally.

This distinction between the scope of the promises again contradicts the findings of traditional source criticism, which generally fails to do justice to the distinctiveness of the two parts of the divine speech, seeing them both as J texts.

D: vv. 16-17:(ויקץ - 'and he woke'): Jacob's First Reaction
Just as the account of the dream is structured to reflect how it was perceived by Jacob, so the different stages of his reaction are narrated as Jacob first wakes and realizes what has happened, then reacts to this realization, and finally, in the light of day, makes a more measured response. Thus there is no need to see vv. 16 and 17 as doublets.

---

67   In general agreement with the thesis of Rendtorff, *Das überlieferungsgeschichtliche Problem des Pentateuch*, ch. 2, though with a greater degree of caution in attempting to relate particular phrases, motifs or clauses to particular stages of the development.

The impression given by the context is that Jacob wakes suddenly, and that it is still night, since morning is only mentioned in v. 18. His first reaction clearly sees the place itself as having some quality, since he is surprised that he did not realize YHWH's presence before he fell asleep. The narrator reports this speech or thought without any theological comment, and we may assume by Jacob's later action that his own perception is accepted by the narrator. The repetition of the noun 'place' links back to the opening verses, just as the final description ('this is the gate of heaven') reminds us of the picture of the ladder stretching between earth and heaven.

The second stage of Jacob's reaction (...וַיִּרָא - 'and he was afraid') is the natural consequence of the first. As Jacob realizes the nature of the place, he shudders with fear in the darkness. He remembers the vision, although he has not yet taken stock of the words spoken to him. This would perhaps explain why Jacob is afraid, even though the vision and speech were meant to reassure him. For the moment we see the natural reaction of a mortal being to an experience of the numinous.[68]

The phrase 'house of God' anticipates the etymology to come. Given the etymological direction of these concluding verses, the reference to YHWH (v. 16a) might seem out of place. Wenham's suggestion that Israelite writers have replaced another name - here El - makes sense of this.[69] Clearly, the writer again wants to affirm that, despite aspects of the passage suggesting Canaanite and other Ancient Near Eastern ideas, it is YHWH who appeared to Jacob.

E: vv. 18-22: (וַיַּשְׁכֵּם - 'and he rose') - the Next Day: Jacob's Considered Reaction
vv. 18-19 pursue the thread of the previous section by bringing to a conclusion the etymological motif. Furthermore, just as the previous section picks up the motif of place from the opening of the episode, so in these verses, the word 'stone' and the phrase 'put under his head' are repeated.

The act of standing the stone upright and anointing it is to set it apart as a sacred symbol, in this case in recognition of Jacob's experience, although also in anticipation of his return. It is likely as well that by his emphasis on this particular stone - at first viewed just as one of several stones of 'the place' - Jacob sees it has having some sacred significance. How far one can

---

68   This does not of itself rule out any traditio-historical explanation for the change from assurance to fear.
69   See above, p. 46.

draw a distinction between the stone as a memorial or witness and the stone as having some inherent special quality is not clear. Certainly there is no attempt by the narrator to counter any possible misunderstanding. All this is very striking given the attitude found elsewhere in the Hebrew Bible, especially, although not exclusively, in the Deuteronomistic writings.[70] The most obvious explanation for this action in the narrative is the idea that in these earlier times, Israel's ancestors differed little in some of their customs from their Canaanite neighbours. Such an idea would hardly be invented, but would most likely reflect a long tradition.

Just as there is no attempt to expand upon the particular quality of the stone, so there is no exposition of what is meant by 'house of God' apart from Jacob's exclamation at v. 17. Given the emphasis on the word 'place' and the uneasy feeling that Jacob continued to have after waking, it would seem most natural to suppose that he saw the place as having some inherent quality that suggested God's presence. Again the author simply narrates.

vv. 20-22: An understanding of the final oath is clouded by the ambiguous structure of the sentence, since grammatically, the apodosis can begin either 'the Lord will be my God' (והיה יהוה לי לאלהים), or with the more concrete 'and this stone' (והאבן). Following most commentators it seems most likely that the former is correct, particularly as, at least formally, there is a change in subject from Elohim to YHWH.[71] Contra some objections, it

---

70   The vast majority of uses of the term מצבה ('pillar') are negative: either as proscribed or condemned or destroyed. Such instances are: Ex. 23:24, 34:13, Dt. 7:5, 12:3, 16:22, Lev. 26:1, 1 Ki. 14:23, 2 Ki. 3:2, 10:26.27, 17:10, 18:4, 23:14, 2 Chr. 14:3, 31:1, Jer. 43:13, Hos. 3:4, 10:1.2, Mic. 5:13. In all these cases it is associated with Canaanite worship, either directed at a Canaanite god or simply following Canaanite practices.

Elsewhere it is found at 2 Sam. 18:18, where its use seems to be neutral, Ex. 24:4, where Moses sets up twelve pillars at the covenant meal at Sinai, and in a prophecy (Is. 19:19), as a positive sign and witness to YHWH.

Apart from that, the word appears frequently in the Jacob story - at Bethel (28:18.22, 31:13, 35:14), but also to mark his final treaty with Laban (31:13.45.51.52), and to mark the place of Rachel's burial (35:20).

71   e.g. Spurrell, G. J., *Notes on the Hebrew text of the Book of Genesis*, Oxford: Clarendon, 1887, 228, Delitzsch, *A New Commentary on Genesis*, 166, Gunkel *Genesis*, 321, von Rad, *Genesis*, 286, Westermann, *Genesis: 12-36*, 459, Blum, *Die Komposition der Vätergeschichte*, 89-91, Waltke and O'Connor, *Biblical Hebrew Syntax*, 526-7, and especially Richter, W., 'Das Gelübde als theologische Rahmung der Jakobsüberlieferungen' *BZ* 11 (1967), 21ff. Fokkelman disagrees (*Narrative Art*, 75-6). Jacob (*Das erste Buch der Tora*, 584) treats the protasis as temporal rather than conditional ('When God is with me...').

is certainly not unheard of for Israel to choose allegiance to YHWH.[72]

The first clause of the condition corresponds to the beginning of those promises made by YHWH in the dream which are more directly orientated to Jacob's situation ('Know that I am with you...'). The second clause also corresponds to these promises, with the repetition of the verbs 'keep' and 'go'. The third clause is added by Jacob: the mention of bread and clothes betrays the very practical need in which Jacob finds himself, only daring to hope for these bare essentials. This concrete dependence could be said to reflect a piety in Israel which sees the need for divine provision even in these fundamental matters.[73] On the other hand, it also points to the desperation of this situation. Furthermore, it can very plausibly be seen as reflecting Jacob's blunt bargaining.[74] In the wider context we can also detect a hint of irony: both bread and clothing have already played a role for Jacob (25:34, also 27:17; and 27:15), and in both previous cases they were the means used by Jacob to carry out his deception; now as a result of that deception (and despite its apparent success), Jacob relies on God to provide these items - not for further deception but for mere survival.[75]

Like the first and second clauses, the fourth and final clause of the protasis refers back to the divine promise (v. 15aβ). In this case however the image is more relational as the reference in the promise to land becomes the family home, and the return is 'in peace', that is, with the threat of revenge and the reality of family disruption removed. This not only applies to the situation with Esau and Isaac, but it will also be pertinent to the

---

72   e.g. Dt. 30:19, Josh. 24, and other parallels in Dt. mentioned below. In his broad ranging study of the genre of the oath, Richter ('Das Gelübde als theologische Rahmung') finds that this type of oath is widespread in the popular religion of Israel. See especially 1 Sam. 1:11, 2 Sam. 15:8, Nu. 21:2.

Against this reading, see Fokkelman, *Narrative Art*, 75-6. It is strange that Fokkelman, who champions a reading of the narrative as a united whole, comments that any indication of a calculating Jacob (implied if v. 21b was the start of the main clause), finds no support in the rest of this passage. It does not occur to Fokkelman to link the action of Jacob here with his actions in other parts of the narrative. This atomistic approach is more reminiscent of the form-critical approach. By contrast, see Alter (*Genesis*, 150): 'Jacob, however, remains the suspicious bargainer - a 'wrestler' with words and conditions.' Also Cartledge, *Vows in the Hebrew Bible and the Ancient Near East*, 166-75.

73   cf. Lk. 11:3.

74   So Cartledge, *Vows in the Hebrew Bible and the Ancient Near East*, 168. Cartledge sees Jacob as expanding the promises made by God and forcing God's hand by making a vow to hold God to his word. Certainly this can be seen as an aspect of the complex motivation of Jacob.

75   Showing the extremely subtle art of the narrative, which through the simple mention of everyday items such as bread and clothing juxtaposes different episodes in Jacob's life.

relationship with Laban.

The actual promise relates to both general allegiance and specifically to the site of Bethel. On a narrative level, the first part, following the first revelation of YHWH to Jacob, depicts the latter's personal and free response.[76] Fokkelman also notes that v. 21b, stating in effect that YHWH will be the God of Jacob, brings to completion the earlier series of YHWH as God of Abraham and Isaac (v. 13).[77] But on another level, Jacob's promise looks to Israel's understanding of its relationship with God. The phrase 'will be my/your God' (אלהים לי/לך היה) is used in the Bible to express the idea of choice, very often explicitly linked with the covenant. In almost all cases the originator is YHWH who chooses his people,[78] although in Dt. 26:17, it is Israel who has declared YHWH to be their God, and in Dt. 29:12-13 there is a mutuality in the covenant. The writer is therefore using a phrase which draws a clear parallel to the covenant between YHWH and Israel, with Jacob acting as a type for later Israel, albeit with a characteristic emphasis on his own initiative.

This stereotypical language by itself would explain the use of the term YHWH (always used in such contexts). Furthermore the term adds to the strong insistence already discerned in the passage, that it is no other than YHWH who has appeared to Jacob at Bethel.

The second and third clauses of the apodosis clearly refer to the site at Bethel and are alluded to at 35:1ff. The switch to first person speech takes the reader once again (as in the description of the dream) to the perspective of Jacob, but it also ensures that the passage ends with a direct note of praise. The promise to tithe is a response to God's provision of food and clothing referred to earlier, and it thereby acknowledges that what Jacob has to give is already given to him by God. Even so the tithe is not specifically mentioned elsewhere in the Jacob narrative and does not have any particular function in this passage. It would seem therefore that its inclusion is meant

---

76   e.g. von Rad, *Genesis*, 286.

77   Fokkelman, *Narrative Art*, 76.

78   Gen. 17:7.8, Ex. 6:7, 29:45, Lev. 11:45, 22:33, 25:38, 26:12.45, Nu. 15:41. It can be seen that the conception is characteristic of the Priestly redaction/source. Other occurrences are 2 Sam. 7:24 (=Dtr?), 1 Chr. 17:22, Zec. 8:8. *BDB*, 44, also notes six other occurrences in Jeremiah and six in Ezekiel. In many cases, it is to be noted that the term is linked explicitly with the covenant.

Westermann (*Genesis: 12-36*, 459) sees a different setting for the phrase, drawing parallels with vows made at 2 Sam. 15:7-9 and Jud. 11:30ff. For him, the phrase calls to mind the cultic tradition within Israel of offering worship at a shrine. Both these passages describe the giving and fulfilling of a vow, but the terminology in these passages is very different, with a particular lack of the phrase אלהים ל היה ('will be my/your God').

to point the reader/listener to a later custom. Most immediately, some connection with tithing at Bethel cannot be ruled out. However in the wider context, there is no doubt that the reader would have found some hint of the Israelite system of tithing in general.

Just as the tithe hints at the religious life of later Israel, so also the phrase 'house of God' hints, even if not primarily or intentionally by an original writer, to the Temple at Jerusalem.[79] However, this aspect of the text should not obscure the place of Bethel itself in the Jacob story, which no doubt had a significance in Israel as well.[80]

Regarding any development behind vv. 18-22, the break at v. 20 may reflect a growth in the text. vv. 18-19, which bring to an end the etymological thread and pick up certain motifs which appeared in the opening verses of the passage, would seem to be a logical conclusion to any original Bethel story, which contains strongly Canaanite elements.

The final two verses point the story forward, although the conditions of Jacob's vow build on v. 15 (except the reference to bread and clothing).[81] Furthermore although there is no contradiction or doublet, the promise that the stone will in the future be the house of God, sits a little uneasily with Jacob's earlier exclamation that his place is the house of God, and with his naming of the place at this stage, although it could be that a cultic act simply reinforces what is already felt to be the case. Certainly it is not

---

79   The proper term for the Jerusalem temple (or any Israelite temple) is בית יהוה ('house of YHWH'). Given the use of the divine name elsewhere in the passage, we might have expected it here. However, the etiological interest of the passage here governs the use of the term Elohim.

On the association of this passage with Jerusalem, see also Schwartz, J., 'Jubilees, Bethel and the Temple of Jacob.' *HUCA* 56 (1985), 63-85.

80   It is of course true that Bethel seems to gain significance in the Bible with the cult set up by Jeroboam in competition to the Jerusalem Temple and Monarchy. However, there is every reason to suppose that Jeroboam was taking advantage of a shrine which was already well established (Judg. 20:18-28, 21:2-4, 1 Sam. 10:3). These references, which bear no element of condemnation, clearly predate the tendency in prophetic and Dtr. circles to condemn Bethel. It follows from this that the tradition of Jacob at Bethel, giving as it does implicit approval to the Bethel cult, would predate Jeroboam. This seems more consistent with the way Bethel is depicted in the rest of the Bible than is Blum's view that Jacob is used by Jeroboam to promote Bethel (see above, pp. 33-4).

81   The link between v. 15 and the oath is another argument against the source critical reconstruction of the passage, since according to those criteria, v. 15 is J whereas the oath is E. Of course, it is possible to reconcile this difficulty by arguing that the oath is a literary creation of E, based on the original form (best preserved by J) which contained a similarly worded promise.

blatant enough to call a doublet.[82]

As it is, the conclusion of vv. 21b-22, by moving from the present response of Jacob to one in the future, calls to mind for the reader later Israelite institutions and ideas - the covenant, the tithe, possibly Bethel as an established place of pilgrimage, and by extension, the Jerusalem Temple - the house of God par excellence.

Conclusion

Historical-Critical Summary

Negatively it has been argued that the documentary hypothesis does not work in relation to this passage, since a careful reading of the passage and study of the structure of different parts has cast doubt on the presence of genuine doublets. This relates particularly to the dream with its united structure and progressive content, and to the differing reaction of Jacob, with immediate and then more measured responses. This is not to rule out any development, but source criticism seems too crude an instrument for subtleties in the text. Furthermore, the study has found contextual reasons for the use of the divine name alongside the more general term Elohim.

Positively, whilst also holding to the principle that our point of departure is the final form of the text and that the end result is an understanding of the final form, I have tried to show that there is scope for a cautious historical approach to the text, particularly using some of the insights of tradition criticism. In the case of this passage, this study supports the widely held view that the passage is the result of a process of development. At the heart of the passage is the interest in Bethel, concluding with the etymology and elements of non-Israelite Canaanite religion. This would have told of the discovery of a holy place, in particular with the revelation through a dream and the appearance of El. In response the recipient, after the natural sense of fear, would have set up the stone pillar and named the place Beth-El. Thus the form of an etiology of a holy place is the starting-point. Regarding the identity of the discoverer, this may or may not have been Jacob, though there is certainly no reason a priori why it should not have been.

After this, the story would have been assimilated into Israelite culture,

---

82   Gunkel notes in passing (*Genesis*, 313) that according to the source critical approach this is the second etymology for Bethel in E. This again reveals a contradiction within an approach which uses inconsistencies to point to doublets and different sources, but at other times is unable to account for them.

possibly as Bethel became a Yahwistic place of worship and/or pilgrimage. The name YHWH would be introduced as part of this process, and if Jacob was not already the main character, this is where his name would be introduced. As the story becomes part of the Jacob story, and then of the wider Pentateuchal story, the promises in the dream are developed, though what lay behind them must remain unknown and we cannot be precise about how these developments happened. It would seem wrong to ascribe all 'Israelite' additions to the same stage since they are quite diverse in style and reference. Furthermore, we cannot make precise links with the Bethel cult at the time of Jeroboam, or any other time. Certainly the passage reflects a positive view of Bethel, but it has been suggested that this could stem from an earlier context before Bethel became contentious. Over and above this though are also aspects of the text which bring our attention to the wider themes of the patriarchal promises and Jacob's journeyings. As a result we are left not with a straightforward etiology, but with a patriarchal narrative of divine assurance and promise with strong etiological motifs.

This view stands in some contrast to that of de Pury who argues that the story of Bethel was always part of the wider Jacob story, although, as mentioned, the above reconstruction cannot rule out the place of Jacob or any content behind the existing form of the divine promises. To try to illustrate his argument, de Pury takes the example of the construction of a motor car.[83] He claims that critics such as Gunkel are not necessarily wrong in wanting to deconstruct the Jacob cycle in the same way that a car mechanic takes a car to pieces. The error is in how these separate parts are to be interpreted: in the case of a car - and, argues de Pury, of the Jacob narrative - the parts are not made autonomously and then subsequently assembled but are made from the beginning to be part of the whole.

Whilst this illustration has the merit of seeing the cycle as both united but with constituent parts, a more suitable illustration for our approach might be that of a cathedral.[84] Such a construction does not come about all at once but over a long period of time. Some elements are created specifically for their part in the building, others might be incorporated, and there are possibly the sacred relics over which the magnificent structure has come to be built. Nevertheless, de Pury presents a note of caution, and reminds us that no story is ever told in isolation but always presupposes a wider

---

83   de Pury, *Promesse Divine*, vol. 2, 515ff. It should of course be noted that by the Jacob cycle, de Pury is referring to an oral precurser to any written form.
84   Alter, R., *The World of Biblical Literature*, London: SPCK, 1992, 69.

context, even if there may be a relative autonomy.[85]

The conclusion offered here supposes that, as long as difficulties and provisionality are acknowledged, some historical work brings benefit. It may be argued that all historical-critical consideration should be laid aside as it obscures a real understanding of the final text. In this context, Fokkelman serves as a reminder of that possibility. Nevertheless I believe that an acknowledgement of the historical dimension has aided an understanding of the final text, in particular to some of the dynamics within it. This will be spelt out in relation to different themes, but in general terms, we have seen that behind the development has been a theological concern. Having some idea of the process of tradition does not obscure theological strands within the passage, but brings them to light, and the final canonical form can be seen as the natural fruit of this process. This is seen most clearly with the most obvious theme, that of God.

God

Given the concentration of divine terms and interest, it is perhaps surprising that many critics rightly see a dual interest in the passage in person and place, but in so doing neglect a most obvious third point, which is language about God. Instead, discussion of the divine is centred on the relation of this language to historical-critical issues or on how it impinges on the person of Jacob or the place of Bethel, or on the religio-historical interest in Canaanite traces in the passage.

God is clearly depicted in the passage: God is portrayed as a character, God appears, speaks, offers reassurance, promises, has a wider purpose of which Jacob is part, accompanies, protects, guides and claims to keep his word. Thus, as elsewhere in Hebrew narrative, God is portrayed in personal terms, with the term YHWH best seen not as a title or attribute but a name. Some aspects, such as God standing, are more obviously anthropomorphic. How we are to interpret these different aspects and attributes relates to the wider task of theology, suffice it to say that there is a given-ness about God and about the possibility of describing God in personal terms.[86]

However, a consideration of this passage in its wider context will sharpen our understanding of how it contributes to an understanding of God. Before the episode, apart from the oracle given to Rebekah before Jacob's birth,

---

85   One weakness in de Pury's argument is that, although he postulates an oral, epic narrative, he is not able to point to any evidence of it in the present text. Thus, it can only remain a hypothesis.

86   See Fohrer, *Exegese des Alten Testaments*, 213ff: 'Das Reden von Gott'.

there is little direct reference to God. Instead, Jacob - with the help of his mother - is left to work out his own destiny, and part of the tension of the previous chapter, as we shall see, is not just whether Jacob will succeed in his deception, but how he should act, if at all. Instead of a clear voice from God, there is the urging of his mother and the blessing of a father extracted through deception. Now at last, Jacob has his first direct experience of God. However, this experience does not last, and whereas we might be led to expect a clear divine lead and protection following the Bethel promises, Jacob will find himself once again caught up in a web of deception, thrown onto his own resources as before. Thus whereas God is often hidden, his voice silent and his purposes achieved through very 'worldly' and human factors, here, the opposite is true - Jacob actually sees God, he is spoken to directly, and God reassures Jacob that he will guide, provide, be with Jacob and fulfill his purposes. Finally, in response, Jacob addresses God directly for the first time (v. 22).

This passage therefore relates to the wider issue of the relationship between the presence and absence of God, and the human and the divine. Although much of Jacob's life suggests that human character and resources are determinative, this passage suggests that underneath all this, the divine plan is being worked out. Part of this dichotomy involves that of grace and sin: in the words of von Rad, 'the fleeing deceiver received such a word of grace'.[87] However, this is only part of a wider mystery of God working in the world: elsewhere von Rad writes how the plans of God 'remained concealed from all relevant persons' even in or through the break-up of a family.[88] In this passage, the veil over the mystery is lifted to reveal, if not the answers to why God's purpose is fulfilled in the way it is, then at least giving the assurance that God is ultimately in control. After the passage the veil is dropped again, except for specific instances or hints. To change the metaphor, the passage stands as a hermeneutical lens through which, with other key passages, we are to read the rest of the Jacob narrative.

Regarding terms used for God, there are clearly several references to the divine: the ladder and the angels of God. But these all point to God himself, and specifically YHWH. We have already noted Ancient Near Eastern ideas. But, we have also noted a strong Yahwistic stamp on the passage. Historically we have seen this tension as springing from the way the text has been adopted and shaped by Israel. This corresponds to the theological tension which both accepts the Bethel tradition (and more widely, the pre-

---

87   von Rad, *Genesis*, 287.
88   von Rad, *Genesis*, 280-1, regarding ch. 27.

Yahwistic patriarchal tradition) and qualifies it by seeing it in a new context.

This seems to be the best way to account for the use of the divine name in this passage. In particular, in v. 16 it would seem that YHWH has replaced El as the name of the deity. The reason behind the replacement would seem to be the concern to emphasize the identity of the patriarchal God with YHWH. Even if an original reference to El does not lie behind our present text, that concern is still a feature of the text. This same concern can also be discerned at v. 13aβ, and 21b which also reminds the reader of covenantal language. The name YHWH at v. 13aα qualifies the non-Israelite character of the vision, and in that position it marks a climax where Jacob sees first the ladder, then angels 'of God', then YHWH himself. Thus the divine name removes any room for theological misinterpretation.

It seems therefore that whereas the writers were prepared to depict Jacob carrying out religious acts that were later seen as unlawful, they were not prepared to allow the impression that Jacob was worshipping any other god than YHWH - even if, according to the wider narrative (Ex. 3:14 and 6:3) that name was not known to the patriarchs.[89] Furthermore, this observation - although not dependent on the historical-critical method - is clearest when we are prepared to accept the historical dimension of the text.[90]

Finally, Jacob was actually able to see YHWH. This forms a parallel to Peniel on the one hand, but also relates to the tradition reflected in Exodus

---

89   This assumes reading both texts in Exodus together as indicating that the name YHWH was hitherto unknown. For a thorough treatment of this issue: Moberly, *The Old Testament of the Old Testament*. Moberly bypasses the question of sources in Ex. 3-4, and argues that the text as it stands is consistent with Ex. 6, and that both passages witness to the view that the divine name was only revealed within the context of Mosaic Yahwism. Regarding the use of the divine name in Genesis, Moberly argues that writers were happy to merge their own perspective with that of patriarchal religion, tolerating what would be seen by later standards as an anachronism. Our reading of this passage supports the view that the name YHWH is introduced quite deliberately. In further support of Moberly, it has been observed that the use of the divine name is not the only way that the passage makes a connection between the patriarchal figure of Jacob and the faith of Israel.

For a critique of Moberly's view: Seitz, C. R., *Word Without End: The Old Testament as Abiding Theological Witness*, Grand Rapids, Michigan: William B. Eerdmans, 1998, 229-47. Seitz himself argues that in Exodus, it is only Moses who previously did not know the divine name. It is however questionable whether this reading, whilst doing justice to a turning-point in Moses' own life, does equal justice to the clear change in the relationship between God and his people that comes about with the Mosaic era. This is supported by the observations made below relating to the idea of holiness.

90   Thus Wenham, in his more historically orientated 'The Religion of the Patriarchs', makes this insight into the text, whereas it is passed over in his commentary.

that a person could not see God and live (Ex. 33:20), and this will be taken further in the next chapter.[91] With regard to this episode, another significant contrast with the book of Exodus is the lack of the language of holiness (קדשׁ). It is of course precarious to argue from silence, but in a passage containing such a strong sense of the numinous and the divine, such a use might have been expected. This is pointed out, for instance, by Westermann, who uses the terms *tremendum* and *fascinosum* in reference to this passage, leaning heavily on the work of Otto's famous thesis on holiness.[92] For Westermann the term 'holy' is only absent because the word itself could only be used after a further development of these ideas. However, a more antithetical reason has been suggested by Moberly who points to the absence of holiness in the patriarchal narratives as a whole and sets up a contrast with the revelation of God as YHWH to Moses where the term is concentrated.[93] Thus a point of contrast can be made between this episode and Exodus 3 since in the latter, the word 'holy' is used for the first time in the story of Israel beginning with the patriarchs. The reason for its absence until then, argues Moberly, is that the term is 'integrally related to the particularity of Israel's relationship with YHWH'.[94] Thus, although the passage contains the quality of the numinous, and the presence of God, the idea of the holy as expressed by the term קדשׁ as used in the Mosaic tradition is not, and cannot be, found, because it is one of those features absent from the patriarchal narratives.

Place (Bethel)

It has been observed in the exegesis how the narrative moves with Jacob from a place of familiarity with its connotations of family home and divine presence at Beersheba to a place of unfamiliarity and anonymity. The fact that its name is kept even from the reader means that we share the perspective of Jacob. Nevertheless the repetition of the term 'place' (מקום)

---

91 It should, of course, be noted that the treatment of this motif is not straightforward in Exodus - see Ex. 24:10-11, 33:11.
92 Westermann, *Genesis: 12-36*, 460. However, in his concluding remarks on the religion of the patriarchs (p. 576), Westermann points out that 'the patriarchal stories are not yet aware of the holiness of God'.
    Otto, R., *The Idea of the Holy: an Inquiry into the Non-Rational Factor in the Idea of the Divine and its Relation to the Rational*, Oxford: Oxford University Press, 1924 (ET of *Das Heilige*, 9th ed.). Otto himself briefly discusses this passage (pp. 131-2), seeing in Jacob's reaction (v. 17) the sense of being somewhere haunted. He sees the same idea expressed at the burning bush (Ex. 3), although there Moses covers his face (Ex. 3:6b).
93 Moberly, *The Old Testament of the Old Testament*, 99ff.
94 Moberly, *The Old Testament of the Old Testament*, 102.

and the definite article tantalizingly hint to the reader that this is not just any place. The same can equally be said of the stone used for a cushion. The next transition is from the place of anonymity to the place of significance, and at least for the Israelite reader, of familiarity. From now on, Bethel will be to Jacob what Beersheba has been to Abraham and Isaac.

This all witnesses to the importance of place in the patriarchal narratives and, more widely, to that of land in the Hebrew Bible. However, beyond this is the suggestion that this place has a special quality, and as we have noted, Jacob recognizes this in the setting up of the pillar and the giving of the name. This quality is not spelt out, but it seems to reflect the idea that it is in this particular place, which Jacob seems to stumble upon by chance, that the divine can be experienced, and perhaps that here, the divine meets the temporal (so, the vision of the ladder) or - in the terms of our wider theme - the human.

However, this idea is set in tension with the idea of God's presence which reaches beyond this place and accompanies his people, in this case Jacob. This is spelt out by the promises relating to God's presence and protection (v. 15), and by the self-definition of God by relationship (with Abraham and Isaac - v. 13aβ).

In a wider canonical context this points to the dual aspects of God's people who travel (the patriarchal narratives, stay in Egypt and exodus, the wilderness tradition, exile) and who have a settled existence in the Promised Land (the preparations for the cult in Exodus and Leviticus, and for social regulation in Deuteronomy, the tradition of Zion/Jerusalem, the monarchy, the Temple). On the one hand the passage emphasizes that God will be with his people wherever they go; on the other hand, is the recognition that this place is special and that Jacob will return here, and the conclusion looks forward to a settled existence and cult at Bethel.[95] Theologically, the passage touches on the tension between the particular and the universal: God's presence focussed in one place versus God not restricted to a place, with both sides of the polarity finding a place in the passage. A similar tension can be found around the building of the Temple - see 1 Kings 8:27ff.[96]

---

95 So Westermann, *Genesis: 12-36*, 460.

96 We already noted in the introduction how Fokkelman tends to play down any idea of the place of Bethel having any specific quality. This tendency can also be found in certain Jewish commentators: Hertz (*The Pentateuch and Haftorahs*, 241-3) writes that the message of the dream is that the earth is full of the glory of God, and he interprets v. 16 as meaning that religion is not restricted to any time or place: 'Praying at any place is like standing at the very foot of God's throne in glory, for the gate of heaven is there and the

This canonical approach rejects the view of Van Seters who only relates this passage to one side of the tension, namely the exile and the need to speak to a displaced people. The reality is more complex than that.[97]

The Human (Jacob)

We have seen above how this passage provides an interpretative key for the whole of the story of Jacob. Structurally this is shown in two ways: in the promise given by YHWH that Jacob will return and in the oath given by Jacob. Together these elements look beyond the incident to an eventual fulfilment in the life of Jacob, thus creating a framework to the Jacob story.[98] In biographical terms, furthermore, it is noticeable that this is Jacob's first direct encounter with God. Again, it should be noted that coming after Jacob's act of deception, this incident highlights God's grace, as does the fact that Jacob's dream is unsolicited by him.[99] Nevertheless there is some ambiguity in the relationship between this incident and chapter 27: does this appearance serve to justify what Jacob did previously? Is God's appearance here dependent on the fact that Jacob has already received the patriarchal blessing? That takes us back to an interpretation of the previous chapter itself, but it would be forcing the point to say that this episode justifies what Jacob has done, although the note of grace here should warn us equally against seeing what will happen with Laban as a punishment. Clearly there is some connection between the blessing received and this incident, but the narrative does not define this closely. Neither is there a clear connection with the opening oracle.

However, as well as representing an incident in Jacob's life, understandable in its own narrative context, the perspective of Israel is never far removed, as is often the case in the Jacob story. This can be seen in two ways: firstly in the promises which would have seen their fulfilment

---

door is open for prayer to be heard,' quoted by Plaut (*The Torah*, 197). However, this contrasts with another tendency to identify Bethel with what was to be Jerusalem (see above, p. 55).

97 Van Seters, *Prologue to History*. Van Seters does acknowledge earlier cultic aspects alongside exilic parts, containing the promises and the vow, which look forward to a future return and centralized cult (pp. 300-1). However, it could just as well be argued that the conclusion of the passage is written from the perspective of an established cult.

98 So Richter, 'Das Gelübde als theologische Rahmung.' 21-52. For Richter, the oath and its eventual fulfilment in ch. 35 are a literary invention of the Elohistic source. However, it must also be the case that the oath itself presupposes the promise given by YHWH.

99 'The fleeing deceiver receives a word of grace', von Rad, *Genesis*, 287.

in later Israel.[100] We have noted how the promises are already partially fulfilled in the life of Jacob, not just those relating to his safe return, but also in an anticipatory way, those regarding progeny, land and blessing. Nevertheless, there is no doubt that these latter promises are only properly fulfilled with reference to the people of Israel.

The second way in which we are drawn into the Israelite perspective is in the use of Jacob as a type for the later Israelite. For instance, it is of course true that Jacob's religious practices do not resemble orthodox Yahwistic practice, but the narrative is at pains to emphasize that it is YHWH that Jacob is worshipping. Jacob is a type, albeit shadowy and imprecise since the writers never deny the discrete nature of patriarchal religion, of the Israelite who worships YHWH, the one true God who has brought his people out of Egypt.[101] This is clearest in the covenantal language of v. 21b, but evident in Jacob's response in general. It is also reflected in the first part of YHWH's promise (v. 15) where the language is close to the piety of Israel, and in the institutions mentioned in Jacob's vow: the promise to build a temple, referring most directly to the later shrine at Bethel, and in a wider context to the Jerusalem temple, and the tithe. It is not possible to see any of this as a purely paradigmatic approach of a later writer wanting to encourage true worship of YHWH at the Temple (as Van Seters argues) since the picture of Jacob's religion is less than orthodox and the writer is happy to let the differences remain. Instead, this approach, which we can

---

100 Here I am using the categories put forward by Moberly (*The Old Testament of the Old Testament*, 138) who borrows them in turn from Christian ways of interpreting the Old Testament. Moberly's argument is that the two commonest methods used for a 'Christian' reading of the Old Testament (the promise-fulfilment model and typology) were already used for an 'Israelite' or 'Yahwistic' reading of the patriarchal tradition, the difference being that in the latter case the methods were applied in the actual rewriting of the tradition.
101 This tendency is strongly reinforced by Rashi, himself drawing on Rabbinic tradition. The word פגע ('came to' - v. 11), carrying also connotations of intercession, indicates that Jacob instituted the custom of Evening Prayer. The fact that מקום ('place') has a definite article means that the place must have already been mentioned - hence it is identified as Mount Moriah (from Gen. 22). This leads to a strong identification of Bethel with the site of the Temple in Jerusalem. This in turn leads to a long discussion about how Mount Moriah can be found at the same place as Luz. Rashi's own suggestion (Rosenbaum and Silbermann eds, *Pentateuch*, 133) is that Mount Moriah was forcibly removed to Luz as the ground shrank before Jacob to bring the two places together. A further popular idea is that Jacob did not proceed straight to Haran from Beersheba but first spent fourteen years studying Torah in the academy of Eber as a preparation for his time of exile (Scherman and Zlotowitz eds, *Bereishis/ Genesis*, vol. 4, 1217).
As already argued, the identification of the site of Bethel with the future site of the Jerusalem Temple, whilst questionable from a strictly historical point of view, is quite natural given both the wider canonical perspective and the mention of the tithe.

conveniently call typological, enables the writers to affirm the parallels in the religion without denying the differences.

In conclusion, to relate this passage to our wider theme of the human and divine, the place Bethel is a point of intersection. In his narrative study Mann aptly shows how the themes of divine and person converge at the place of Bethel:

> The Bethel story is to the Jacob cycle what the charge to Abram was to the Abraham cycle (12:1-3)...In both passages the patriarchs stand at the threshold of a journey, but their points of origin and destination are reversed...Jacob is going where Abraham forbids Isaac to go (24:6,8), and is the only patriarch to court disaster by going East. Thus the threshold on which Jacob stands is fraught with danger, both behind and ahead. But the place on which he stands, or lies, is a threshold of a different order; it is the 'gate of heaven' (vs. 17). Yahweh is there in this 'awesome place'. Bethel is both literally and figuratively an intersection of the divine and human paths. Jacob is standing at a strange door which opens in three directions: behind is his past of failure and alienation; ahead is his future of both hope and uncertainty; and over above, coming down to meet him, is the presence of God.[102]

---

102 Mann, *The Book of the Torah*, 55.

Chapter 3

Peniel
(32:23-33)

Introduction

Questions in Relation to the Text

This passage is notoriously difficult to interpret. For those interested in historical-critical approaches, there is widespread agreement that the passage has a long pre-history, but also an acceptance that the development is so complex that it is extremely difficult to reconstruct it. For those interested in theological meaning, there is the highly unusual picture of God (or is it really God?) entering into a struggle with a human, and of seemingly being on the verge of defeat. In all, there are huge ambiguities and fundamental questions.

From a historical-critical perspective, Martin-Achard mentions the following difficulties or incoherences:[1]

- v. 23 suggests Jacob has crossed the stream; v. 24 seems to deny this.[2]
- Who comes out on top in the struggle? v. 29 suggests that Jacob has won; v. 31 shows him relieved to have escaped death. Von Rad, with others, sees this tension reflecting the complex prehistory of the text where an earlier account of Jacob defeating a divine being has been 'concealed' by additions, at the expense of the coherence of the narrative.[3]
- Two mentions of a blessing (v. 29b, v. 30), - Martin-Achard sees this as a doublet. This of course assumes that the giving of a new name is indeed a blessing.
- The coming of dawn is mentioned three times (vv. 25, 27, 32).

---

1   Martin-Achard, R., 'Un exégète devant Genèse 32:23-37.' In Barthes, R. et al. *Analyse structurale et exégèse biblique*, Neuchâtel, 1971, 47.
2   Verse numbers given here refer to the Masoretic Text (Hebrew). In English versions, the passage starts at v. 22.
3   von Rad, *Genesis*, 320-21. Likewise Seebass (*Der Erzvater Israel und die Einführung der Jahweverehrung in Kanaan*, BZAW 98, Töpelmann: Berlin, 17), for whom this is the clinching factor regarding the question of sources.

- In one case, the place is called Peniel, in the other Penuel.

In addition, the following questions are raised:

- The passage offers several etymologies: for the name Peniel (v. 31), the name Israel (v. 29), and for the food tabu. Westermann considers that the word-play between יעקב (Jacob) and ויאבק (wrestled) reflects an original etymology for the place of Jabboq.

The question raised by these etiological elements is which, if any, are central and which are secondary. This question generally reflects the view that this text is a simple etiological tale, originally formed around one etiology.

- What are we to understand by the 'blessing' given to Jacob? Is it some power extracted from a demon, in the way one might rob it of some special knowledge or superhuman power,[4] or is it the blessing of God?
- Linked to this, who is the opponent of Jacob: a river demon, Esau, God, an angel, a psychological experience or nightmare?
- What is the relation of the passage to the wider Jacob story, especially chapters 32 and 33?

Historical-Critical Approaches

Gunkel, following the example of many, is able to reconstruct two parallel stories.[5] The Yahwistic source relates Jacob crossing the Jabboq with family and possessions. A stranger wrestles with him until sunrise and Jacob dislocates his hip. Jacob asks the name of the stranger, receives no reply, but is blessed. He calls the place 'Peniel', marvelling that he has come away alive, albeit limping.

In the Elohistic story, Jacob remains on the north side of the river, it is he who hits the figure on the hip, and the figure pleads that Jacob let him go since dawn is coming. For this reason Jacob learns that the figure is divine (whereas in J, the divinity of the figure is revealed by its refusal to reply). Once Jacob realizes this, he extorts a blessing (thus displaying his characteristic 'presence of mind'), and as a blessing, he is given the name 'Israel' with the explanation that he has prevailed over gods (Elohim).[6] The place is not named by Jacob, but is already called Penuel, and the E account ends with the explanation of the food tabu. In this form, it is the demon who

---

4   Westermann, *Genesis: 12-36*, 519.
5   Gunkel, *Genesis*, 347ff; reference is also made to *The Folktale in the Old Testament*, Sheffield: Almond Press, 1987 (ET of *Das Märchen im Alten Testament*, 1917), which represents Gunkel's later views - see J. Rogerson in the introduction to the English translation (esp. p. 16).
6   Gunkel, *The Folktale in the Old Testament*, 84.

barely escapes before the rising of the sun.

However, Gunkel's main contribution is not in separating two sources but in attempting to highlight the original folktale elements behind both accounts. In particular, he finds that the concept of a divine being, beaten by Jacob (preserved in E and, argues Gunkel, in Hosea 12:5) is the most ancient, and certainly pre-Yahwistic: the 'god' described here is not YHWH, but a demon, possibly a river demon. The tale thus reflects other folktales of demons who savagely attack human beings at night, but whose power vanishes at daybreak. Eventually, this story came into Israelite circulation and the names Penuel, Jabboq and Jacob were added, though it was incorporated into the Jacob-Esau cycle at a later stage still, as demonstrated by the very different portrayal of Jacob elsewhere.[7] In his commentary, Gunkel detects vestiges of an originally mythical, legendary saga, with Jacob portrayed as a giant; however Gunkel's later and more revised view is that the story is essentially a folktale about spirits or demons.

Clearly, Gunkel's interest lies in tracing an original tale, and the ideas behind this. There is no real attempt to draw theological conclusions, either for the reader today, for the Pentateuchal writers or for Israel. The only application which he does make in the commentary is a passing acknowledgement of the wealth of allegorical readings that this passage has encouraged.

Thus, questions facing the reader are resolved by the historical method: alleged repetitions derive from different sources, and even the giving of a name is seen as the doublet of the giving of a blessing. Ambiguity is also 'solved' in this way, so that in one source, Jacob (or the hero) wins, whereas in the other, he escapes with his life. The nature of the blessing and the identity of the attacker are determined by the original, folktale genre.

Although von Rad generally accepts the idea of continuous sources in the Pentateuch, he does not accept that this passage contains parallel strands, the only real doublet being v. 23 and v. 24b.[8]

Von Rad is a clear advocate of the historical approach and accepts Gunkel's view concerning the original pre-Yahwistic saga of a nocturnal attack on a man. He further argues that a historical understanding is essential:

---

7   'The courageous god-vanquisher and the Jacob who trembles before Esau are actually quite different figures.' Gunkel, *Genesis*, 353.
8   von Rad, *Genesis*, 319ff.

This knowledge about such a long history is not, however, only a concern of a special science, but it concerns everyone who wants to understand the story; for only then can the reader be preserved from false expectations of a hasty search for 'the' meaning of this story.[9]

This last clause however shows that whereas Gunkel is happy simply to discover the 'original' story, von Rad has a wider concern to show the depth of meaning and ambiguity in the present text, and that for him, the historical method is an indispensable tool to this end:

It is therefore all the more amazing that Israel found this ancient framework and imaginative material, which derived from the crude, heathen past, completely suitable to represent Yahweh's work with Israel's ancestor. For the narrator's opinion is...that in and behind this 'man', this nocturnal assailant, Yahweh himself was most directly at work with Jacob.[10]

Unlike Gunkel, von Rad is concerned to give voice to the 'Yahwistic' narrator, and in particular, to uncover the range of theological meaning.[11] This is shown in his exegesis where he identifies pre-Israelite elements but then reverts to the perspective of the later narrator. Like Gunkel he sees an earlier conception of Jacob nearly defeating a heavenly being, now modified by additions (v. 25b, 32b). He then notes how the final narrator was happy to leave such ambiguity open.

For von Rad, most theological interest lies with the elements of blessing and the giving and concealing of names. Again, he sees that both the elemental grasping for blessing and the belief in the power of names are vestiges of the ancient tale, but he also shows how these themes have become central to the Yahwist's concerns. The blessing now is clearly from God, but the request for a blessing is still 'a primitive human reaction to an encounter with God', being 'the most elemental reaction of man to the

---

9   von Rad, *Genesis*, 319.
10   von Rad, *Genesis*, 324.
11   In many respects, von Rad's approach is anticipated by K. Elliger 'Der Jakobskampf am Jabbok. Gen 32:23ff als hermeneutisches Problem', *ZTK* 48 (1951), 1-31. Like von Rad, Elliger sees the work of the Yahwist in giving a theological emphasis to a much older story, with the real interest of final form of the story lying with the nature of God and God's grace and mercy. Elliger goes on to give an arguably very Lutheran interpretation of the attack by God on Jacob: God's attack is an act of judgement but it also becomes the place where Jacob is spared, justified from past sin and given a new identity. Thus this event is a type for the Cross where Christ receives the judgement deserved by humanity, but where sinful humanity also finds justification (pp. 30-31).

divine'.[12] Clearly the concept of 'primitive' is loaded and ambiguous, but von Rad's use of the term here is instructive: whereas for Gunkel, what is primitive reflects an ancient way of looking at things, now superseded by newer ways of understanding reality, for von Rad 'primitive' is something which remains in human nature even in our technological age. This means that he is able to relate the text to our own experience in a way that Gunkel does not.

Von Rad notes that the connection to v. 29 seems loose at first - perhaps leaving us to infer that the text was not always one unit, but he is more concerned to show an inner continuity in the passage as it now is. As with blessing, the verse reflects an ancient view that to know the name of a divinity is to be able to summon or even manipulate it. Again though, von Rad sees embedded in this question about the name 'all man's need, all his boldness before God', and especially 'the longing for God'.

Von Rad then goes on to comment on the blessing that God does give to Jacob with characteristic passion:

> But how far removed from the petition itself is the final fulfilment, and what lies between this petition and its fulfilment (v. 29b)!...Thus it is clear again that our narrative is far removed from all those sagas which tell of the extortion of a divine nature by man and of the winning of a blessing.[13]

A related shift in emphasis is noted earlier: the notion of 'prevailing' once referred to a struggle with a demon, and the astonishment engendered was at the suicidal courage of Jacob (would not the astonishment have been more at the strength and cleverness of Jacob who had no choice but to defend himself?), but now the astonishment is reversed, so that we wonder at the fact that God let himself be coerced in such a way by Jacob's violence.

In an extended epilogue, von Rad goes on to comment on how the story has been radically and daringly adopted, and then argues how a historical perspective prevents one from finding the 'one' meaning of the passage, with breaks in coherence actually adding to the depth. He then shows how we are to relate this passage to the wider context of the Jacob narrative (something Gunkel fails to do), but also to the Yahwist's salvation-historical perspective. In view of the giving of the name of Israel in this passage, such a broad Israelite perspective is surely required of the text itself.

---

12   von Rad, *Genesis*, 321.
13   von Rad, *Genesis*, 323.

Thus von Rad's approach has similarities to that of Gunkel, but more striking are the differences. He has sought to bring to bear findings of historical investigation for theological use, and in so doing has even offered what is close to a synchronic reading, and one which here anticipates the canonical approach. He has tried - arguably with considerable success - to offer a reading which is both sensitive to a diachronic perspective, but is also concerned with a synchronic and theological understanding. The question that this approach poses is whether the historical starting-point is really as necessary as von Rad claims - especially as scholars who eschew any historical discussion are also able to see ambiguity and paradox, and a great many scholars of the historical school do see ambiguity in a much more negative light, as a problem to be solved (as seems to be Gunkel's presupposition).

Like von Rad, Westermann finds no evidence of parallel sources, whilst accepting that the passage has a long prehistory stretching to pre-Israelite times, being attached to the river Jabboq.[14] However, Westermann differs from von Rad and Gunkel in seeing certain elements as much later than the Yahwistic writer, in particular, verses which suggest that Jacob was wrestling with God (vv. 28f - Jacob's new name, v. 31b - Jacob's conclusion that he has seen God face to face). References to the food tabu (v. 26b and v. 33) are also later.

This creates the problem that the verses which have most given occasion for 'profound and extensive theological explanations' are those which are 'secondary'.[15] For Westermann it is impossible to understand the narrative as a whole from this perspective, and he makes the point that the theological meaning of these additions is to be studied separately. Interestingly, at no stage does he do so himself.

Regarding the Yahwist, he took the old tale and inserted it at this point in the Jacob story. In this form, the river demon tried to stop Jacob crossing the stream. This has to be the original plot since the Yahwist did not hold the view that YHWH was only active at night or feared the breaking of day. Jacob survives with the help of God and so has experienced that God is with him. 'He can now go on to meet his brother.'[16] Thus Westermann does consider the passage in a wider literary context, unlike Gunkel, although it is not the context which now exists.

From what has been noted, it is clear that Westermann regards certain

---

14 Hence the wordplay יבק- אבק -Westermann, *Genesis: 12-36*, 515.
15 Westermann, *Genesis 12-36*, 520.
16 Westermann, *Genesis 12-36*, 521.

parts of the text as an organic part of the whole, and other parts as additions to be discarded and treated separately. This must seem arbitrary, since there is no justification for his assumption that the 'Yahwistic' version, itself only a scholarly supposition, is the version which carries theological or literary weight.

In this sense, Westermann comes some way between Gunkel and von Rad. Gunkel is interested in the very beginnings, von Rad in the text as it is, albeit with its traces of historical development, whereas Westermann has chosen somewhere in between. Moreover, Westermann sees little room for ambiguity or depth of meaning in the way that von Rad does, with the result that he does little justice to the text as it is and to the way it has clearly made an impression on exegetes through the ages.

Text as Unity

This can be seen in two very different ways: on the one hand, the text may be seen as being a unity from its very conception (so Blum), and so to treat this particular text as a single unit would result from a historical judgement. On the other hand, the text may be treated as a unity, irrespective of what it once might have been (so Barthes).[17]

Blum is clearly concerned to understand this text both as a literary unity and as an integral part of its literary context.[18] However, it becomes clear that this is because of his view that this text was conceived from the start as a single unit integral to the wider narrative.[19]

Regarding literary context, he highlights several links: for instance, the words פנים ('face') and עבר (translated 'cross', 'sent across', 'pass' in

---

17   Barthes, R., 'La lutte avec l'ange: Analyse textuelle de Genèse 32:23-33.' In Barthes, R. et al. *Analyse structurale et exégèse biblique*, Neuchâtel, 1971, 27-39.

18   Blum, *Die Komposition der Vätergeschichte*, 143ff.

19   A similar view is taken by Wahl, *Die Jakobserzählung*, 280. As with the Bethel incident, Wahl sees mythical elements as better suited to the post-exilic period. However, he gives no specific reason for seeing such connection, apart from the comment that 'mythological motifs and mythical expressions clearly flourished in post-exilic Israel in reaction to a restrictive monotheism' (p. 286 - own translation).

In response, it should be noted, that as with the Bethel tradition, Wahl takes no account of allusions to this tradition in Hosea. Furthermore, Wahl can be accused of setting up a false dichotomy: because his declared aim is to test which parts of the Jacob story go back to an actual historical event involving an historical Jacob, his judgement becomes inevitably sceptical. For instance, he asks rhetorically how credible it is that two men could spend the whole night in a struggle, concluding that there can be no connection to an actual struggle (p. 282). The alternatives seem to be that either the story actually happened or that it was made up by some post-exilic author. This hardly does justice to the traditional-historical approach.

NRSV), the wider time frame, and the theme of blessing underlying the Jacob-Esau story. Added to this is the deliberate contrast between the nocturnal struggle with God and the peaceful daytime encounter with his brother. These are all elements which none of the above scholars have really highlighted. In particular, Blum discusses the theme of blessing. On the face of it, the interest is in the outcome of the struggle, but the author uses the motif of the sunrise and the ambiguity in v. 26 about who is really defeated to point the reader to the 'truer' meaning of this passage, which links with the struggle for blessing and its acquisition behind the Jacob-Esau narrative as a whole. Ambiguity is used by the author to point to the wider context which deals with the question of Jacob's blessing, seen in a positive light in chapter 27, but as more problematic in chapter 33.

Blum clearly has a point in relating the question of blessing in the Penuel incident to that in the rest of the narrative, as opposed to seeing the concept here as being so totally different. However, there is also a sense in which the Penuel scene leaps out of its literary context. Blum accepts some possible tradition behind the literary text, with some etiological link between the struggle and the name 'Israel'.[20] We are then left with the question of how much this tradition has already taken shape. Is it not more likely that the rest of chapters 32 and 33 were composed or modified in the light of this incident, which after all, has a lot more depth, or that the two elements were brought and worked together? It seems that Blum has brought out an essential aspect of the narrative, but has not exhausted its meaning.

Barthes uses the passage to demonstrate a structuralist analysis, which is consciously different from an historical analysis (which investigates the origins of a text) or an analysis which looks at how the text is composed.[21] Especially it means eschewing the traditional theological concern for meaning or truth.[22]

Barthes looks at the text from several perspectives: a sequential analysis, and, under the category of structural analysis, an actantial and then a functional analysis.

The sequential analysis looks at the sequence of events in the text and discovers three basic stages: passage (i.e. the crossing), struggle, and mutation. Regarding the passage (crossing), there are two possible readings:

---

20 Blum, *Die Komposition der Vätergeschichte*, 145.
21 Barthes, 'La lutte avec l'ange', 28.
22 'Le problème, du moins celui que je me pose, est en effet de parvenir à ne pas réduire le Texte à un signifié, quel qu'il soit (historique, économique, folklorique ou kérygmatique), mais à maintenir sa signifiance ouverte.' Barthes, 'La lutte avec l'ange', 39.

one, that Jacob crosses the stream and then encounters the figure; the other, that he encounters the figure and then is free to cross. We have already seen that this has been noted by other scholars, but, rather than seeing this as a difficulty or obscurity to be cleared up either by reference to contradictory sources (Barthes is unconcerned whether there are sources or not) or redaction, he simply spells out the resulting ambiguity.[23] The ambiguity leads to two possible readings: in the one, Jacob is left alone before crossing and so has to undergo an ordeal by combat before reaching his goal. In the other, Jacob crosses first and then remains alone in solitude, making the combat a religious event and the change of names a baptismal experience. Both readings, one folkloristic, the other religious, are to be read alongside each other.[24]

The struggle itself is also marked by ambiguity: who is the stranger and who is the subject of the verbs? This ambiguity is resolved, but only retroactively. There is also a paradox in the way that the struggle is resolved: there is a decisive blow, but it does not succeed. Instead, the outcome is different than we would expect, and this introduces the idea of reversal: the weaker one defeats the stronger, but in return he is marked ('marqué') on the thigh. Barthes is able to see this idea of marking as significant to the life of Jacob as a whole. From the beginning, Esau, as the first-born, should have been the one marked out, but this marking out is reversed as Jacob supplants the older (Gen. 27:36), something anticipated in the birth where Jacob is grasping Esau's heel. The idea of marking here links to the theological theme of election.[25] In this text then, God (the stronger) is a substitute for Esau (the older) who is displaced by the younger (Jacob). This reading is close to that of Blum, who as we have seen, sees the blessing received by Jacob as parallel to the blessing he receives at the expense of Esau elsewhere.

Mutation or 'nomination' is the third and final element of the sequence. There are numerous changes which result from this text: the physical change to Jacob's body (as he acquires a limp), a new name and status for Jacob, a new name also for the place, and a new food tabu. Each of these involve a transition ('passage') which of course underlines the whole event.

---

23   Barthes, 'La lutte avec l'ange', 32.

24   'Le théologien souffrirait...de cette indécision; l'exégète la reconnaîtrait, en souhaitant que quelque élément, factuel ou argumentif, lui permette de la faire cesser; l'analyse textuel...goûtera cette sorte de *friction* entre deux intelligibles.' Barthes, 'La lutte avec l'ange', 32.

25   Barthes himself indicates that the reading could contribute to an understanding of the socio-economic relations between Edom and Israel.

Structural Analysis - The first model is based on the work of Greimas, and is called an actantial analysis. Characters, or even some inanimate objects, are placed into the category of one (or occasionally more) actant, an actant being a role within the narrative. This particular text has a pattern which is familiar in mythology: there is the Subject (Jacob) who is the subject of the quest, the Object of the demand (the crossing of the stream), the 'Destinateur' (God) who issues the challenge, the 'Destinataire' (Jacob), the Opponent (God) who opposes the Subject, and the Helper who assists the Subject (in this case, Jacob himself). It is not unusual for a character to have more than one role, but that the 'destinateur' should also be the Opponent is very rare and indeed seems to break the rules, as it is virtually impossible for the Originator to also be the Opponent. This accounts for the shock that the text causes.

The second model, based on that of Propp, is a functional analysis. Here Barthes shows how the narrative has many elements common to folktales. Again, the role of God is unusual, since the role he has in the narrative is structurally that of the evil character.

Conclusion

Barthes' approach is clearly unhistorical and general, in that he does not relate the passage either to the history of Israel or its literary conventions, or to the Ancient Near Eastern culture. Instead, he relates the passage to general patterns common to all popular folktales. Clearly this rests upon the view that all popular literature betrays common underlying patterns. This is indeed a sort of form criticism, but one which compares the form of this text not to texts from a close cultural and historical proximity, but to universal forms (and so there is no discussion of an original setting). But more than that, Barthes is interested in the peculiarities of this text which are sharpened when it is set against general patterns. Thus the role of God is especially unusual as he turns out to be not only the Originator of Jacob's quest, but also his Opponent. Barthes does not see it as his place to develop the significance of this, but simply to note that it virtually breaks the rules of folktale syntax. Likewise, the discussion of 'marquage' and especially the marking of Jacob's thigh, relates to the wider motif of Jacob being marked out in opposition to his elder brother. In both this episode and in the wider narrative, Jacob overcomes the stronger or older - in one case, God, in the other, Esau.

The problem with Barthes' approach is that it is difficult for the trained exegete to assess fairly. One criticism often levelled at this sort of approach is that it merely states the obvious in somewhat convoluted and technical jargon. In a sense Barthes may not disagree, since he is claiming to show what is already in the text, simply spelling out explicitly what the reader senses implicitly. He is certainly not aiming to point to hidden truths or meanings in the text, seeing his task as descriptive rather than constructive. It is perhaps for the exegete to use some Barthes' insights in the constructive task of relating the text to any theological or historical perspective. The extent to which this can be done will enable us to assess Barthes' work.

An initial response would suggest that Barthes' work is of variable value. It has already been acknowledged that he enables us to see in clearer profile how unusual the role of God is in this story, and he confirms views that this text has parallels in this respect, which might encourage us to search for an underlying significance in this.[26] However, in discussing the ambiguity in the description of Jacob's crossing the river (either before or after the struggle), the exegete is left feeling dissatisfied. Barthes anticipates this when he writes that the exegete will search for a way of solving what is perceived as a problem - after all, surely the text cannot say that Jacob both crossed the stream and did not cross the stream! Barthes is simply content to spell out the ambiguity (contradiction?), and shows how the two possibilities give rise to two ways of seeing the struggle, either as an ordeal or a religious experience. But we are left with the question: can a text simply bear that amount of contradiction? Should we not at least consider whether Barthes has misread the text, and may not some understanding of the conventions of the Hebrew writers help us to read the text in a better way? In this case, Barthes' method is perhaps restricted in refusing to consider the conventions of the writers. It may be that there is no alternative reading (or only a solution on a diachronic level - which still leaves us with having to make sense of the text synchronically), but one wonders whether Barthes is too ready to jump to this conclusion - we do not even know whether he has considered the text in the original Hebrew. Furthermore, it is not clear that an ambiguity leads necessarily to two alternative understandings of the struggle in quite the way Barthes suggests.

This leads to another objection which is his claim that theologians or exegetes find ambiguity difficult. We have already seen that von Rad is able to find ambiguity in the text without wishing to 'solve' it, and that for him, it is an historical approach which allows this. Certainly, one of the claims of the champions of the historical method is that these methods have freed exegetes from harmonizing approaches to the Bible, and allowed us to see

---

26   See below, p. 91.

different perspectives in sharper profile, and there is undoubtably some force in this claim. In a similar fashion, Barthes drives a clear wedge between seeing a text as open ended in its meaning and discovering a kerygmatic (or historical) meaning. Certainly, some approaches could be seen as reductionist, especially those which tie the meaning of a text to some supposed historical setting, but this is something the canonical approach has sought to overcome by showing how the scope or 'meaning' of a text has been widened by being incorporated into a new, less specific context. In addition, a theological approach does not rule out seeing the text as open ended. On this point, Barthes has made a false dichotomy.

In short, then, Barthes may be of help in showing more clearly certain features of the text, but it is also clear that his approach does not rule out other methods, and is perhaps an additional tool which needs to be used alongside others and which must not be used uncritically.

Regarding the other approaches, we have seen how the traditional source critical approach has largely been left aside by recent works. This seems correct as it seems that only vv. 23 and 24 are in any sense a doublet. For the rest, there is no compelling case for seeing two parallel stories. It is perhaps true that where source criticism isolated two competing versions - one where Jacob is almost defeated, the other where the divinity is almost defeated - it has thrown into sharper relief the ambiguity of the narrative itself: to say, for instance, with v. 29 that Jacob is the victor does not do full justice to the whole text, which suggests that the outcome is not so clear cut. The fault of source criticism has been to translate this ambiguity into historical terms, delineating clear sources.

Gunkel and Westermann both show an interest in earlier stages of the text, and make any understanding of the text as it now stands a secondary concern. For Gunkel, interest lies in uncovering the original (oral) saga and identifying legendary or folktale elements. For Westermann, the interest is in finding the (written) narrative as it was first incorporated into the Yahwistic narrative.

These approaches may be criticized on two accounts. Firstly, the search for earlier stages is at the expense of an understanding of the final form, and the choice of a certain stage as the one to be investigated is somewhat arbitrary. On the other hand, the work of Gunkel in particular may be helpful in understanding the text as we now have it, as an understanding of the process may help us see the finished result in a better light (so, von Rad). The second criticism is that this sort of approach is always hypothetical and results can rarely be assumed. In particular, Westermann's approach should be strongly questioned. He is able to reconstruct an earlier version only by seeing those elements of the text which suggest that Jacob's opponent was God himself as much later. This sort of argument is inevitably circular. In particular, he argues that the renaming of Jacob is close in time and thought to the Priestly source (see Gen. 35:10), but this ignores the fact that P finds it necessary to include another account of the naming of Jacob. Surely, it is more likely that the Priestly writer or redactor in chapter 35 has chosen to reinterpret a much older tradition? One also wonders whether a writer so close to P would really have wished to conceive such a daringly anthropomorphic picture of God who not only wrestles with, but is also defeated by, the patriarch.

I have tried to show how von Rad combines an historical approach whilst seeking to interpret the text as it is. Overall, he shows restraint in attempting to isolate an original text from later additions, and this means that his exegesis is less dependant on hypothetical reconstructions. At this point, von Rad is very close to the later canonical approach. There is a tendency to see ambiguity resulting from the prehistory of the text, but von Rad goes beyond pointing this out by seeing the passage as a literary unit in its own right.

Finally, Blum sees things in the text that the other scholars have not, in particular that the passage is embedded into the wider narrative. However, this leads Blum to jump to a diachronic judgement that the text must have been composed for the context and, inversely, judging by Blum's method elsewhere, we can assume that if he had judged that the passage had an independent origin, he would have been less concerned to approach it synchronically. In particular, he forces the question: should links with the wider context immediately bring us to make historical judgements? Is it not feasible that this passage and the surrounding narrative (and wider picture of Jacob) had a mutual effect on each other, and that the writers shaped their material as appropriate? Even Blum accepts that some tradition must have preceded this narrative, and this suggests that the alternative of viewing some passages as old stories incorporated fairly well untouched into the wider context against that of viewing other passages as constructed de novo for the context is too clearly made.

A Reading of 32:23-33

The passage can be structured as below:

vv. 23-24   - Introduction to the scene
v. 25   - The struggle
v. 26   - Attempt to break stalemate with 'touch' to the thigh
vv. 27-30   - Dialogue, themes of blessing and name
v. 31   - Naming of place
v. 32   - Jacob leaves, bearing the mark of his encounter
v. 33   - Explanation of food tabu.

From this it is clear that the main part of the struggle is barely described. Instead the emphasis lies on the outcome and especially on the conversation. Central to the structure of the passage (and indeed, it will be seen, to the interest of the passage) are the demand and giving of a blessing, and the names of the protagonists.

It therefore seems that the passage is built around the giving and non-giving of names, with the struggle itself providing the startling background for this theologically important theme.[27]

---

27   It may be that we can go further in detecting a chiastic structure to the passage:
vv. 23-25 which set the geographical location and the time, and the background to the dialogue.

  a - Jacob is injured on the thigh (v. 26)
  b - request to be released, for the dawn is coming (v. 27a)
  c - demand for blessing (as condition) (v. 27b)
  d - request for name (and answer) (v. 28)
    - giving of new name with explanation
  d'- request for name (and refusal) (v. 30a)
  c'- blessing is given (v. 30b)
  (naming of the place and explanation - v. 31)
  b'- sun risen, and Jacob crosses (v. 32)
  a'- Jacob limps on thigh (v)
  Final etiology (continuation of the thigh motif).

It has to be admitted that some caution has been called for in detecting chiastic structures, and also that in this case the pattern is not exact. However, there may be several reasons for this: the writer only has a certain amount of freedom, because the plot demands a certain logic in the order, there is always the possibility that the writers were dealing with traditional material and so felt a certain need to preserve some elements, and variations in a pattern may be intended to bring out contrasts, an obvious example being that whereas Jacob answers God by giving his name, his opponent refuses to disclose his.

Exegesis

vv. 23-25a clearly present a difficulty. v. 23 suggests that Jacob crosses the Jabboq with his family, v. 24 suggests he stays alone. v. 25a makes it clear that whichever side Jacob is on, he ends up alone. Few readers will be satisfied with Barthes' suggestion that we let the ambiguity remain. It could be that in this case a diachronic explanation is to be found, for instance that v. 23 was the original itinerary note, and v. 24 was later added to make a bridge with the Peniel episode. As the text now stands, v. 23 functions more like a notice over the whole episode, with v. 24 starting to narrate the actual episode in detail. One effect of the repetition is to emphasize the word 'cross' (עבר), a frequent motif in chapters 32 and 33.[28] Whatever we are to understand textually, the narrator is silent as to Jacob's motivation in wanting to be alone.

v. 25b describes the fight very succinctly. There is no clue as to who the 'man' (איש) might be, and this remains a mystery until the very end. We are left, with Jacob, to consider various alternatives: a night or river demon, a stranger, an angel, Esau - least of all, perhaps, would we consider God.[29] The temporal phrase at the end of this verse (עלות השחר) means that the day is just beginning to break. It is therefore not a doublet with v. 32. Instead, v. 32 is the next stage as the sun rises. This motif of increasing light replacing the darkness reinforces the gradual realization of Jacob as to what has really been taking place, the objective description of night turning to day reflecting Jacob's subjective point of view.

v. 26 brings us to the resolution of the struggle. In the next two verses there follows a sequence of verbs with no explicit subject, and until the end of v. 29, it is not always clear who is who.[30] The lack of proper nouns is not unusual in Hebrew narrative but here adds to the tension and the picture of the two combatants being evenly matched. It also increases the confusion over the event and the outcome.

A stalemate is reached, so the combatant tries to break it by playing a trick on Jacob. Whether this is a magic touch or a strong blow to Jacob's

---

If it is true that chiastic patterns tend to emphasize the central elements, then there is no question that here, the requesting and giving (or refusal) of names is central. Around this is placed the theme of blessing.

28   Blum, *Die Komposition der Vätergeschichte*, 143.

29   So Barthes, 'La lutte avec l'ange', 37.

30   The sequence is made up of the characteristic pattern of 3ms waw-consecutive verbs, with no explicit subject.

thigh is not clear.[31] The reader can see an irony in the wider context of Jacob's life as the one who usually plays tricks on others is here on the receiving end.

v. 27 assumes that the attempt to break the stalemate has failed. It is not immediately clear why the opponent should need releasing with the rising of the sun, though once we realize his divine nature we understand the need to conceal identity. It is probable that behind this lies the ancient motif of demons being active only at night, but to the later reader there may be the hint of the idea that it would be dangerous for a human to see God in broad daylight (see v. 31). In this case, the paradox would be that the very opponent who is fighting with Jacob is also concerned not to see him perish.

As it is, we still do not know who it is that Jacob is dealing with. Certainly, the demand for a blessing suggests that Jacob has some idea of the divine nature of his opponent, and his demand for a blessing could, from his point of view, represent the idea of trying to extract some power. It is probably wrong to interpret the idea of blessing given solely in these terms, but equally, the nature of the struggle suggests that this element is present. Alternatively or additionally, Jacob could have in mind that his opponent is Esau, and that this is some sort of reenactment of the struggle for the blessing.

vv. 28-29: At the end of v. 28, we are at last clear about which character is which, although not yet about the identity of Jacob's opponent.

v. 29, with the giving of the name Israel, is clearly important, but before considering the significance of the verse in this episode, there are several issues to be addressed.

Excursus: the Giving of the Name Israel

i. Etymology - this verse offers a clear etymology for the name Israel (ישראל), by which the name is linked to the rare verb שרה, itself generally defined as 'struggle', 'strive', 'persist', 'exert oneself', 'persevere'.[32] Hosea 12 seems to reflect this where the verb is used in v. 5 (MT -שרה), but the

---

31   On a metaphorical level it has been suggested that 'thigh' is a euphemism for sexual organs, and that the injury to the thigh could refer to the fate of Jacob's offspring (e.g. S. Gervitz, 'Of Patriarchs and Puns: Joseph at the Fountain, Jacob at the Ford.' *HUCA* 46 (1975), 52-3; L. M. Eslinger, 'The Case of an Immodest Lady Wrestler in Deut 25: 11-12.' *VT* 31 (1981), 273-4; Hamilton, *Genesis 18-50*, 331.

32   *BDB*, 975.

form וישר is used in the next verse. Despite the rarity of the verb שרה, the
Biblical account (reflected in Hosea) interprets the name 'Israel' as a
compound with a verb with the noun אל (El), where v. 29b suggests that
'God' is the object of the verb.

However, this has been questioned on at least two fronts. First, there is
the problem that, when read without the explanation of v. 29b,
grammatically it makes much more sense to see 'El' as the subject of the
verb, in which case the name would mean 'God strives', and this has been
the interpretation of a number of scholars.

There is then the further questioning of whether we can accept the
meaning of the verb at face value. Many other suggestions have been made,
the most popular of which has been 'reign', 'hold sway'.[33] However, it is
difficult to be certain what the verb actually means. There is also the further
question of whether it is a jussive or imperfect.

In terms of making sense of the text as it is, this debate is of little
consequence. Within the context of Jacob's struggle the verb itself is
intended to carry the meaning of 'struggle' or 'contends'.

ii. Significance - a cursory view of approaches to this verse shows a wide
range of method and presupposition. Gunkel claims that 'Elohim' would
have referred to the demon that this incident originally described, and that
the statement was a way of proudly describing Israel as victorious and
invincible.[34] There is however no consideration of how this now refers to
God. Von Rad also perceives an original reference to a demon, but
acknowledges that now the reference is to God. As well as marvelling at
Jacob's suicidal courage', the wonder shifts to the fact that 'God let himself
be coerced in such a way by Jacob's violence'.[35] Westermann sees v. 29 as
later, since the name Israel presupposes the establishment of Israel with its
twelve tribes, but he does not really consider the theological significance of
this verse.[36] More emphasis is given by Fokkelman:

> V. 29 is a monologue, a solemn 'order of baptism', spoken authoritatively...A
> well-established nature, a long-fixed route of life must be turned back
> radically...The evil and long-awkward name of Jacob is thrown away and

---

33   For this I am following the review of Zobel, H.-J. ('ישראל', *Theological Dictionary
of the Old Testament*, vol. 6, 397-420).
34   Gunkel, *Genesis*, 350.
35   von Rad, *Genesis*, 322.
36   Westermann, *Genesis 12-36*, 518.

exchanged for a beautiful, theophorous name.[37]

As for the significance of the name, Fokkelman refuses to consider this apart from the present context. From the context he sees the verb contained in the name (שרה) as meaning 'fight', but also sees 'God' as the subject. He then applies this understanding to the narrative - it may mean 'God fights with you, because he is forced to by your stubbornness and pride [in resisting God's way of blessing Jacob and trying to extract the blessing in his own strength].[38] But the name can also mean 'henceforth God will fight for you, for he appreciates your absolutely sincere and undivided commitment'.

This overview of different approaches to v. 29 suggests that the more a reader is prepared to consider the verse in its present context, and not simply to seek to identify its original Sitz im Leben, the more they will find of significance. Gunkel and Westermann's view that this verse has a separate origin and reflects a celebration of Jacob's/Israel's strength against any opponent, whether divine or human, may be true as far as it goes, but it hardly begins to do justice to what von Rad sees as the marvel that the reader now feels, once we realize that it is indeed with the God of Israel that Jacob has been struggling.

By contrast, Fokkelman tries to take seriously both the context and the internal structure of the name Israel since he recognizes that 'El' ought properly to be regarded as the subject, but he also tries to apply this literal meaning to the story of Jacob.[39] However this interpretation seems forced and does not really do justice to the etiological form of the statement, where the giving of the name is grounded in *Jacob's* struggle with 'God and men'.[40] In fact Fokkelman's interpretation of v. 29b rests solely on the literal meaning of the word Israel, whereas in reality, the correspondence between a name and its etiology is often imprecise. This means that we are not forced to look for a complete harmony in all the elements of a text in such a way that, as in the case of Fokkelman's reading of v. 29, we fail to do justice to the literal reading and the genre of each element. Of course, there may be some justification in seeing in the name Israel some

---

37 Fokkelman, *Narrative Art*, 215-6.

38 Fokkelman, *Narrative Art*, 217.

39 Fokkelman accepts that the 'folk-etymological' meaning of Israel might not be the same as the original sense of the name.

40 The etiological nature of the statement is demonstrable by the giving of a new name, together with the conjunction כי + verbal clause, and the root of the new name being repeated in the explanatory clause.

understanding of God who 'fights' for his people, but this element is at the most secondary within the context of the Jacob narrative.[41]

An alternative interpretation is to translate the statement differently, such as suggested by Hamilton. This follows closely the LXX and Vulgate readings by translating the phrase 'because you have struggled with God, and with men have you succeeded'.[42] In favour of the more traditional understanding, this alternative does not take account of the structure of the final verb, which most naturally translates 'and have prevailed'.

To return to the passage, the etymology in v. 29b does not correspond exactly to the structure of the word Israel where 'El' would be the subject, but this is not untypical of etymologies and probably indicates that the verse has been introduced in order to relate the episode to a wider perspective. Thus, the explanation of v. 29b can be understood on various levels. It clearly refers to this particular episode. On a broader level, it is not inappropriate to understand the reference to 'men' as Esau, whom Jacob is about to meet, and as Laban.[43] The phrase 'with God', although referring to this episode, could also be seen as a reference to Jacob's life and the way he has sought to extract God's blessing by his own means.[44]

But the verse has a wider context still which is that of Israel. This passage contains the first mention of the name Israel in the Biblical story.

---

41   See Jacob (*Das erste Buch der Tora*, 642-3): on one level, the word ישראל does refer to Jacob as a 'Gotteskämpfer', fighting against 'einem Übermenschlichen'. However, from a broader perspective, Jacob is fighting a 'Gotteskampf': in other words, the divine is working and fighting in Jacob in his war on the side of God. This relates to the understanding of Israel as fighting a holy war.

42   Hamilton, *The Book of Genesis: chapters 18-50*, 335. This is also suggested by Anderson, F. I., 'Note on Genesis 30:8', *JBL* 88 (1969), 200, supported by Eslinger, L. M. ('Hos 12:5a and Gen 32:29: A Study in Inner Biblical Exegesis.' 95). In favour of this, is the resulting chiastic structure and rhythmic balance.

43   In this way, Dillmann, seeing a reference to Jacob's conflict with Esau which clearly is still unresolved, reads the phrase ותוכל as a promise that Jacob will indeed overcome his brother (Dillmann, A., *Die Genesis*, 3rd ed., Leipzig: S. Hirzel, 1892, 364). Nevertheless, this reading should be set aside the actual resolution of the conflict with Esau, where any concept of victory seems to be undermined by Jacob's subservient behaviour and Esau's graciousness.

44   Notwithstanding Alter's caution in interpreting the word אלהים, which he calls a 'high concentration point of lexical ambiguity' with possible meanings of 'divine being' or even 'princes'. Furthermore, argues Alter, the reference to Jacob's struggle with divine beings is not necessarily a reference by Jacob's opponent to himself (*Genesis*, 182). Nevertheless, this caution seems unnecessary given the antithesis of the word with 'men', and a less than full understanding of the term אלהים does not really do justice to the striking character of this passage, nor to Jacob's own amazement in v. 31.

This giving of the new name of Israel is clearly a turning-point, and is meant to be seen as significant not just for Jacob, but also for his descendants. Any interpretation of this episode needs to take account of this perspective. It is remarkable that Israel, or at least this tradition within Israel, should see its origins in such an ambivalent incident. Indeed, far from serving to exalt the patriarch as Gunkel or Westermann suggest, this incident seems to further question his motives and religious attitude.[45]

This approach of seeing the verse as relating first to the entire Jacob narrative, and then to Israel is taken by von Rad:

> This event did not simply occur at a definite biographical point in Jacob's life, but as it is now related it is clearly transparent as a type of that which Israel experienced from time to time with God. Israel has here presented its entire history with God almost prophetically as such a struggle until the breaking of the day. The narrative itself makes this extended interpretation probable by equating the names Jacob and Israel.[46]

v. 30: Jacob now asks his opponent his name. Because of his new name and its explanation, Jacob, as the reader, has no doubt guessed, or is close to guessing, who his opponent is. The importance of names is well attested in Biblical tradition, and it is natural for the mortal human to want to know the name of the divinity. It may also be that underlying this request is an ancient idea that possession of a name means the ability to exert power over a divinity.[47] Such an idea would certainly be consistent with the issues of

---

45 Perhaps such a concern contributes to one interpretation of the statement in v. 29, which does not see the stranger as giving Jacob the new name at this point but as simply announcing that Jacob 'will be called' Israel (i.e. named Israel) at a later point (i.e. in ch. 35) - Rashi in Rosenbaum and Silbermann eds, *Pentateuch*, 160; also Jacob, *Das erste Buch der Tora*, 639. Thus this statement is a prophetic declaration. In the wider context of the Jacob narrative it is certainly true, as we shall argue, that ch. 35 can be taken as a confirmation of Jacob's new name, and of certain promises, and that this is done in a much less ambiguous manner. However, the distinction between promising that somebody will be given a new name in the future and actually giving that name must be somewhat strained - especially as 35:10 also employs the imperfect tense - see also Gen. 17:5.
46 von Rad, *Genesis*, 325.
47 So Gunkel, *Genesis*, 350-1. By contrast, Hamilton (*The Book of Genesis*, 336) denies that the passage has any suggestion that Jacob wishes to know the name in order to exert power. However his clear distinction between this passage and 'parallels from primitive religion in which demons and numens played a large part', does not do justice to the oddity of this passage and the issue of power and force which is already raised. Whereas we can agree that the request for a name is a natural part of Biblical theophanies, and is in itself a request for information, it would not be inconsistent with Jacob's character to want to use such knowledge for his own benefit.

struggle and strength which this passage so clearly depicts, even if the idea is not explicit.

In terms of the structure of the passage, vv. 29 and 30 are pivotal and similar in highlighting the theme of names. However the differences betray the difference between the two combatants. God's question to Jacob is direct, as is the answer. Jacob's question is more polite (שאל - 'asked' - usually refers to a request), and the verb הגידה ('tell' or sometimes 'reveal') may suggest the divine nature of the name. The other difference is of course that Jacob gets no answer. Thus in this verse there is no doubt that God is not fully letting Jacob control him, and he preserves his freedom.

There is a striking parallel with Ex. 3:13-14 at this point, where God does not refuse to disclose his name in answer to Moses' request, although the explanation of its significance is still open ended. In the case of the Peniel story, the situation is the reverse, as a new name is given in relation to Jacob. Taking the contrast further, Jacob exclaims that he has seen God face to face and lived (v. 31), whereas Moses hides his face for fear of seeing God (Ex. 3:6). Indeed, with both Moses and Jacob, the theme of seeing the face of God has a significance. In the case of Moses, there is certainly an ambivalence towards the idea. In Exodus 33 both sides of a polarity are expressed: that it is not permissable to see the face of God and live (v. 20), but also that Moses' close relationship to God meant that God spoke to him face to face (see also 24:11). In the Jacob story, there is not quite the same ambivalence: YHWH appears to him in a dream (28:13), and now again he sees God at night. As we shall see, for Jacob, the theme also relates to the sphere of human relations.[48] Whether deliberate or not, the contrast may be an indication of differences between the patriarchal relationship with God, which in some ways is less mediated but which does not know the name YHWH, and the Mosaic understanding where God reveals his name, but with it comes a new understanding of holiness.[49] On the other hand, Jacob

---

48   See below, p. 196.

49   Above, pp. 47, 60-1. See conclusions of Moberly, *The Old Testament of the Old Testament*, also Fischer, G. (*Jahwe unser Gott: Sprache, Aufbau und Erzähltechnik in der Berufung des Mose (Ex. 3-4)* Freiburg, Schweiz, Universitätsverlag/Göttingen: Vandenhoeck & Ruprecht, 1989), on the understanding of Ex. 3-4 as a turning-point, which picks up much of the patriarchal narratives, and looking forward to the development towards Mosaic Yahwism.

Calvin (*A Commentary on Genesis*, vol. 2, 201) also makes a contrast, although for him the much greater contrast is with the Christian dispensation: 'It is to be observed, that although Jacob piously desires to know God more fully, yet because he is carried beyond the bounds prescribed to the age in which he lived, he suffers a repulse.'

is astonished at being able to see God, just as he experiences a sense of awe and trembling after the Bethel experience.

Finally Jacob is blessed. To repeat the quotation from von Rad:

> How far removed from the petition itself is the final fulfilment! Jacob first has to reveal his name and his nature, he has to receive a new name, and he has to give up the question about the unknown assailant's name. Thus it becomes clear that our narrative is far removed from all those sagas which tell of the extortion of a divine nature by man and of the winning of a blessing.[50]

This distance suggests that, although on the face of it God is forced to respond, the coercion is only apparent, and it is on God's terms that Jacob is blessed. This impression is even clearer in the next verse.

v. 31: If Jacob is unable to give a name to God, he is at least able to name the place where he has experienced God (see also 28:19, 35:15). There is an interesting parallel between the explanation clause here and in v. 29 which has a very similar structure.[51] However, the meaning of the two is opposite: in the one, Jacob is told that he has struggled and prevailed; in the other, even the act of seeing means that he has barely escaped with his life. Thus the statement that Jacob has prevailed has to be read alongside his own perception. His amazement reflects the reader's amazement that God could let himself enter into a struggle in this way.[52] It could be that the

---

Reference to Ex. 3:14 is made by Vawter (*On Genesis*, 351), although he sees the answer given to Moses ('I am who I am') as a statement of God's ineffability, and so having the same force as the refusal to Jacob. As stated, there is some truth in this, but nevertheless there is surely some importance in the revelation of the name YHWH to Moses, especially when read alongside Ex. 6.

Another parallel is Jud. 13:17-18. In this case the human being (Manoah) asks for the name (here, it is revealed that the character is an angel), which is again refused. Likewise there is a repetition of the motif of seeing God and dying (v. 22). Thus the episode is closest to that in Genesis both in the refusal to reveal the name and in the explicit amazement and awe at having seen the 'face of God'. However, vv. 16 and 21 make it clear that it was not the name YHWH which was withheld but the name of the angel, and thus the refusal to disclose the name is in part to prevent Manoah from honouring the angel rather than YHWH. Furthermore, this incident is not so pivotal or charged with the same theological concentration as the incident at Peniel.

50 von Rad, *Genesis*, 323.

51 כי + qtl verb form + waw impf. consec.

52 von Rad, *Genesis*, 322. Hamilton (*The Book of Genesis 18-50*, 337), pointing to the repetition of the verb נצל from v. 12, denies that Jacob's speech denotes surprise at having seen God and yet surviving. Instead the repeated verb denotes that Jacob sees in his preservation here, the assurance of a preservation against Esau the next day, and so his

different understandings of the outcome of the struggle betray some diachronic development but the two statements now stand alongside each other, creating a sense of ambiguity.

v. 32: The episode is over, and it is daytime. Just as the beginning of dawn marked the beginning of the dialogue, so daylight marks its end. There is a further inclusio with v. 23 and the mention of night, which marked the beginning of the episode. The whole episode has been a gradual process from darkness and confusion to light and at least some clarity about what was going on. This is emphasized by the preposition (לו - 'upon him'). The word 'passed' (עבר) takes us back to the beginning of the struggle, where it was used several times, and likewise the reference to Jacob's limp refers back to v. 26, where the injury is sustained.

There is no more reference to any confrontation or dialogue, and we do not even read of the disappearance of the mysterious figure. In a sense the conversation and the subsequent realization that Jacob was really dealing with God have overtaken interest in the struggle itself. We might even be tempted to think that Jacob was only dreaming except that in his limp he carries a permanent mark. What matters now is not so much the struggle itself, but the changes that it has brought about: Jacob's limp, his new name, the place name, darkness to light. All of this is underlined by the motif of passage (עבר), as this has been a place of transition. The fact that Jacob is left with a limp again emphasizes that his victory is not as clear cut as we might think.[53]

v. 33: Just as the struggle has left a strong impression on Jacob, so it leaves an impression on his descendants. This actualization of the event ('to this day') again shows how this episode is not just to be seen as an event in Jacob's life, but has a link to the life of Israel. Furthermore, just as the previous verse has the first occurrence of the name Israel, so now there is the first occurrence of the phrase 'Israelites' in the Bible.[54] As with other parts of the story, it is likely that this part is a tradition which has been brought in or has been made for the wider story, but any original context has been lost and was not regarded as consequential by the narrator.

---

surprise is at the answered prayer. However, Hamilton seems to contradict this insistence later on (p. 346): 'The surprise in ch. 32 is that Jacob saw God, and yet his life was spared.'
53   The suggestion that the lameness is to be seen as a tacit judgement on the crafty Jacob is probably overstated (McKenzie, J. L., 'Jacob at Peniel: Gen 32:24-32', *CBQ* 25 (1963), 75).
54   בני-ישראל - literally, 'sons of Israel'.

Conclusion

Historical-Critical Summary

As with the passages already studied, we have seen no justification for a division along traditional source critical lines. Nevertheless, an acknowledgement of some historical development has helped to show some of the depths of this passage, and this study has tried to show that a cautious use of historical tools has helped understand the final form.

Although there is evidence that this passage is embedded in its wider narrative context through various motifs, there is nevertheless something startling about the passage, and its complexity and density, together with a strongly anthropomorphic picture of God, suggest that it has a different origin from the surrounding narrative.

Those origins are now well and truly concealed, but the picture of some sort of divine figure struggling with a human at night and seeming to surrender some sort of blessing, would seem to be a residual element of an original tale. The suggestion that an original wordplay between אבק ('wrestle') and יבק ('Jabbok'), now not so prominent in the text, may have given this a local setting at the Jabbok ford is also plausible.[55] This may also explain the association of the figure of Jacob (יעקב) with the place.

However the Israelite writer(s) have shifted the emphasis of the text even more to the theme of blessing and, in particular, interest has moved to the names of the two opponents. In addition, the passage now contains the bewildering idea that it is God himself that Jacob has faced in struggle. Furthermore, the two explicit etiological motifs, one regarding the name Israel, the other regarding the eating customs of the Israelites are perhaps best seen as ways of appropriating this ancient story rather than original features.

This development of a once independent, non-Israelite story into an episode in the life of Israel's patriarch, best accounts for why the passage is clearly distinct from its narrative context on the one hand, but is also woven into the narrative fabric on the other hand, being represented as a turning-point for Jacob, and even for Israel. Beyond this, little more about the development of this strange tale can be said.

---

55 Westermann, *Genesis 12-36*, 515.

God

As in the story at Bethel God is depicted in anthropomorphic terms in that God is a character in the narrative who stands, speaks, has a form. This anthropomorphism is taken even further in that God wrestles with a human, almost as an equal, and on the face of it is coerced by that human.

However it would be wrong to form from this any conclusion about the lack of theological sophistication on the part of the writer. On the contrary we have seen that behind this simple depiction of a struggle lies all manner of ambiguity which, even if partly a result of historical development, cannot simply be resolved by recourse to tradition history.

Part of the ambiguity centers around the motif of concealment and darkness. Although this passage may be said to represent the presence of God in contrast to the absence of God within much else of the Jacob narrative, presence is here ambiguous and partly concealed. Even at the end, when it is clear that God has been present, there is still a feeling of confusion as to what has really taken place. Thus although on the face of it there is the resolution of the ambiguity of which figure is which, and who the mysterious figure really is, the passage as a whole raises still deeper questions.

One indication of this is the fact that instead of a clear-cut promise (such as given at Bethel) there is the giving of a name, which although of great significance and privilege for Jacob, is complicated by the double-edged etymology: it is praising Jacob in a fashion, but is nevertheless a strange way to go about it.

A deeper level of ambiguity is the question of who has really won, as the two statements of vv. 29 and 31 stand in some tension. Behind this is some suspicion that God has allowed himself to be beaten. Jacob does seem to come away as victor, but we feel that there is more to the story than has been revealed. In particular, the conclusion of von Rad is most appropriate that behind all this, is the wonderment that God should put himself in such a position.[56] For the theologian, this leads to consideration of how God works through an apparent position of weakness: on the face of it God has been defeated, but in this display of weakness, his plans not just for Jacob but for his descendants have moved closer to fulfilment.[57]

---

56   von Rad, *Genesis*, 322.
57   From a Christian perspective, there is some scope for considering the passage from the Pauline idea of God's power revealed in weakness (1 Cor. 1:25). See Brueggemann, *Genesis*, 271; also, from a devotional perspective, Tugwell, S. (*Prayer: Living with God*, Dublin: Veritas Publications, 1975, 63-64):

Another level of ambiguity is in the activity of God as made clear by the actantial analysis of Barthes who points to the startling and paradoxical case of the originator of the quest turning out to be also the opponent. In terms of the story, Jacob has to cross the stream if he is to return home as commanded by God (31:3), but now he faces a lethal obstacle who turns out to be God. This causes us to wonder at the nature of God who both commands but then seems to obstruct.[58] This idea is also taken up by Hermisson who sees the motif of 'das Dämonische' (demonic) in God, not just in this story but also in such events as the demand that Abraham should give up his only son (Gen. 22:1ff), the testing of Job (Job 1:6ff) and in some prophetic imagery.[59] To this could be added the strange threat to Moses after his call to return to Egypt (Ex. 4:24ff), the angel standing in the way of Balaam (Nu. 22:22) and the killing of Uzzah (2 Sam. 6:7). Such stories and motifs in their own way point to the ultimate freedom of God, and paradoxically, although depicting God in the most anthropomorphic of terms, they actually serve as a corrective against any attempt to limit God to any predictable pattern.[60]

The obscure hint given in Genesis becomes too appallingly explicit in the New Testament, with the Son of Man literally given over into the hands of men (Mt 17:22), to do with him whatever they please. And somehow - and this is the deepest mystery of all - the contemplation of that victory of man over God is what brings countless men, heart-broken, shattered, unmade, humbly seeking forgiveness and new life from the God who made himself known in such weakness...Really to meet the weakness, the poverty, the humility of God, while we are in the full flood of our strength...surely that is what 'disables' us, giving us a new name, leading us into a light so brilliant...and making us incapable, at least to some extent, of simply resuming our career of ambition and way of strength.

See also earlier comments of Elliger ('Der Jakobskampf am Jabbok', 1-31) - above, p. 69.
58   This paradoxical picture of God's work lies behind Calvin's reading (*A Commentary on Genesis*, vol. 2, 195-6):

It is not said that Satan, or any mortal man, wrestled with Jacob, but God himself: to teach us that our faith is tried by him...Therefore, what was once exhibited under a visible form to our father Jacob, is daily fulfilled in the individual members of the Church; namely, that, in their temptations, it is necessary for them to wrestle with God...[but] we do not fight against him, except by his own power, and with his own weapons...for he, both fights *against* us and *for* us.

59   Hermisson, H.-J., 'Jakobs Kampf am Jabbok (Gen 32:22-33).' *ZTH* 71 (1974), 259.
60   Similarly de Pury (*Promesse Divine*, vol. 2, 102). De Pury situates this theological concern with the Yahwist, who has transformed an earlier story of Jacob defeating a river god. In its present form, the story holds together the idea that God cannot be manipulated with the idea that Jacob is nevertheless blessed: 'A Penuel ont été sauvegardées à la fois la souveraineté et la fidélité de Dieu.'

Thus on all these levels there remains a degree of concealment. On the one hand the passage again points to the action of God in Jacob's life, but on the other hand it intensifies the tension felt elsewhere of God's presence and absence. As a result this passage is not a revelatory counter-point to the wider narrative, but reflects in itself the tension between the divine and the human felt throughout the narrative. In a way, therefore, it is a commentary on much of Jacob's life.

This motif of concealment also relates to the refusal of the stranger to disclose his name. As noted in the exegesis, the passage contrasts with Exodus 3, where Moses is given the name YHWH in answer to his request, but where he covers his face for fear of seeing God. In relation to a comparison with the Bethel incident, we noted that part of the contrast is the entrance of the concept of holiness (קדש) into the life of Israel in the book of Exodus, and the contrast in this passage further illuminates differences between the relationship with God as portrayed in the patriarchal narratives and as portrayed from the time of Moses.[61]

Finally this concealment and ambiguity gives justification to speculation as to who this figure could represent. Any reading of the passage has to do justice to the literal understanding that the figure is identified with God, but such an identification should not be seen as closing the question. To quote one commentator:

> As the text stands, it is clearly none other than YHWH in human form (32:30). But the fact that the story is so suggestive of these other interpretations [i.e. that the figure is a spirit, Esau, a projection of Jacob's subconscious]...makes it likely that in a sense they are all true, as they all belong to the immediate or wider context of the story. God confronts Jacob not only in human form, but as Esau, whom he fears, as a night spirit, belonging to the time when his fears are at their sharpest, as a river spirit because he is crossing a perilous boundary in to the territory of Israel, and as the embodiment of the deepest hopes and fears of his own mind. The writer boldly incorporates these folkloristic motifs in order to try to convey something of the mysterious depth of the occasion.[62]

---

61   Interestingly, both this passage and Ex. 3 mark significant turning-points. In the former case, it is the introduction of the name 'Israel'; in the latter case, the name YHWH. These are both important for the individuals concerned (Jacob and Moses) but also for Israel.
62   Moberly, R. W. L., *Genesis 12-50*, Sheffield: JSOT Press, 1992, 31. This open-ended approach would therefore allow for the identification of the figure with Esau or an angel of Esau as found in much Jewish commentary - see Scherman and Zlotowitz eds, *Bereishis* vol. 4, 1437; also Jacob, *Das erste Buch der Tora*, 643:

The fact that God could appear to Jacob in human form again shows an interweaving of the human with the divine, with a significance beyond this incident, since the episode is an indicator of the wider story. This interweaving is, of course, spelt out in the declaration of v. 29b.[63]

Jacob

As noted above, this passage is a commentary on the wider narrative, sharpening the ambiguous nature of the divine presence in Jacob's life. Conversely, as well as providing an illustration of the nature of the divine, this incident also provides a comment on Jacob himself as highlighted in v. 29.[64] Thus we have already noted how the struggling 'with God and men'

> Auch er ist ein 'Satan'...der 'Satan' ist auch ein Gotteskämpfer, er vertritt immer eine gute Sache, ein relatives Recht. Und das war Esaus Sache. Er durfte mit Recht auf den Bruder ergrimmt sein, der ihn betrogen hatte...So ist der Gottesbote der Geist, das Recht Esaus, der Schatten, der Jakob zwanzig Jahre verfolgt hatte und sich jetzt riesengroß erhebt. Mit Einem Worte: es ist die eigene Vergangenheit und Schuld, mit der Jakob 'ringt'.

In particular the episode is in response to Jacob's prayer for help, where the 'angel' acts in a similar way to Job's 'Satan', testing Jacob's resolve and testing God's plan for Jacob to become Israel. As it is, the outcome of the episode prefigures Jacob's reconciliation with Esau. Furthermore, argues Jacob (p. 642) the injury inflicted upon Jacob by the angel is to be the key to Jacob's salvation from Esau, since it is the sight of Jacob struggling to bow seven times with his injured leg that will disarm Esau, diffusing his anger.

For a psychological understanding of the figure, see also Alter (*Genesis*, 181): the figure is 'the embodiment of portentous antagonism in Jacob's dark night of the soul. He is obviously a doubling of all with whom Jacob has had to contend, and he may equally well be an externalization of all that Jacob has to wrestle with within himself.'

To this list of possible interpretations, Kunin adds that of Jacob's father (*The Logic of Incest*, 129).

63   In the wider context of the Jacob story it is noticeable that YHWH already has revealed his name (28:13). It would therefore seem unusual for Jacob to ask now about the name. One could reconcile the two passages by arguing that in 32:30 Jacob is still not sure who his opponent is, and so he is asking about the identity of the opponent rather than about the name of God per se. No doubt Jacob's ongoing uncertainty is a factor behind the request, but there is also the emphasis on the name itself, and to reduce Jacob's question simply of wanting to know who the person is does not do justice to the wording of the request or to the high importance of names themselves, particularly in relation to God. It seems better therefore to see this incongruity as arising from a historical tension.

64   Alter, *Genesis*, 180:

> The image of the wrestling has been implicit throughout the Jacob story: in his grabbing Esau's heel as he emerges from the womb, in his striving with Esau for birthright and blessing, in his rolling away the huge stone from the mouth of the well, and in his multiple contendings with Laban. Now, in this culminating moment of his

can refer to the Laban and especially the Esau episodes, and how Jacob's attaining of both the birthright and the blessing from the eldest son, Esau, is in some sense a rebellion against the prerogative of the first-born, and thus even against God. But there is equally the mystery that God allows Jacob to triumph, both in his struggle for supremacy over Esau and over himself in this episode, and just as Jacob does not come from this episode unscathed, neither does he come from his procurement of the blessing in chapter 27 unscathed. From the perspective of Jacob, the human perspective, it would seem that he has to get his way by his own means and that there is no outside help to rely on. But from a wider perspective, hinted at here, God is using Jacob's very self-assertion to achieve his own ends, and the fact that in this passage an explicitly Israelite perspective is drawn in, shows that these ends reach far beyond the life and fate of the individual Jacob. Indeed for Jacob, in his lifetime, to be the chosen one is indeed a mixed blessing.

But this passage also represents a turning-point. As noted above, this is highlighted by the repetition of the word עבר (cross/sent/pass), but is especially indicated by the new name which Jacob receives. Fokkelman's comment that this is a 'baptism' where the 'evil' name is exchanged for a 'beautiful, theophorous name' needs some qualification in the light of what has been noted about the double-edged nature of the etymology; yet this passage, and the giving of the name does mark a departure for Jacob, and does represent a great, undeserved privilege.[65] This raises a question as to

---

life story, the characterizing image of wrestling is made explicit and literal.

65   Fokkelman, *Narrative Art*, 215-6, already quoted above. For Fokkelman, as for many commentators, this episode represents a great conversion experience. Driver , S. R. (*The Book of Genesis*, 8th ed., London: Methuen, 1911, 297) writes:

> The moment marks a great spiritual change in Jacob's character. He feels his carnal weapons become lamed and useless...as the result of his struggle his natural self is left behind, he rises from it an altered man...and so we may notice that from this point in his history we hear no more of him as practising craft and deceit: he is still indeed (chxxxiii.) politic and resourceful; but he becomes more and more...the type of a just and God-fearing Israelite.

A further spiritual dimension pointed to is that of Jacob's feeling of guilt and his experience of God's grace (so Dillmann, *Die Genesis*, 364).

    However, caution needs to exercised in these applications, especially where concepts such as guilt, forgiveness or even conversion are not explicitly found in the narrative.

    The same applies to the idea that this incident represents a cleansing or confession of guilt, a suggestion made, for instance by Wenham (*Genesis 16-50*, 296) who argues that

how much things really do change for Jacob in the light of this incident, and could apply equally to Jacob's fortunes and to his inner character. This is something we shall have to address when we come to look at the wider story. Nevertheless, judged in its own right, there is no doubt that we are meant to see here a deep experience of Jacob that has a lasting effect on him.

Furthermore this passage is both a turning-point and perhaps an exercise in self-understanding for Israel. The fact that the word 'Israel' appears for the first time, and twice at that, indicates that something new has occurred, as for the first time Israel as a named, clearly defined entity has appeared. What is surprising - and something which we shall encounter again in the Jacob story - is that it is at such a moment as this that 'Israel' should enter the stage of human history. It comes at a point where Jacob is at his most vulnerable, left alone; and it is given in the context of a struggle with - that is, against - Israel's God. This shows on the part of the bearers and shapers of Israel's traditions an ability to examine its own beginnings in a self-critical way. It could of course be argued - as Gunkel and Westermann indeed do - that v. 29 is a proud statement of invincibility, but that does not take account of the mood of the passage as a whole, especially of Jacob's own assessment at the end.[66] Even so, we can perhaps detect some degree of admiration at the hero's tenacity and strength, albeit muted by a strong suspicion that Jacob has indeed been fortunate to escape.

Moreover, the actual etymology for the new name of Israel, that Jacob has striven with God and men, could be said to relate to Israel itself. In this way the passage bears witness to a people, or least the bearers of its traditions, which sees its very origin, and perhaps continued existence, in terms of a struggle against other peoples and even against its own God, that is, of a people fighting against the odds, stubbornly refusing to give in, falling back on its own resources, even faced with what seems to be a hostile God against whom it has to fight for survival, but perhaps also a people which, in spite of itself and appearances, has been spared by God. This comes in part from a recognition of sin on the part of Israel, but more

---

by making Jacob speak out his own name, the angel is forcing him to make a statement about his cheating nature and that this therefore amounts to a confession of guilt. Terms such as guilt or confession probably go beyond what the text allows, especially as the explanation of Jacob's new name seems almost to make a virtue of Jacob's struggle with Esau and Laban.

66 Gunkel, *Genesis*, 350 and Westermann, *Genesis: 12-36*, 518. However, both Gunkel and Westermann interpret this verse independently of the passage itself. Compare Elliger ('Der Jakobskampf am Jabbok', 21), who sees the way the name is introduced to show that 'Israel' is 'kein Ehrenname mehr'.

widely, of the mysterious workings of God. As with Jacob, to be chosen is
a mixed blessing, to be marked out means to be wounded and to carry a
limp.[67] Such an understanding no doubt takes us beyond the confines of the
passage itself, but this is the sort of passage which invites just such a
reflection.[68] To fail to make such a wide connection is to misunderstand the
nature of this strange story.

To conclude this section, the above comments can be taken one step
further in drawing a contrast between the human and the divine in this
passage. Our considerations have gone in two directions: on the one hand,
the divine has been expressed in the terms of concealment and mystery,
particularly at the mysterious grace that God should be - or seem to be -
defeated or coerced by Jacob. This is expressed in Jacob's own remark (v.
31). On the other hand, the human is expressed in terms of the courage,
strength and persistence of Jacob, expressed in the statement of v. 29. The
first aspect lends itself to considerations about the nature of God, with the
motif of concealment but also grace, and the idea of God showing himself
weak in the face of human strength. The second aspect lends itself to
reflections about human spirituality, where the idea of 'wrestling with God'
is often explored in the realm of prayer or life, but also about how faith may
involve situations where the believer seems to be thrown onto their own
resources or even onto fighting against what might seem to be the divine
plan. The one aspect is a consideration about the working of the divine; the
other, about human striving.

In broad terms, both of these work in tension through Jacob's life - on the
one level, it is the story of human achievement involving human strength,
deception, cunning; on the other level, it is the story of divine providence
working in the life of this individual, albeit in a hidden way, though where
Jacob and the reader occasionally see evidence of the divine at work.

---

67   Levenson, *The Death and Resurrection of the Beloved Son*, 59 - see above, pp. 23-4.
68   For a reflection on how the passage relates to the experience of the Jewish people:
Leibowitz, N., *Studies in Bereshit (Genesis)*, 3rd ed., Jerusalem: World Zionist
Organization, 1976, 369-7. McKay, H. A. ('Jacob Makes It across the Jabbok: An attempt
to solve the Success/Failure Ambivalence in Israel's Self-Consciousness.' *JSOT* 38 (1987),
3-13) relates the passage to the experience of the exilic community and their anxieties about
returning to the land of Israel. Certainly this is a valid application of the passage but to
translate this 'success/failure ambivalence' into historical terms in order to 'solve' it goes
against the whole approach taken in our own reading, as is the use of such a reading to
ascribe to the passage in its developed form an exilic origin.

PART 2

THE HUMAN STORY OF JACOB

Chapter 4

The Struggle for Blessing:
Jacob and Esau Part 1
(26:34-28:9)

The first part of Jacob's life is centred on his struggle with Esau for blessing and supremacy. Although prefigured in the opening scenes, the struggle reaches its most dramatic climax in the deception by Jacob of his father Isaac.

As well as the usual introductory historical-critical questions, we shall also address the moral question raised by the passage. This is a necessary question to ask as it relates to the genre of the passage, and so affects how we are to read it. As often the case, the work of Gunkel is a useful starting-point for both these aspects.

A Note on Chapter 26

Before looking at chapter 27, brief reference should be made to the inclusion of material about Isaac in chapter 26 between the two episodes involving Jacob and Esau. Most commentators coming from a historical-critical perspective simply treat the chapter in its own right, passing over its present context. There is little doubt that the passage has been placed in its present context by a redactor of the overall cycle.[1]

Furthermore, the break in subject matter from the fraternal conflict provides an interlude before continuing with the intense drama. Wenham develops this idea by pointing out that as well as showing links with other parts of the patriarchal narratives, the episode serves as a foil for what is to come.[2] Chapter 26 depicts a rather timid Isaac, trying where possible to avoid conflict, who nevertheless is the recipient of the divine promise and

---

1   See Fishbane, M., *Text and Texture: Close Readings of Selected Biblical Texts*, New York: Schocken Books, 1979, 42, on how this episode fits into the wider structure.
2   Wenham, *Genesis 16-50*, 185ff.

finds peace.[3] The wealth which he acquires also makes tangible the
'blessing' over which the brothers are to fight. This attitude of Isaac also
contrasts with the active Jacob who gets what he wants by deception and
conflict: 'If Isaac could achieve so much without manipulating people, why
do Jacob and Rebekah have to resort to the tactics about to be described?'[4]

Introduction

Mainly because of historical-critical questions as seen above, there is no
unanimous definition of the limits of this passage. The heart of the passage
are the scenes between Isaac-Esau, Rebekah-Jacob, Jacob-Isaac and Esau-
Isaac. The subsequent verses spell out the consequences of what has
happened with no clear episodic markers. However, it is clear that, literary-
historical questions aside, 28:10 marks the next major episode.
Furthermore, 26:34-35 have more in common with what follows them than
with the preceding chapter and, as we shall see, act as a framing device with
the closing verses of this passage. Thus we shall be considering Gen. 26:34
- 28:9.

Source Criticism

Gunkel offers a detailed argument in favour of a source critical approach.[5]
He starts with the probability that strands of both J and E are present since
this episode is presupposed by both sources elsewhere. For him the main
indication of sources is that Jacob uses two methods of disguise (and thus,
Gunkel presupposes, they are a doublet). From this, he detects two parallel
accounts: in one, Jacob puts on the goat's skin (v. 16), Isaac tests the
identity of the person before him by feeling, and although he recognizes the
voice of Jacob, he believes that he is feeling Esau's arms. This act of
deception has been thought up by Rebekah. Because Isaac has already heard
Jacob's voice, once he realizes he has been tricked, he immediately knows

---

3   By contrast, Hamilton (*Genesis: 18-50*, 190) sees a reversal of fortunes for Isaac
between ch. 26 and ch. 27: 'Both chs. 26 and 27 are laced with the theme of deception. The
difference is that Isaac is the deceiver in ch. 26 but the deceived in ch. 27. The villain
becomes a victim, and nemesis is at work in his life as much as it is in the life of his
younger son.'
4   Wenham, *Genesis 16-50*, 188.
5   Gunkel, *Genesis*, 298-300; among other such attempts: Delitszch, *A New Commentary
on Genesis*, 147; Procksch O., *Die Genesis*, 2/3rd ed., Leipzig: Deicherische
Verlagsbuchhandlung, 1924, 166.

that it is Jacob who has carried out the deception (v. 35). In the second version, Jacob puts on Esau's best clothes. Isaac tests the identity of the person before him by kissing and by the sense of smell. Consequently, when Isaac learns that he has been deceived, he does not know at first who has tricked him (v. 33).

Apart from 26:34-35 and 27:46-28:9 other commentators are far less confident in identifying sources. For instance, von Rad seems undecided,[6] and Westermann sees some repetition (vv. 33-38) but denies that this points to parallel sources, arguing instead for additions to the text.[7] Blum sees the only repetition in v. 44b and 45a.[8]

Thus much scholarly opinion has turned from that reflected by Gunkel. Regarding the presence of doublets, it is far from clear that the different disguises and Isaac's different reactions are genuine repetitions, and what little repetition there may be in the passage (e.g. v. 44b/45a) is hardly cause for dividing the whole passage into two continuous sources. Furthermore, we shall see that the passage is well structured and flows smoothly. Regarding other traditional criteria for source division, there are hardly enough occurrences of YHWH or Elohim for this criterion to have any weight. In v. 20, where both terms occur, they are not interchangeable, but 'your God' (אלהיך) is appositional and descriptive to YHWH. The other occurrence of both words is in the first blessing (v. 27 and v. 28), but it is notable that Elohim has a definite article, and so would not fit neatly into a pattern of other so-called 'Elohistic' texts. There is no reason for supposing that the two terms are not simply a poetic variation, or that they vary for some other, inexplicable, reason.

This leaves the question of 26:34-35 and 27:46-28:9. Here there is much more of a case for seeing a separate source. The first set of verses neither follows smoothly from the preceding chapter about Isaac which is closed by the etymology of Beersheba, nor makes any mention of Esau who is suddenly reintroduced. Furthermore the theme of these verses - that of intermarriage - does not correspond to the tightly knit narrative that is to follow. However, these verses do correspond to the final verses which

---

6   von Rad, *Genesis*, 276; also Skinner, J., *A Critical and Exegetical Commentary on Genesis*, Edinburgh: T. & T. Clark, 1910, 368-9. A more recent attempt to apply source critical methods to this passage is undertaken by Schmidt, L., 'Jakob erschleicht sich den väterlichen Segen: Literaturkritik und Redaktion von Genesis 27,1-45.' *ZAW* 100 (1988), 159-83. The case here is built especially around the repeated mention of Isaac blessing (v. 23b.27) - see exegesis below.

7   Westermann, *Genesis 12-36*, 436.

8   Blum, *Die Komposition der Vätergeschichte*, 79ff.

reintroduce the theme of intermarriage, with 27:46 resuming the upset that Esau's marriages are causing to his parents. Furthermore the blessing which Isaac gives to Jacob is of a very different style to his earlier blessing and is more similar to promises found in the patriarchal narratives.

In particular there is a strong case for regarding these verses as part of the Priestly source in Genesis. This is because of the proper nouns Paddan-aram, Bethuel and the term Aramaen, all concentrated in Gen. 25:19-20. This impression is confirmed especially by 28:1-4 where Isaac's blessing corresponds closely to the divine promise of 35:9-15. Wenham argues against ascribing this passage to P, by claiming that the distinctiveness of the vocabulary is due to the genre of the passage rather than its source.[9] However, he seems to underestimate the accumulative effect of all the terms, and in particular he passes over the term El Shaddai (v. 3 - see especially Gen. 17:1, Gen. 35:11, Ex. 6:3) and underestimates the difference in style and theme between these verses and the main part of chapter 27. As we shall see, it is true that these verses show connections with chapter 27, but to say that they 'echo' or 'are modelled on' them, as Wenham does, certainly is not to say that they originate from the same hand. Thus in all probability these verses belong to the same strand as Gen. 35:9-15 which is commonly ascribed to P.

Form Criticism and Tradition Criticism

Gunkel's interest is in the characters of Jacob and Esau, and as in Gen. 25:21ff he concludes that these characters are based on very old legends, representing types of the shepherd and the hunter.[10] He does not attempt to work out who these figures actually were (i.e. whether they actually existed or were thought to have existed as mythical characters), but they are not of specifically 'Israelite' origin. This can be seen in that the sagas do not match historical details regarding Israel and Edom, where in reality, Israel is supposed to have been not cowardly but warlike and brave, and where Edom was reputed for its wisdom (Jer. 49:7, Bar. 3:22). Gunkel therefore argues that the references to Israel and Edom are much later.

In the original tale, the hunter is the first-born and despises herd farming, but the shepherd attains the upper hand through his cleverness, which means that he gains the better land and pasture and consequently dominance over his brother. One can see how this reading reflects a possible tension between the cultures of man as hunter and, perhaps, an emerging culture of

---

9   Wenham, *Genesis 16-50*, 203.
10   Gunkel, *Genesis*, 308.

man as settled husbandman or farmer - a contrast which is universally valid. But as the text then found its way into Israelite hands, it acquired references to the struggle with Edom: Edom is understood to be the older people, yet Israel has the better land.

Von Rad's historical interest and method is slightly different, although his conclusions are similar to Gunkel.[11] Since the story depicts the characters as tribal ancestors, they can be taken to be tribal recollections. However, the Jacob stories are situated in an area defined by names such as Peniel, Bethel and Shechem, covering central Palestine and a small part east of the River Jordan, whereas Edom was situated much further south. Consequently, the Esau of chapters 27 and 33 is traditionally not Edom, but represents the hunter people whom the people of Jacob (the tribe which saw Jacob as their ancestor) met as they colonized East Jordan and whom they as shepherds recognized as having a different way of life from their own. It is later, when the stories are transferred to the Judean south that the connection was made between Esau and Judah's great rival Edom. For von Rad, therefore, the hunter-shepherd contrast is not general as for Gunkel but rooted in a specific cultural encounter between two tribal groups.

Westermann sees the long traditio-historical development of a single, independent, oral family story from the 'patriarchal period'.[12] With most exegetes he argues that the blessings were added later since they presuppose relations between tribes and peoples rather than within a family. The identification of Esau with Edom is very much secondary.

Over and against these views Blum claims that the ethnological meaning of the story is part of the substantial and original meaning. In chapter 25, the understanding of Jacob and Esau as being Israel and Edom respectively is the presupposition not only of v. 23, but of the whole section, since the description of Esau is aimed at the names Edom and Seir (v. 25). Blum argues that this is also the case with chapter 27. His evidence not only rests on the blessing (which most would see as later), but is also more securely rooted in the plot. He points to v. 11b where the description of Esau as 'a hairy man' is both vital to the plot but also refers back to 25:25, both of which again should be seen as a reference to Seir.[13]

Blum, however, avoids claiming that the two brothers are straight-forward allegories, and that the meaning of the stories can simply be translated back into ethnological terms. For example, the motif of the

---

11 von Rad, *Genesis*, 276.
12 Westermann, *Genesis 12-36*, 435.
13 The word 'hairy' (שער) contains the same Hebrew letters as the name Seir.

younger getting the better of the older should not be seen to mean that Edom was an older nation, but is simply a common motif. Thus the ethnological perspective does not exhaust these stories, and the reader can see other dimensions by refocussing to another 'depth of perspective'.[14] Unfortunately, what these other perspectives might be is not really spelt out, since Blum's main concern seems to be the historical and traditio-historical context.

Some similarity can be found with Van Seters who sees the chapter as being written by the Yahwist himself, with the blessing as an integral part.[15] As well as exploring the content of the blessings, Van Seters is interested in the relationship of chapter 27 to Gen. 25:21-34, and he concludes that the former is based upon the latter, developing many of the motifs found in the opening story.

In conclusion, whereas most scholars have played down the national-historical aspect of the text, Blum stresses its importance by attempting to show that it belongs to the earliest part of the text. Irrespective of his historical-critical judgments, he has shown that the ethnological perspective is an important part of the text as it is. Nevertheless, it should be pointed out that the ethnographic dimension is far from dominant, especially as in itself, the word 'hairy' (שער - v. 11) is not an obvious allusion to Seir. Regarding the view of Van Seters, this depends to some extent on how one sees the relationship between this passage and chapter 25, but also his wider thesis of the pervading Yahwist writer. In respect to chapter 25, I suggested that it may have contained traditional elements which had been shaped by a final redactor of the Jacob story to form an introduction, a view with which Van Seters disagrees.[16] Also to be questioned is the extent to which the influence behind the wording of the blessing can be traced, since Van Seters sees a derivation from royal ideology.[17] Nevertheless, both Van Seters and Blum have shown that Gunkel's account of the origins of the story can no longer be taken for granted despite its widespread support. It remains open to question whether chapter 27 was originally an ancient tale of two brothers of contrasting lifestyles or whether it was conceived as a literary work deliberately incorporating folkloric motifs. In either case, we must also take

---

14   Blum, *Die Komposition der Vätergeschichte*, 72.

15   Van Seters, *Prologue to History*, 282-8.

16   See above, p. 24-5.

17   Van Seters, *Prologue to History*, 288. Van Seters argues for the same influence here as for the promises in the Bethel passage. However it remains to be shown how ch. 27 and the promise and vows in 28:1,0-22 (see p. 298) are all creations of the same writer (J), given obvious differences in style and content.

seriously the fact that this family story - whatever its origins - is told in such a way that it also has something to say about the relationship between Israel and its neighbours.

The Moral Question

One of the reasons why Old Testament theology is so complex and problematic is the problem of how the above mentioned questions of source and tradition affect any attempt to make theological sense of the narrative. This is especially the case with a question which confronts the reader of this passage: how are we to appraise the deception by Jacob, and for that matter, his mother? Is it to be condemned or praised? The reason why this is complicated by the historical agenda is that it forces us to ask a preliminary question: was it a concern of the original writer(s)?

For Gunkel, the answer is that it was not, and thus, by implication, it should not trouble us too much either. He begins by criticizing both those who 'piously' try to justify the moral standpoint of the story on the one hand, and the modern 'anti-Semites' on the other, who feel bound to use such stories to denigrate the people of Israel (and the Bible itself).[18] He feels that both sides are battling in vain. On the one hand, Gunkel agrees that the story shows no moral sense, but even seems to delight in Jacob's action. But on the other hand, he says it is anachronistic for us 'moderns' to judge earlier people by our standards. At this point his own view on the development of religion comes out: 'There was a period in Israel, too, in which morality and religion were not yet closely linked in the way we now consider self-evident.'[19] Consequently it is 'unhistorical' and therefore inappropriate for us to raise moral questions.[20]

---

18 Gunkel, *Genesis,* 300. Unfortunately, Gunkel goes on to say that we may see in the ancient Hebrew's pleasure in trickery, a tendency which - 'as everyone knows' - has been inherited by their most recent descendants - a view to which Ehrlich (*Randglossen zur Hebräischen Bibel,* 134) takes great exception. Part of Ehrlich's criticism is of the assumption that later generations are any more moral than earlier ones. This touches on the evolutionary view of religion - assumed also by Driver: 'it may be also, because, as Gunkel observes, the moral sense has been educated gradually,' (*The Book of Genesis,* 255).
19 Gunkel, *Genesis,* 301.
20 Brueggemann (*Genesis,* 229) holds a position which has some similarity to Gunkel's in that he observes that the narrative makes no attempt to explain or justify, and concludes that it simply tells the story as it is, reflecting a reality of calculation and coveting. The text therefore gives us no cause for reflection on the morality of Jacob's action. However, unlike Gunkel, Brueggemann does not see the text as simply cheering on the side of Jacob in his deception, and, with von Rad, as we shall see, he sees above all else, the mystery of the divine choice.

Von Rad is deeply dissatisfied with Gunkel's approach, and characteristically seeks to bring theological fruit out of a historical-critical approach.[21] His own reading points out the seriousness of the episode, and he states that the crime against the blind man would not only be a crime against humanity, but also against God, citing Lev. 19:14 and Dt. 27:18.20. He also points out that the story does not have a happy ending as Gunkel suggests, but that the family is divided and bankrupt - 'None of that would have caused the ancient reader to laugh.'[22] He then goes on to consider the issue of personal guilt, but sees the main concern of the narrator as 'to awaken in the reader a feeling of sympathetic suffering for those who are caught up mysteriously in such a monstrous act of God and are almost destroyed in it.'[23] The passage inevitably makes us consider the idea of guilt and motivation, but the ultimate question is how God takes (or even brings about?) such a morally ambiguous human act and incorporates it into his plans.

However, two later commentators wish to go further in looking at the guilt or innocence of Jacob and Rebekah. Fokkelman, like von Rad, argues that the lack of an explicit moral statement does not mean that the passage has no moral interest, but he goes further in seeing Jacob (and Rebekah) as clearly guilty in the eyes of the narrator since the actions lead to the destruction of the whole family.[24] Although there is a divine plan, the characters still have moral responsibility, and, overall, each shares some guilt: Esau for earlier despising his birthright (25:34), Isaac for opposing God's will in wanting to bless Esau - he thinks that Isaac will have known from Rebekah that the blessing of Abraham is destined for Jacob. These moral conclusions are not to be found as such within the text, but 'It is one of those insights which the narrator leaves to our own discernment, relying on a wise reader/listener'[25]

Jacob is most clearly in the wrong, his guilt expressed in Esau's complaint in v. 36[26] and in the words of Isaac in v. 35 ('Your brother came with guile..'). But Fokkelman reserves his strongest censure for Rebekah,

---

21   von Rad, *Genesis*, 279-81.
22   von Rad, *Genesis*, 280-1. So also Procksch (*Die Genesis*, 170): 'Mit dieser Erzählung hat J ein Kunstwerk von gedrungener Tragik geschaffen.'
23   Likewise Speiser, *Genesis*, 213.
24   Fokkelman, *Narrative Art*, 115ff. Fokkelman is reflecting a more traditional approach of Christian commentators - e.g. Keil-Delitzsch (*The Pentateuch*, 279-80): 'In this way a higher hand prevailed above the acts of sinful men, bringing the counsel and will of Jehovah to eventual triumph, in opposition to human thought and will.'
25   Fokkelman, *Narrative Art*, 118.
26   'There is no doubt that the narrator shares this view.' *Narrative Art*, 119.

'the originator of all the misery and the one responsible in the first place,' since 'she denies her husband and marriage, she contrives to deprive Esau of his being for her darling's benefit, she urges Jacob to his vile deceit. She is the only one guilty with respect to all the others.'[27] If we object that Rebekah and Jacob are merely carrying out God's plan, Fokkelman claims that their guilt is for wanting to carry it out in their own way, even being prepared to use evil means to achieve their purpose. The ends do not justify the means.

If Rebekah is the most guilty party for Fokkelman, she is a saint for Allen:

> It is my thesis that on the level of spiritual call she can be viewed as handmaiden, vessel, prophet, sacrificial victim, suffering servant - in short, as the point where God's will became known on earth at a certain time in salvation history.[28]

Allen claims that modern, and particularly Protestant, exegesis has been chiefly condemning of Rebekah, reflecting a tendency to devalue the writings of the Old Testament and the strong ethical nature of Protestantism. This contrasts strongly with much Jewish or early Catholic commentary, and her own work draws strongly from the influence of these approaches.[29]

In contrast, Allen points out that Rebekah is the first person in the Biblical story to offer herself in reparation for someone else ('On me be the curse my son' - v. 13). Her first reported words are the generous offer of water to the servant of Abraham, she then goes on to offer hospitality, and throughout chapter 24 it is emphasized that she is the one chosen by God. Allen offers the possibility that Rebekah had an inner sense of the religious significance of the event, and it is Rebekah who is sensitive to the struggle of the twins in her womb. Allen also wonders whether it is in fact Rebekah

---

27 Fokkelman, *Narrative Art*, 119-20.
28 Allen, 'On Me Be the Curse My Son!', 160.
29 On insights offered by various Jewish commentators, see the main commentary below. On the whole Rashi and similar commentators tend to avoid the wide-sweeping questions of the morality of Jacob's acts, whilst maintaining a broadly positive view of him. Nevertheless, particular comments on specific phrases do hint at a wider perspective - see for instance Rashi on 32:21: 'It shall no longer be said that the blessings came to you through supplanting and subtlety but through noble conduct and an open manner.' (Rosenbaum and Silberman, *Pentateuch*, 160). See also Maher, M., 'The Transfer of a Birthright: Justifying the Ancestors.' *PIBA* 8, 1984, 1-24, who reviews attempts by rabbinic commentaries (and early Christian) to put the action of Jacob in a positive light.

who is the necessary link between Abraham and Jacob, since she seems to play a much more active role than Isaac who does not receive a specific call or test from God. She also allowed herself to be passed off as Isaac's sister to save his life (26:8).

Regarding chapter 27, Allen considers the possible moves open to Rebekah, and concludes that she takes the best option open to allow the divine plan to be fulfilled. She also takes seriously the 'fear and trembling' that Rebekah must have felt at this stage, and her words of v. 13 show that her decision was a courageous and holy act - 'Abraham was willing to sacrifice his beloved son, and Rebekah was willing to sacrifice her life'.[30] In conclusion she writes,

> Therefore, if we view the complete circumstances of Rebekah's life, her sanctity can stand as a model of profound significance for women and men of today. She serves as a model of courage, immediate acceptance of grace, long-suffering, and willingness to die for God. In her own response to God, she is a mother of the faith. More concretely, she is the mother of Jacob, i.e., of Israel.

Conclusion of the Moral Question Raised by Chapter 27

The commentators considered here have taken us through a whole range of opinion - from a refusal to consider the question of morality by regarding it as unhistorical and anachronistic, to moral judgments in favour of or against Jacob/Rebekah, to an acceptance of the moral element but a hesitancy to resolve an ambiguity, preferring to point to the startling way that God works through such situations.

To deal first with the question of historical interpretation, this needs to be tackled on two levels. The one level is whether Gunkel is historically correct in asserting that the original writer and audience had no moral qualms with this story. This is by no means clear, and much recent work has argued that Hebrew narrative is more sophisticated than some commentators have acknowledged. The absence of explicit comment should not lead one to suppose that there is no interest. On the other hand, this absence does suggest that it is perhaps equally wrong to give such a strong weight to what may be hints of moral condemnation. The moral element, if it is there, is unobtrusive and leaves some room for ambiguity.

The second level of this historical concern is the hermeneutical question of whether we can be content with 'discovering' the original intention. This

---

30   Allen, 'On Me Be the Curse, My Son!', 171.

not only assumes a lot more confidence in the results of a form critical approach than we can actually have, it also ignores the concern to see this text as part of a wider literary context in which it now has to be read. It is somewhat arbitrary to pinpoint one (hypothetical) stage in this development and to regard this as the one stage to be interpreted. Thus even if it could be proved that the 'original' form of this story had no moral concern, it now forms part of a collection of religious writings which clearly do have moral concerns.

Where Gunkel may have been helpful is in making us wary of imposing our particular views on the text. As mentioned above, von Rad is helpful in both acknowledging a moral question but also in refusing to resolve what is an ambiguous question. In particular Fokkelman seems too quick in his outright condemnation of Jacob and Rebekah for wanting to force God's plan with their own evil means. This outright moral condemnation does not do justice to a passage which seems more to pose questions than to offer clear-cut answers.

The same may be said about Allen, although by focusing on Rebekah's acceptance of any curse (can one say 'guilt'?), she does not play down the ambiguous nature of Rebekah's act or make light of it. What is perhaps less clear is the extent to which Rebekah's particular course of action is to be commended. The text itself is silent and perhaps part of the tension is caused not just by whether Jacob (and Rebekah) will succeed, but also in whether she has chosen the right course. Whereas Allen sees a parallel with the testing of Abraham (ch. 22), at least in that episode the voice of God is clearer; the problem here is that there is no voice from God, just as there is no authorial voice to tell us what to think.

This brings us close to von Rad's interpretation, though Allen has helped us to focus the problem a little more closely. The moral ambiguity can be stated thus: on the one hand, Rebekah knows the divine will in its general terms, and her dilemma is how she (and, by extension, Jacob) should play a part in its fulfilment. Furthermore, her action does eventually result in the blessing of Jacob and consequently of Israel, though that is not to say that this was the only way this could have resulted.[31] On the other hand, she encourages her younger son to trick his brother and father. Given the wider Torah context with its command to respect parents and the protection of the blind (Lev. 19:14, Dt. 27:18), and given the break up of the family which

---

31 Although it might be more accurate to state that her action *was followed* in the long term by God's blessing, since even the causal connection between the two might be unclear.

follows, we are left questioning the conduct of Jacob. We can also see that Rebekah's part in this episode is more than incidental, especially as in the wider narrative context, it is she who carries the knowledge of the divine plan. In the words of Allen, she can be described as 'the mother of the faith' or 'the mother of Israel', but it is a faith full of ambiguities, uncertainties and flaws. That Israel should see in this incident and in the incidents around it, its own beginnings is a testimony to a willingness of itself or at least of the bearers of its religious traditions to be self-critical to the utmost. On top of this we should also note with von Rad that the interest of the passage is as much with the ambiguous nature of God's work, as it is with the conduct of the people drawn into God's purpose.[32]

The Relation with Gen. 25:29-34

One final question to be considered is how this passage should be seen alongside 25:29-34, and about the relation between birth-right (בכרה - *bcrh*) and blessing (ברכה -*brch*), whether one implies the other, and if so, why Jacob needs to repeat his deception. This implies a traditio-historical question, but also the synchronic question of how to read the two together.

On the one level, the two episodes fit together as part of the development of the plot, and an explicit link is made at 27:36. In the first case, Esau loses his birth-right, strictly speaking by bargaining. For birth-right, see earlier excursus.[33] The blessing of the second episode is seen as the transmission of power.[34] Commentators are divided on how much religious significance

---

32   Mann (*The Book of the Torah*, 51), commenting on the opening scene of the Jacob cycle, notes that, if Jacob appears unscrupulous, then the character of Yahweh appears to be even more so:

> Moreover...the cycle resists any attempt at discerning whether the corresponding inscrutability in the character of *Yahweh* comes as a result of having to deal with such shady people or, on the contrary, it is Yahweh's incomprehensible will that invisibly directs the human characters.

33   Above, pp. 21-4.

34   Van Seters (*Prologue to History*, 284) emphasizes this distinction. The legal right of the first-born has already been decided (25:29-34). What is at stake now is the blessing, dealing with 'such matters as future prosperity, fertility, and prowess over one's foes' which Isaac had meant to bestow upon Esau not because he was the firstborn, but because he was the favourite. It is of course true that the two are not exactly the same, and they can be read together, but it is difficult to hold a clear distinction especially as it is never spelt out what birth-right means in terms of the patriarchal story, where it would seem to relate to the patriarchal promises in general, as would surely the blessing. Furthermore, in the story itself, the oldest-youngest contrast does play a role, both in the narrative (v. 1) and in the words of Jacob (v. 19) and Esau (v. 32).

the blessing should have, but most who consider this passage in the wider context have no doubt that we should understand it as the blessing of Abraham, containing the divine promise.[35]

As to why there seem to be parallel stories of deception, Fokkelman notes that in chapter 27 the birth-right has become a claim, something disputed. It is used only in speech - vv. 19, 32; 33; otherwise the more neutral term 'elder son' (בן הגדל) is used. Thus the struggle for blessing is based upon the claim of the first-born, which is disputed. Presumably the reason it is disputed is because of the earlier incident. However, this does not really answer the question of whether Esau's selling of the birth-right in that incident was effective, indicating that he was genuinely giving up any claim to it, and more importantly whether this had any consequences for the paternal blessing.

Overall, it would seem that behind the two episodes are two independent traditions, which have now been to a greater or lesser extent worked together. This does not make it impossible to read them as one story now, but it does explain why they seem to repeat themselves in some ways and why the relation between the birthright and the blessing is not clear. From a historical-critical perspective this seems to make most sense.

A Reading of 26:34-28:9

For the most part, the passage is clearly structured into scenes, each with two characters and each narrating a simple development. However at the end of the passage this tightly-knit scenic structure is loosened.

The basic structure is as follows:

> scene 1: Isaac and Esau (vv. 1-4),
> scene 2: Rebekah and Jacob (vv. 5-17),
> scene 3: Isaac and Jacob (vv. 18-29),
> scene 4: Isaac and Esau (vv. 30-40),
> scene 5: Rebekah and Jacob (vv. 41-45).

Around this are placed 26:34-35 and 27:46-28:9 which present the action

---

35   Although see below, p. 121 (footnote 70).

in a different perspective.[36] v. 46 is pivotal in this arrangement in providing a logical link between the main plot and the concluding verses.

Exegesis

26:34-35: Introduction

These verses provide a sudden change of subject from the incidents centred around Isaac. The fact that Isaac is also troubled by Esau's behaviour might sit a little uneasily with the fact that he shows no sign of disapproval of Esau in the coming scene and that the old parental preferences (25:28) are still intact. Nevertheless these two verses may also hint at the passivity of Isaac who has not acted to guide Esau's marriage.[37] As they stand these verses, by showing disapproval of Esau, send out a hint to the reader that what is to come should be seen in a wider context.

27:1-4: Isaac and Esau

Elements are introduced which will be vital to the action: Isaac's blindness, the proximity of his death and the need to pass on the blessing.[38] Although Isaac is near death, the depiction of him and his attitude to his approaching death is relaxed. This may be a cultural reflection of a matter-of-fact or solemn approach to death, but it also contributes to the detached authorial voice which will contrast so strongly to the emotions felt by the protagonists.

The use of 'my son' (בני) by Isaac introduces the ambiguity which will run throughout the passage about which 'son' is to be blessed and which one Isaac is talking to. It also betrays Isaac's clear favouritism since Esau is simply 'my son', leaving Jacob out of the reckoning. In terms of what is conferred by blessing, there may as well be only one son.

The reply of Esau to Jacob ('here I am' - הנני) recalls another significant

---

36   Fokkelman (*Narrative Art*, 97) sees 27:46-28:5 as a sixth scene, although the tension is no longer maintained, nor the restriction of two characters to the scene. This also leaves v. 6ff out of the picture.

37   Wenham, *Genesis 16-50*, 205.

38   Among reasons given for Isaac's blindness in Jewish tradition are that it was caused by the incense offered by Esau's wives to idols; it was brought about by God to enable Jacob to obtain the blessing; as a punishment for failing to restrain Esau's wicked deeds; so that Isaac would not have to witness these deeds. (All cited in Scherman and Zlotowitz, *Bereishis*, vol. 3, 1114.) Also see Maher, 'The Transfer of a Birthright: Justifying the Ancestors', who adds a comparison made with the blindness of Eli (1 Sam. 3) and the behaviour of Eli's sons (p. 8). Also Kunin: 'His physical condition also can be taken as symptomatic of spiritual blindness. He is blind to God's choice.' (*The Logic of Incest*, 113)

moment for Isaac (Gen. 22:1.7) - see comment at v. 18. It is interesting what is assumed by this situation: commentators point to the ancient idea of blessing and its association here with the word נֶפֶשׁ, containing the idea of the whole of a person's life, including their energy and vitality.[39] Furthermore, the whole tension of this episode depends upon a common assumption that the family blessing is passed down from one father to one son.[40] Paradoxically, this is spelt out nowhere else in the patriarchal narratives.

The description of the meal links this passage with the meal in the earlier passage where Jacob and Esau conflict over their position. Gunkel also points to what he sees as the original sacrificial context of any such meal.[41]

Thus these opening verses both introduce the factors which will be significant to the dramatic plot, and they take the reader back to a time associated with this conception of blessing and family relations.

vv. 5-17: Rebekah and Jacob

The opening scene portrays what we are meant to see as an age old event between father and son proceeding according to custom, but now the intervention of the mother brings about the drama. Although Rebekah was listening from the outset, the narrator withholds that information until now. Appropriately, we are now reminded of the preferences shown in chapter 25: Isaac and his son (27:5a), and Rebekah and her son (v. 6a).

Throughout this episode, and indeed in the last episode of the chapter, it is Rebekah who guides the destiny of Jacob. This is particularly marked in the syntax with the mention of Rebekah interrupting the smooth flow of verbs in the Hebrew text.[42] The introduction of Rebekah brings about the complication.[43] As in chapter 25 there is no disclosure of motive: either for

---

39   The word נֶפֶשׁ is simply translated 'I' in NRSV. Likewise, Alter (*Genesis*, 137) simply sees the use of the word נֶפֶשׁ as intensive synonym for the personal pronoun.

40   Wenham (*Genesis 16-50*, 205) thinks that it is unusual that Isaac wants to see only one son and bless him alone. This brings an element of culpability on the part of Isaac who has ignored Esau's unfavourable marriages. Similarly Jacob, *Das erste Buch der Tora*, 577. Certainly Isaac acts with a certain secrecy which may deserve some criticism and which indeed backfires. Nevertheless, some caution is needed since it is not really possible to state what the correct conventions might be.

41   Gunkel, *Genesis*, 302.

42   The sequence of $w + x + qatal$ is twice broken by the mention of Rebekah.

43   So Willi-Plein, I., 'Gen 27 als Rebekkageschichte: Zu einem historiographischen Kunstgriff der biblischen Vätergeschichten.' *TZ* 45 (1989), 327-8. Through this disruption, the 'Vätergeschichte' becomes the 'Rebekkageschichte'.

Kunin sees the role of Rebekah as part of a wider depiction of women as 'ambiguous

her preference of Jacob over Esau, or for her resolve to act. Westermann suggests it is her sense of the injustice at a system in which only the elder son inherits the blessing.[44] Another reason, is that she is seeking to put into effect the will of God.[45]

Her speech does not reveal her motives or inner feelings, but they do show an urgency and an authority, to both of which Jacob responds. One feature of biblical narrative which Alter points out is the tendency for one character to repeat the direct speech of another, often almost word for word save for a few differences.[46] These differences seem to be minor but can be revealing about the person who is speaking. In this case, Rebekah recounts to Jacob the words spoken by Isaac to Esau, but the urgency of the situation (note the insistent הנה - 'behold' - in the Hebrew text) caused by the lack of time is shown in the relative brevity of her description of what Isaac said, compared with the more detailed instructions of Isaac himself. She limits herself to telling Jacob all that he needs to know for him to see the urgency of the situation. There is however one addition: the blessing is to take place 'before YHWH' (לפני יהוה). Gunkel sees this as the relics of an older custom of the blessing or an oracle being preceded by a sacrificial meal to a deity (cf. the meal of Balaam in Nu. 23).[47] Certainly there is something to be said for the motif of eating before a solemn event which, by its nature, involves YHWH. In fact this may reveal a parallel to the Balaam narrative. However, it seems more likely that the phrase is a deliberate reminder of what is at stake.[48] It takes the reader beyond the confines of a family incident, and the divine name YHWH in particular reminds the reader that it is the God of the people of Israel involved here. Significantly, it is

---

and dangerous' (*The Logic of Incest*, 118). This is part of his argument that in the biblical narrative, the wife is by definition an outsider brought into a family to preserve against incest. As an outsider she represents a potential danger because she challenges existing structures and relations.

44   Westermann, *Genesis 12-36*, 444.

45   So Allen, (see above pp 107-8); Procksch also points out the similarity between Jacob, 'der kühle Rechner' and his mother: 'Er ist ohne Sympathie geschildert, der echte Sohn seiner Mutter, der Schwester Labans', (*Die Genesis*, 338).

46   Alter, *The Art of Biblical Narrative*, ch. 5.

47   Gunkel, *Genesis*, 309.

48   So Westermann, *Genesis 12-36*, 438: 'I think that the phrase is...intended as a balance between the narrative (Isaac blesses) and the pronouncements (Yahweh blesses).' Certainly, Rebekah's mention of YHWH seems to make Brueggemann's assertion that there is no indication that Rebekah knew what she was doing seem rather puzzling (*Genesis*, 235). Brueggemann makes this point to show how the human actors merely serve to further the divine plan. However true this might be, the assertion by itself tends to flatten the human side of the events.

Rebekah rather than the patriarch Isaac who emphasizes this.

The authority of Rebekah is revealed in the words she uses in her commands (see vv. 8, 13b, 43a). Key words are 'my son' (בני), 'obey' (שמע), 'my word' (קלי), 'command' (צוה). To the narrator and his reader, the words 'command' and 'obey' would normally apply to the correct attitude to God and to the Torah. Rebekah, it seems, is assuming - rightly or wrongly - for herself a similar authority. All that Jacob has to guide him are these insistent words of his mother. Furthermore the urgent and repetitive use of 'my son' (בני), used with these other terms, reflects the way wisdom addresses the reader in the Book of Proverbs.[49]

Rebekah's instruction for Jacob to fetch two kids from the flock is a practical necessity because of the limited time available before Esau's return, but also points to the difference between the two lifestyles described in chapter 25. This contrast is even brought out in the appearance of the twins, with the reference to Esau's hairy appearance also found in 25:25.[50]

Jacob's objection in v. 12 is more out of fear of the plan failing than because of any moral scruples, and once Rebekah offers to take any consequences he seems to accept.[51] The lack of any explicit moral comment by the narrator does not preclude any moral interest. The reader faces the question of whether Jacob is doing the right thing, especially since his father is elderly and blind, and whether he will succeed. The lack of any

---

49 Other similarities with wisdom motifs might be the connection of the meal (מטעמים) with deception (Prov. 23:3), and the word חלק ('smooth') and its cognates used to describe someone as deceitful (e.g. Prov. 2:16, 7:5, 28:23, 29:5, 20:19, 26:28). The phrase מטעמים is used three times, with the clause 'such as I/he loves', underlining the statement of 25:28 that Isaac's predispositions are governed by his stomach. Perhaps the addition of wine to the meal (v. 25b) reflects the same set of ideas.

50 Hendel (*The Epic of the Patriarch*, 83) points to this contrast, but makes the point that in Israel, it is only domesticated animals that are suitable for sacrifice to God. Here, he comes in close agreement with Gunkel's observations regarding the sacrificial overtones of the meal. He also makes the point that by putting on the animal skin, Jacob 'becomes' Esau, but also how in this case, and in other ancient passages, the person becomes the animal being sacrificed. So also Ackerman, S. ('The Deception of Isaac, Jacob's Dream at Bethel, and Incubation on an Animal Skin.' G. A. Anderson and S. M. Olyan eds, *Priesthood and Cult in Ancient Israel*, Sheffield: JSOT Supp 125, 1991, 119.) It is not clear how much of this is pertinent to the reading of the text as it stands, though it could be that there is some link between the contrast of domestic and wild and the practice of only sacrificing domestic animals. This would add to the interest which Rebekah and Jacob show in the divine aspect of this episode (see on v. 7, and also v. 20) and add another dimension to Jacob's preference for a domestic lifestyle.

51 Pace Scherman and Zlotowitz, *Bereishis*, vol. 3, 1030-1: 'Deception went against his very grain. Jacob remains the eternal epitome of truth yet he was being asked to deceive.' See also comment on v. 19. Similarly Leibowitz (*Studies in Bereshit*, 265).

direct authorial or divine voice makes this question sharper. The nearest we have are those words of Rebekah which seem to claim an urgency and authority paralleled elsewhere only by the commands of God, but we are left wondering whether she is genuinely speaking with a divine authority or whether she is misleading the ancestor of Israel.

In this context Rebekah's offer in v. 13 is extremely bold and forceful. It seems to be more than just the reflection of an ancient belief that a curse could be 'magically' deflected. If the latter idea is present, it is a motif now used to show the seriousness of Rebekah's plan.

The description of Jacob's action in v. 14 is brief, emphasizing the speed with which he executes his mother's instructions, and the greater significance of Rebekah's part as her actions are described in greater detail. The taking of Esau's robe in v. 15, adds to the motif of Jacob taking the place of his elder brother and there is no disturbance to the flow of text with the introduction of this additional means of deception.

vv. 18-29: Isaac and Jacob

Isaac's reply to his son is full of irony. There is a parallel to v. 1b where Isaac opens with 'my son', and Esau responds 'Here I am'. Now the parallel to Genesis 22 is even clearer since it is Isaac who is speaking, and in both cases where he uses this one word he is unaware of what is to happen. At the beginning of his life and at the end, Isaac is not in control of the circumstances around him and finds himself being misled. The haunting question ('Who are you, my son?' - מי אתה בני) shows that Isaac knows that a son is standing before him, but he is not sure that it is Esau. The three Hebrew words skilfully and ironically underline the tension of this whole section and the doubt tormenting Isaac.

Isaac's question also forces Jacob into an explicit lie. By announcing himself with the address 'my father', he did not have to lie in the strict sense, but now he has to say that he is Esau.[52] Isaac's ongoing uncertainty forces Jacob into an even greater lie: it is YHWH who has helped him. On the face of it, this is a lie of even greater seriousness,[53] but there may be an

---

52 Rashi tries to exonerate Jacob by arguing that the words spoken by Jacob can literally mean 'I am he that brings food to you, and Esau is your first-born [עשו בכרך]', (Rosenbaum and Silbermann eds, *Pentateuch*, 124). However, see Ibn Ezra's trenchant dismissal of this, (Strickman and Silver eds, *Ibn Ezra's Commentary*, 262). For Ibn Ezra, Jacob's stratagem must not be taken too seriously.

53 'Jacob's second and more horrendous lie, the mawkish, sanctimonious, incredibly hypocritical attribution of his here and now presence to the beneficent designs of Yahweh.' (Vawter, *On Genesis*, 303.)

ambiguity: is it perhaps true that God - through the cunning of Rebekah - has indeed helped Jacob?[54]

Isaac is still not convinced, and so the tension increases. In v. 23 he seems satisfied enough to bless Jacob. Thus Isaac, the human agent, who on the face of it, is reversing the divinely inspired oracle uttered at the twins' birth, unwittingly becomes the means by which its words are fulfilled.[55] As so often in the Jacob story, the human is made to fulfill the divine purpose. On the face of it, v. 23, and especially the last clause, may seem to be a doublet as the statement that Isaac blessed Jacob is not followed immediately by the words of the blessing. However the verse can make perfect sense in its context, marking Isaac's decision to bless Jacob, based on his sense of smell. It therefore acts as a summary statement or 'proleptic summary'.[56] In addition, Westermann argues that the phrase 'and he blessed him' indicates the beginning of the blessing ritual involving acts of identification (v. 24), eating (v. 25), physical contact (v. 26), and the words pronounced (v. 27ff).[57] This seems to make sense of the text as it is, with v. 23 indicating the point at which Isaac leaves his questions and begins to bless Jacob. Certainly, the question of v. 24a seems either like a final attempt to reassure himself or a formality, unlike the earlier, more probing enquiries.[58] There is a contrast throughout of the different senses: Isaac is unable to use the sense of sight, and he puts greater trust in the sensual elements of smell and touch than of hearing.

The blessing itself is fairly unique among the patriarchal narratives and much of its language and imagery is similar to that of Deuteronomy or, in particular, Numbers 24. Westermann sees specific parallels to the Balaam narrative in the introduction of the blessing where in both cases the blessing begins with what the speaker can perceive, in one case by sight, in the other by smell; another parallel is the way that a blessing of fertility gives way to

---

54 Note also: 'Such words of [God] were not of the kind likely to have been spoken by the rough Esau. The name God was probably rare on his lips. Hence Jacob's statement arouses his father's suspicions,' Hertz, *The Pentateuch*, 232.

See also Plaut, *The Torah*, 190-2, who quotes the midrashic tradition that Jacob's reference to God gave away his identity, but also suggests that Isaac let himself be deceived, albeit subconsciously. For Plaut, the deception is only on the surface: Esau knows he is not the chosen one in any case, and Isaac subconsciously wants to be misled.

55 So Ryle, H. E., *The Book of Genesis*, Cambridge: University Press, 284.

56 Ska, J. L., 'Sommaires proleptiques en Gen 27 et dans l'histoire de Joseph.' *Bib* 73 (1992), 518-27.

57 Westermann, *Genesis 12-36*, 439. So also Hamilton (*Genesis:18-50*, 218): 'The imperfect of *barak* here can only be an ingressive perfect.'

58 Ska, 'Sommaires proleptiques', 521.

a prophecy of dominance over other tribes. Clearly there is a connection between possession of fertile land and military supremacy. Von Rad notes that Isaac is excited by the 'smell of the Promised Land'.[59] The blessing ends with a third parallel to Balaam's prophecy with the so-called 'counter-curse'. A third example of this, though with slightly different wording, is in Gen. 12:3. These express the irrevocability of God's promise or blessing and express the centrality of the patriarchs and their descendants in the outworking of God's blessing among the nations.

v. 29 clearly sees Jacob and his descendants as dominant. No doubt Edom would not be far from any application of these words. However the scope of this blessing cannot be reduced to a reference to Israel's subjugation of Edom, since its wording never leaves a more general field: the subjugation is of people*s* (v. 29a), and Jacob's brother*s*, and so its meaning cannot be exhausted to one specific historical event. This final 'counter-curse' also keeps the scope of the blessing to a more general scope.

vv. 30-40: Isaac and Esau

This third scene spells out the implications of the blessing of Jacob and the fact that such a blessing cannot be reversed.[60] As Isaac realizes what has happened there is an explosion of emotion. All the words of the first clause in v. 33 are employed in bringing this out, and the intense description of emotion contrasts strongly with the earlier, and more typical restraint of the author. The same applies to Esau's reaction, and the assonance of the '-i' sound in the Hebrew text at the end of v. 34 emphasizes the desperation that there should be something left for him.[61]

On Esau's insistence, Isaac does what he can. It is wrong to describe vv. 39b-40 as a curse, as no vocabulary associated with this form is used. However, although these lines do have the form of a blessing, it is a 'blessing' empty of promise.[62] The first words emphasize this as they repeat word for word the opening words of the first blessing. In this case though

59   von Rad, *Genesis*, 278.

60   Jacob questions this (*Das erste Buch der Tora*, 568). Instead Isaac recognizes the hand of God in his error.

61   'Esau's sobs, which are described as 'bitter' (*mara*), recall the earlier emotions he brought upon his parents..(26:35),' (Hamilton, *The Book of Genesis: 18-50*, 224). This reaction of Esau contrasts with his deferential tone when he first approaches his father, not suspecting what has happened (v. 31). This is unlike Jacob whose speech to his father is more direct, revealing his sense of urgency (Alter, *Genesis*, 141).

62   An 'anti-blessing' (Coats, G. W., *Genesis, with an Introduction to Narrative Literature*, Grand Rapids, Michigan: Eerdmans, 1983, 204).

the particle before the word 'fatness' (מִשְׁמַנֵּי) is privative (translated *'away from* the fatness of the earth') rather than partitive (*'of* the fatness of the earth').[63] Again, this description matches how Israel may have perceived Edom, but this historical perspective does not obscure the narrative logic of the episode.[64] Nevertheless, it should also be noted that there is a hint of hope for Esau's descendants and, implicitly, of ominous warning for Israel.

vv. 41-45: Rebekah and Jacob

These verses are less tightly constructed than the previous scenes. Their function is to spell out the result of the deception, and to form a link both with the next episode of Jacob's life as he flees to Haran and with the motif of flight and return which finds its conclusion in chapter 33.

The result of Jacob's deception is clear as the family is hopelessly divided. It is Rebekah in particular who suffers from this, as demonstrated by a rare outburst in v. 45b. The narrator is silent as to how Rebekah learns of Esau's plan, something he says only 'to himself' (בְּלִבּוֹ), and the verb used (נגד√ - simply translated 'were told' in NRSV), with overtones of divine revelation, may cause us to wonder whether Rebekah has had divine warning.[65] Her words to Jacob are just as authoritative as they were before, except that there is also a note of personal desperation which may well correspond to the earlier acceptance of any curse from this episode but which also has similarities to Rebekah's exclamation before the birth of the twins.[66] Even so, she does not realize for how long Jacob will be absent, or that she will never see him again - or maybe she does, but wants to hide this painful knowledge from her son, lest he hesitate in leaving her.

The beginning of v. 45 ('until your brother's anger...') does seem to be a redundant repetition of the previous clause, and may well be the reflection of some unevenness.

vv. 46-28:9: Jacob's Departure

Without these verses, the story would end with Jacob fleeing without his father's knowledge in order to save his life. v. 46 introduces another reason

---

63 Pace Willi-Plein, 'Gen 27 als Rebekkageschichte.' 321, and Alter, *Genesis*, 143.

64 For relations between Israel and Edom, see 2 Sam. 8:12-14; also 1 Ki. 11:14ff, 2 Ki. 8:20, 22.

65 Ibn Ezra considers this possibility, but rejects it in favour of the idea that Esau had simply confided in one of his friends (Strickman and Silver eds, *Ibn Ezra's Commentary*, 272).

66 So Alter, *Genesis*, 145.

for Jacob to leave: the need to find a wife from his own people. This motif is introduced in a very smooth way and is consistent with Rebekah's prominent role as already shown.[67] Finally Isaac is nudged into doing something about the marriage of at least one of his sons, as his own father had done for him. Thus on the face of it, Jacob's departure is not with quite so much shame.[68]

Another function of these verses is to make more explicit the divine nature of the blessing given.[69] In this sense the blessing given is not a

---

67   'To save Isaac from the knowledge of the true reason why Jacob was leaving his home, Rebekah pretends that he is going to Haran in search of a wife,' (Herz, *The Pentateuch*, 238). Again, an indication of Isaac's weakness.

Leibowitz (*Studies in Bereshit*, 286-90) points to the explicit remark in v. 5 that Rebekah is mother of Jacob *and Esau* to show that in sending Jacob away, she is also saving Esau, from committing the crime of fratricide.

68   The smooth transition to this conclusion and the way that these verses pick up motifs from the earlier narrative might suggest that these verses, although from a different source, are shaped around the earlier narrative, but this is of course part of the wider, much contested debate.

Certainly it is false to insist either that a consistency between these verses and ch. 27 means that they are from the same hand (so Wenham, *Genesis: 16-50*, 204); or that marks of a different hand mean that the verses were written 'entirely without reference to xxvii. 1-45', so that 'there can be no question that it forms part of a different representation of the current of events,' (Driver, *The Book of Genesis*, 262).

69   This reading denies the argument made especially by some Jewish scholars that a clear-cut distinction should be made between the blessing given earlier and this blessing. For instance, in Scherman and Zlotowitz (*Bereishis*, vol. 3, 1020-9) it is argued that Isaac had intended to give to Esau the first blessing which concerned material wealth and power, whilst reserving for Jacob the more spiritual blessing of Abraham. This is why it is only in the second episode when he is knowingly blessing Jacob that Isaac refers to the patriarchal blessing. Similarly Jacob, *Das erste Buch der Tora*, 574-7, Leibowitz, *Studies in Bereishis*, 275-8.

In practical terms, it is difficult to envisage how Esau's descendants might have had lordship over other nations and the descendants of his brothers (27:29), whilst Jacob enjoyed God's blessing. Furthermore, both blessings involve living in a land of plenty, albeit articulated in differing ways. On a broader level, it is surely false to make a clear distinction between material and spiritual spheres of life. Thus whatever hermeneutical considerations govern the solution offered here, and granted some difference between the more material blessing in ch. 27 and the blessing in 28:3-4, the passages themselves do not allow for such a clear-cut distinction.

See also Mann, *The Book of the Torah*, 54, who considers the above question but, on the basis of Isaac's invocation of God in 27:27b.28a and of the counter-curse (cf. 12:3) is inclined to see here the operation of the patriarchal blessing.

doublet of 27:27ff but more an interpretation of it.[70] These words spoken by Isaac make it unquestionable that it is the patriarchal promise, the blessing of Abraham (v. 4) which Jacob has gained. Thus a stronger link is made with the wider patriarchal story. Furthermore because of the straits in which Jacob finds himself, there is a strong contrast between the vast scope of the blessing and the reality of Jacob's predicament. This reflects the similar contrast in the Abraham story where Abraham is promised a vast number of descendants but remains for so long childless.

The verses 28:6ff return to the sorry Esau. Given that he attempts to take a positive step and that he now sees that he might have some cause for blaming himself, we can perhaps detect the germination of a seed of hope that his anger is not so total and that in the cold light of reason he might be more ready to excuse his brother. Again then, these verses show links with the rest of the narrative. Most importantly, they indicate that Esau's fate is not wholly undeserved. True, there is no attempt to soften Jacob's deceitful behaviour, but by framing the behaviour around this motif of intermarriage, the narrator provides a wider perspective.

Finally, however, this is not done in such a way that Esau is despised or seen as being outside the scope of divine favour. Lamentably he tries to make amends, again without the active guidance of the father who allows him to make his own mistakes, but the narrator continues to show an interest in Esau by recording his marriage. Furthermore, the link with Ishmael is more than coincidental, since Ishmael is also a 'forgotten first-born': pushed aside in the story of divine favour but not beyond all reach of divine providence.[71]

Conclusion

Historical-Critical Summary

We have seen that most of the passage is a tightly-constructed series of scenes, each of two persons. Within this there is little scope for marking out sources, although there may be some suggestion of traditional development behind the well-shaped plot: the blessings stand out as they introduce the nations of Israel and Edom, and it could be that this ethnological aspect

---

70 Gross, W. ('Jakob, der Mann des Segens. Zu Traditionsgeschichte und Theologie der priesterlichen Jakobsüberlieferungen,' *Bib* 49 (1968), 340-1) sees 28:3 not as a blessing but an expression of hope that Jacob will be blessed, realized in ch. 35.
71 Syrén, *The Forgotten First-Born*, 121ff.

grew out of the story. On the other hand, some form of blessing is necessary to the story and so an argument seeing the blessings as secondary has to accept some earlier version of the blessing. It could just as easily be argued that the story as a whole was composed around the traditional blessings.

If not necessarily an indication of traditional development, then at least a hint of an original relative independence of the story may be the way that the narrative takes for granted, and thereby assumes that the reader will, a set of circumstances which the wider context of the patriarchal narratives does not: that is, that the family blessing is passed down by the father to one son. This clearly is not the case if we look to either side of the family tree. In the case of Abraham, we read of no blessing given by him to Isaac. It is true that there is a conflict between Ishmael and Isaac which is similar to this, and also that God blesses Isaac after Abraham's death, but that there has to be such an ordeal as this passage is not self-evident. On the other side, Jacob does also pass on a blessing near his death, but this time it is shared between all his sons. Theologically this is understandable since all the children of Jacob are now inheritors of the patriarchal blessing, and the fact that such divisive family feuds are avoided, or at least avoidable, is to be seen as a positive development. Literarily this difference in the assumed conventions of blessing shows the relative independent character of the different parts of the patriarchal narrative. This is particularly the case when compared with the way the transition is made from Abraham to Isaac, since here the difference cannot be accounted for by purely theological or thematic terms.[72]

However we have also seen that there is now a frame around the earlier narrative, most probably from the Priestly source. These verses do not obscure the real force of the passage, but add a different perspective by introducing the matter of Esau's ill-considered marriages and the need for Jacob to marry within the clan. Particularly in the case of 27:46 it is difficult to make a clear distinction between the main story and these verses since Rebekah still has the proactive role and the verse makes most sense in the light of v. 42a, and so for this reason v. 46 is sometimes seen as redactional. Rebekah's role might also be hinted at by the phrase 'and his mother' in 28:7, with a possible reference to Rebekah's part in his departure (v. 43), in parallel to Isaac's formal sending. Furthermore there are links with other parts of the main narrative of the Jacob story - cf. the emotions expressed

---

72   Even if valid, Speiser's comparison of the blessing scene here and Hurrian texts does little to throw light on the dynamics within the passage as it is, as Speiser himself notes that any reminiscence of an ancient convention is now lost by the Biblical writer (*Genesis*, xli and 212-3).

in 27:46 with 25:22 and 27:13 - in all these cases there is the sense that Rebekah is particularly sensitive to the pain caused by strife. It is also to be noted that by themselves, these verses from the Priestly source give no account for why the younger son should be given the blessing instead of the elder.[73] Note also that the theme of going to Laban, in order to find a wife, is consistent with the bulk of the Jacob-Laban story. Thus these verses provide added cement between the two cycles. All this suggests that a distinction between a final redactor and a separate Priestly source might be unclear.[74]

In addition these verses make more explicit the spiritual significance of the blessing given to Jacob, and how this blessing relates to the wider patriarchal promises. As argued in the commentary, we have seen how the blessing of 28:1ff serves to confirm the earlier blessing and to spell out these themes, whilst also arguing against a clear distinction between different sorts of blessing.

The Story of Jacob and Esau within Israelite Scripture

The story draws on motifs and experiences common to all mankind, such as that of fraternal rivalry, and of the contrast of a more stable, domesticated lifestyle and the hunter lifestyle, especially when read alongside Gen. 25:27-34. Furthermore, in the blessing given to Jacob (27:27), there is a clear emphasis on the importance of the land.

In addition though, there is a concern to understand Israel in relation to other peoples and to its God.[75] Much discussion about the place of Edom in the passage often centres on false premises, with the importance of

---

73   So Alter, *Genesis*, 147.
74   See also Alter, *Genesis*, 147, who accepts that these verses come from the P source, but who sees them offering not a contradictory but an alternative explanation. By contrast, see Emerton, J. A., 'The Priestly Writer in Genesis.' *JTS* 39 (1988), 397.

For a much more negative appraisal of these verses, see Brueggemann, *Genesis*, 236ff, who sees them as an inappropriate 'intrusion' into the primary narrative, being unrelated to what precedes or follows. He sees the Priestly writer as departing from story to teaching - 'and negative at that'. Our reading has attempted to show the contrary, that these verses are related to the 'primary' narrative. Furthermore, Brueggemann's claim that 'this is the only theological criticism of Esau in the Genesis narrative' takes no account of 25:34.

75   Fretheim, T. E. ('The Jacob Traditions: Theological and Hermeneutic', *Int* 26, 1972, 423) sees this as a major aspect of the Yahwist's presentation of the Jacob tradition: 'Israel should see herself in Jacob - recipients of God's grace', especially as Esau is depicted as the better man with the natural claim (also Brueggemann, *Genesis*, 234-5). However, Fretheim's claim that the Yahwist was wanting to show that Jacob/Israel is blessed in order to serve other peoples would seem to go beyond a reading of the Jacob story itself.

Edom-Israel being tied to the question of diachronic precedence. This assumes that what is central to our concern is determined by what is original. It cannot be denied that as it is, there is a clear concern to see in Israel's early history, the beginnings of its relations with its neighbouring peoples, in particular with Edom, and to interpret these relations in theological terms. The narrators saw 'Israel' - whether the united monarchy, the Southern Kingdom or the surviving community - as having a special and privileged place in history.

However, this story is now part of the wider Pentateuchal story of promise. This means that as they looked back on the patriarchal period, the Biblical writers were concerned to see a time of promise, looking forward to at least the partial fulfilment of the Mosaic covenant. On the one hand there is the recognition that things were different, as we have seen in the almost unspoken 'acceptance' by the narrator of the convention of passing the blessing from father to one son in a way that excluded others from this specific divine blessing. On the other hand, it is clear that it is the blessing of YHWH that is being passed on, something made explicit in the inclusion of the divine name at important points: in v. 7 where Rebekah spells out what is at stake in this blessing, and in v. 27 in the blessing itself. What happened on Isaac's deathbed was to have consequences for endless generations. This is even more emphasized in the P strand (28:3ff).

The Divine-Human Contrast

Given the above, it is surprising that this incident, so important for those who saw themselves as Jacob's descendants, should be told with such frankness. This points to an understanding, as von Rad has sought to emphasize, of God working through incomprehensible ways, in ways where his will prevails even where families are torn apart and fathers deceived. The divine will is worked through human failings. To see God involved in even these events, points to a faith seeking to see God as the determining factor of all history, and it is this which points to a monotheistic faith, the same faith which could see YHWH's work even in the destruction of Jerusalem and the Temple along with the exile of his people.

On the other hand the human side of the story is not lost as protagonists are never reduced to mere puppets. Just as the work of God is seen as complex so are the workings of our human characters. The structure of the story into episodes of two characters reflects secretiveness and hiddenness of motive. We are often left wondering about the feelings and real motives of each character. Is there scope in the text to see a reluctance on the part of Jacob, based not just on the fear of being caught? Is he simply out for his own gain or aware of some divine purpose? How are we to identify with Esau? How much does Isaac really know and why does he act secretly? Can we really assume that he does not know about the earlier oracle? Or does he know deep down that Jacob is the one to be blessed and is he really deceived so easily? And what about Rebekah, whose role is particularly striking: is she trying to ensure that the divine will is being fulfilled, or is she simply expressing her favouritism? And has Rebekah got the desired end right (that Jacob should be blessed), but failed to trust that God will himself bring about the fulfilment of the oracle?[76]

What is truly perplexing about this story is that Jacob and the reader never really know. The story sits within an ambiguity: on the face of it, it is a clear deception and attempt to go against the will of the father, but the reader is also aware of the wider context, where God has declared through an oracle that Jacob is to receive the blessing. It is certainly difficult to know what weight to place on this oracle when reading this story. It would have been so much easier if Isaac had received the divine oracle at the birth of the twins, but as it is, Rebekah has to carry the burden of this knowledge without knowing how it is to be fulfilled, or whether it is her place to play a part. Thus as well as asking whether Jacob will succeed in his deception, we are faced with the even more perplexing and lasting question of whether he has done the right thing. It is wrong to argue that this story does not have a moral concern, since just as it is part of the Pentateuchal story of promise, so it is part of Israel's book of Torah.

It is this lack of a clear voice from God to guide Jacob that makes Rebekah's role so tantalizing: is her voice the voice of the divine, the authority of YHWH (something which the authority and wording of her speech might suggest),[77] or is she a false guide, leading Israel's ancestor astray? However, the consequence of such a possibility is to bring into disrepute the very calling of Jacob and therefore Israel.

With regard to the Bethel and Peniel incidents, we have already had occasion to note certain points of contrast between the religion of the patriarchs as depicted in the story of Jacob and that of later Israel.[78] In this passage, a further possible point of contrast is that we see here a Jacob without the firm guidance of the Torah. However as well as this point of contrast, indications are also that Israel was encouraged to see types for itself in the patriarchal characters. In this text, this can be seen in the

---

76 So Calvin, *A Commentary on Genesis*, 88.
77 Willi-Plein even suggests that Rebekah is a *dea ex machina* ('Gen 27 als Rebekkageschichte.', 331).
78 pp. 47, 60-2, 86.

etymological motif with the word-play between the name Jacob and the verbal root עקב ('supplant' - v. 36). By seeing in Jacob a type for Israel, the narrators were not afraid of showing that 'Israel' had no special merit, that its faith could be just as shot through with ambiguities as was Jacob's, and that their election by God over other nations was truly a mystery. It is of course true, that humour deflates some of the severity of the passage, but this humour is far from being the jubilation imagined by Gunkel.[79]

Finally, of course, there is the question of culpability and its consequences - not only whether Jacob has committed a crime against his brother, his father and ultimately his God, but also of what might arise from this, perhaps his fears of v. 12 coming back to haunt him. We have already hinted that there is no evidence of this at Bethel,[80] but we shall have to bear the question in mind in the next longer episode of Jacob's life.

Thus this episode shows how difficult it is for the protagonists to discern the divine will and act appropriately. Rebekah and Jacob might be aware of the wider plan, but they are left to see its fulfilment through. Isaac and Esau do not even see the wider plan: Isaac's blindness is a metaphor for his lack of insight into God's plan, and Esau's ill-chosen marriages demonstrate his ignorance. The passage is more than a straight-forward denunciation of Jacob and Rebekah. This is emphasized by the opening and closing references to Esau and the added motive and circumstances for leaving. Instead the passage shows again that the Jacob story is a complex interplay of the divine will and human fallibility, personality and effort.

---

79   Gunkel, *Genesis*, 300-2.
80   Above, p. 63.

Chapter 5

The Struggle for Justice:
Jacob and Laban
(29-32:1)

Introduction

This long section dealing with the stay that Jacob makes with his uncle
Laban provides a long break between the two main episodes of the Jacob-
Esau plot. However, it is to prove far from a relief from the theme of
conflict. Furthermore the Jacob-Laban story is both preceded and followed
by the divine appearances already discussed which set this very human
conflict in the context of the divine encounter with Jacob.

In itself the Jacob-Laban narrative forms a fairly coherent and self-
contained whole. Nevertheless certain circumstances are assumed, such as
the family relationship, elements from the divine encounter at Bethel, and
there is a certain mirroring of the relationship between Jacob and Esau.
Furthermore the Jacob-Esau story forms a bracket around the Jacob-Laban
story. This appearance of a self-contained cycle on the one hand, and the
connections with the wider Jacob story on the other hand, suggest a rather
complex development behind the text.

The narrative can be divided into the following parts:

29:1-14	- The meeting at the well
29:15-30	- The deception of Jacob by Laban
29:31-30:24	- The birth of Jacob's children
30:25-43	- Jacob's deception of Laban and increased wealth
31:1-32:1	- Jacob's flight, the final confrontation and treaty.

The Meeting at the Well (29:1-14)

Historical-Critical Issues

Due to coherence and unity in the passage, there is little enthusiasm for dividing it into sources. Regarding other redactional development, Blum finds the hint of a tension between v. 1 ('the people of the east' - בני-קדם) and the place Haran (v. 4), since elsewhere the former term relates to the people who live in the desert to the east of Transjordan, whereas Haran is located in Northern Syria.[1]

However, a similarity with other well scenes, particularly in Gen. 24:11-33 and Ex. 2:15-22, has led to some discussion of form. For instance Westermann sees an independent oral narrative form lying behind the separate stories, and suggests that their family context goes back even to the patriarchal period.[2] However he does not attempt to discern an original form, and it is noticeable that even Gunkel satisfies himself with noting a connection between the three passages.[3] Von Rad is even less adventurous.[4] This is a little surprising since it is often held to be axiomatic that where there are such doublets, the task of form criticism is to discern the 'original' form behind the Gattung, and to identify later elements (compare the discussion on the passages narrating the 'endangering of the ancestress'). In this case, perhaps little is made of the connection because it does not present what might be seen as the problem of doublets.

A more fruitful approach is suggested by Alter using the idea of 'type scene'.[5] His concern is less to find the one elusive and hypothetical form behind the scenes, as to explore the manifold variations of a pattern. His use of the concept of type scene circumvents the tricky question of history, and is more concerned to do justice to the texts as they stand. He sees the 'betrothal' stories as an example of this, and invites us to see how variations in the stories, as adaptations of commonly understood conventions, highlight certain themes or motifs. For instance, in the case of chapter 24, the most striking variation is that the future husband, Isaac, is not at all present and that Rebekah plays a significant part. This clearly reflects their

---

1   Blum, *Die Komposition der Vätergeschichte*, 103, also Van Seters *Prologue to History*, 277. (This is especially reflected in references in Judg. 6:3.33; 7:12; 8:10.)
2   Westermann, *Genesis 12-36*, 463.
3   Gunkel, *Genesis*, 318-9.
4   von Rad, *Genesis*, 288-9.
5   Alter, *The Art of Biblical Narrative*, 51ff, and briefly, *Genesis*, 152; also Wenham, *Genesis 16-50*, 229ff.

portrayal elsewhere.[6] The role of YHWH is also more noticeable in this case. Regarding Exodus, Moses responds to an injustice shown to the shepherdesses, and there is no initial intention of finding a wife.

In this reading of the version in chapter 29, we shall use Alter's model of the type scene to draw attention to what is distinctive here.[7]

Exegesis

v. 1: The journey itself is passed over cheerily by the narrator as the interest is concentrated onto Jacob's arrival.[8]

vv. 2-3 set the scene by describing the sight that greets Jacob, the particle 'behold' (והנה) marking a change to the perspective of Jacob.[9] However v. 3 goes beyond Jacob's point of view as the narrator describes the custom of the local shepherds in using the well. Whereas Moses sees the injustice of the shepherds at the well, here Jacob encounters the complicating conventions and obstacles, just as later he is to find family and social conventions and agreements whilst staying with Laban a key hindering factor. Jacob's flouting of the convention in v. 10 likewise reflects this aspect.

The mention of the stone reminds us of the stones and the column from the Bethel episode, and perhaps hint that we are already seeing the beginning of the fulfilment of God's promise to Jacob.

vv. 4-8: The question about Laban's well-being (שלום) perhaps reminds us of Jacob's desire to return to his father's house in peace (בשלום), expressed in his oath to God at Bethel (28:21).

Jacob's enthusiasm is set off by the reluctance of the shepherds: it is Jacob who starts the conversation, and his questions are met first with very abrupt answers, and then the device of deflecting Jacob's attention to Rachel as soon as she arrives.[10] Their inertia is heightened by the fact that

---

6   See also Teugels, L., "'A Strong Woman Who Can Find?' A Study of Characterization in Genesis 24, with some Perspectives on the General Presentation of Isaac and Rebekah in the Genesis Narratives.', *JSOT 63* (1994), 89-104.

7   For Alter's treatment of the same passage: *The Art of Biblical Narrative*, 54-6.

8   The idiom 'lifting his feet' (not reflected in NRSV) gives the impression of optimism, briskness or agility (so Rashi - Rosenbaum and Silbermann eds, *Pentateuch*, 134). This expression is paralleled by Jacob 'lifting his voice' in v. 11 (Alter, *Genesis*, 151).

9   Alter, *The Art of Biblical Narrative*, 54.

10   Sherwood, S. K., points out that, with the exception of this text, the interrogative מאין ('Where do you come from?') is always directed to the person arriving on the scene, and that this reversal underlines Jacob's initiative and activity. (*'Had God Not Been on My*

they are unwilling or unable to act before all the flocks are present.[11]

vv. 9-12: The interest of Jacob seems divided between Rachel and the sheep, (at this stage, we do not even know what Rachel looks like). In fact it is interesting that he sees to the sheep before speaking to Rachel. Family ties are also emphasized: Rachel is the daughter of Laban, the brother of Jacob's mother, and the sheep belong to Laban, the brother of his mother. When Jacob waters the sheep, he is doing so because they belong, again, to Laban the brother of his mother.[12] Thus his motivation is family interest (unlike Moses who has no family connection). The unblocking of the well and flowing of the water accompany the sudden warmth of Jacob to his cousin and his tears. The images of the well (important for fertility), flowing water and emotion have sexual undercurrents.[13] The unblocking of the well is also an indication of how Jacob will bring prosperity to Laban.

Finally, the removal of the large stone suggests once more Jacob's strength and enthusiasm, again in contrast to the inertia of the other shepherds. This is consistent with the picture we have of the struggling Jacob at Peniel, and of the stones he sets up elsewhere. Fokkelman also points to the symbolic value of Jacob removing the stone as removing an obstacle, and it is no doubt significant that of the well scenes considered, only Jacob has to remove a large stone.[14] This picture of Jacob contrasts with his portrayal in relation to Esau, where Esau seems to be the more powerful, and Jacob relies on cunning.

vv. 13-14: Jacob meets Laban. In the patriarchal story this is of course not the first time that we meet Laban. In chapter 24 he seems equally enthusiastic though there is the hint that Laban is as much enamoured by the expensive bracelets given to Rebekah (24:30), and we see there also a reluctance to let the servant go immediately. However, on the face of it, there is as yet no hint of the future troubled relationship between Jacob and

---

Side': An examination of the Narrative Technique of the Story of Jacob and Laban: Genesis 29,1-32,2, Frankfurt am Main: Peter Lang, 1990, 39.)

11   Note the impersonal form of the verb used to describe the act of unblocking the well (וגללו - v. 8), rather than the first person plural we might have expected (cf. v. 3 where the verb probably does refer to the shepherds). Certainly there is a reluctance to claim responsibility for such heavy work and one wonders whether they were waiting for Rachel to do the job.

12   Bar-Efrat, *Narrative Art in the Bible*, 117.

13   Hinted at by the pun between 'watered' in v. 10 (וישק) and 'kissed' in v. 11 (וישק) - Alter, *Genesis*, 152.

14   Fokkelman, *Narrative Art*, 125.

Laban.[15] vv. 13b-14a are a little intriguing: what are 'all these things' (v. 13b)? This rather vague phrase could refer to what has just happened or to Jacob's past. Does the vagueness of this phrase hint at a reticence on the part of Jacob to disclose everything about his past? And is Laban's conclusion (cf. Gen. 2:23) simply a recognition of kinship, or of affinity in character, or might he even see the possibility of some covenantal bond based on family relationship?[16] Is there some irony in his reply which we can appreciate once we know that deceit is indeed a family trait?

Conclusion

Regarding the origins of this passage, it is difficult to detect any development behind the written form. The passage clearly has in view what is to come, and is intended as an opening scene, lulling the reader into a false sense of ease and drawing on images which will be significant for the Jacob-Laban narrative. It also presupposes the relationship between Laban and Rebekah, and there are hints of the earlier Jacob story. All this suggests that this passage was never an independent or even self-contained story.

We have seen that in this passage, a comparative study of 'type scene' has proved more fruitful than a traditional form critical study. The use of the well type scene emphasizes the importance of family interest for Jacob. Furthermore, undercurrents of fertility or sexuality look forward to the birth of the sons and the breeding of the flocks, as well as the prosperity Jacob will bring to Laban. In addition, in contrast to chapter 24, there is no mention of the divine. Partly this reflects Jacob's nature which is to rely on his own striving, but it may also reflect a greater difficulty in detecting the

---

15   Rashi comments:

> HE RAN TOWARDS HIM, thinking that he was laden with money...AND EMBRACED HIM - When he saw that he had nothing with him, he thought, "Perhaps he has brought gold coins and they are *hidden away* in his bosom!"...HE KISSED HIM - he thought, "Perhaps he has brought pearls (or precious stones in general) and they are in his mouth!" (Rosenbaum and Silbermann eds, *Pentateuch*, 136).

With the benefit of hindsight (and remembering the meeting of Laban with his distant family in ch. 24), there is justification for questioning Laban's motives - also Wenham, *Genesis: 16-50*, 231.

16   See Brueggemann, W., 'Of the Same Flesh and Bone (Gen 2:23a).' *CBQ* 32 (1970), 537-8; also Hamilton, *Genesis: 18-50*, 256.

work of God in the Jacob cycle than in the Abraham cycle.[17]

However, most striking is the absence of a marriage to end this scene.[18] Whereas the wedding is the clear outcome of the well scenes in Genesis 24 and Exodus 2, it is not in sight here. Clearly this is unusual since it was Jacob's (ostensible) purpose in travelling, and there has been an open expression of affection with possible sexual overtones between Rachel and Jacob. But the passage finishes not with Jacob achieving his goal, but with a month's stay with his uncle. The removal of a stone will seem easy compared to the barriers Jacob will face before he can reach the goal of marrying Rachel, let alone of returning home in peace.

Although Bethel is not mentioned explicitly, there are hints of it. We have already seen a recurrence of the stone motif as Jacob's night time dream is followed briefly by this daytime vision, and the omission of journey details emphasizes this connection. The daytime vision and action would seem to indicate God's protection and accompaniment. But the lack of a marriage means a delay in the fulfilment of God's promise. God seems to be present with Jacob through the guiding of circumstances (as with Abraham's servant), but that presence will become more elusive and problematic for Jacob.

Also noticeably absent at the well is Laban, not to mention his sons. Seen together with the inertia of the shepherds, the impression will develop of the laziness of Laban and his sons, especially as they are next mentioned grumbling (31:1). There is no explanation as to why Rachel has the job of shepherding, and what seems insignificant now, will again become more suggestive as Jacob's troubles increase. This sense of laziness, and the strenuous and rushed activity of Jacob after a long journey contribute to an ongoing portrayal of Jacob as a scrupulous worker who makes things happen - this theme will continue to develop throughout the coming narrative, and will contribute to the divine-human contrast.[19]

---

17 Vawter (*On Genesis*, 319) thinks that the lack of explicit mention of providence is not so much a denial of the work of God but emphasizes Jacob's preference for steering his own course rather than looking for a sign as Abraham's servant. This is true and adds to the theme of human endeavour in the Jacob story, but nevertheless, as we shall see, the 'hand of Yahweh' will prove to be more ambiguous in Jacob's stay in Haran.
18 Although Alter does not hesitate to call this a 'betrothal' type scene he neglects to spell out the irony that the actual betrothal is missing.
19 This hard work is an important aspect of Jacob's defence in his final confrontation with Laban - Alter, *Genesis*, 152.

Marriage and Deception (29:15-30)

Historical-Critical Issues

There is a sense in which this unit is part of the preceding since it brings to a conclusion the marriage of Jacob and Rachel, closing the betrothal type scene, albeit after complication and delay. However the break at v. 14 also marks a certain independence.

Within the passage itself there is little evidence of different sources or additions, the exception being the references to the maids of Leah and Rachel respectively (vv. 24 and 29), which prepare for the following episode with the birth of Jacob's sons.

Within the text, v. 16 with its mention of Rachel as Laban's daughter is often seen as an unnecessary repetition from the earlier episode. However its function is different here as it draws attention to the contrast between the sisters and sets the tone of the ensuing events.

Exegesis

vv. 15-20: On the face of it, the tone of these verses has some similarity to the gentle optimism of the previous episode, even if the length of Jacob's service seems excessive.[20] However, even at this stage Laban's craftiness comes to light. Previously we read of his enthusiasm as he greets Jacob as a relative, then a month passes by. Now the tone has imperceptibly changed as Laban, whilst ostensibly offering something to Jacob ('your wages' - מַשְׂכֻּרְתֶּךָ), smuggles in the concept of 'service' (עבד). Jacob is easily taken in and seems to make things even worse as he suggests not only his payment, but also the length of service! Thus what on the face of it seems to be Laban's plausible suggestion that Jacob should have some reward turns their relationship into one of employment and service. Laban's self-interest is also revealed as he is obviously pleased at the prospect of his

---

20 It may seem odd that Jacob has to do anything in order to be able to marry Rachel, but it seems to have been customary to pay something over to the father in compensation for the marriage of a daughter (see Westermann, *Genesis 12-36*, 466-7, and von Rad, *Genesis*, 290). Thus Isaac had to do nothing to marry Rebekah because the servant was able to offer expensive gifts, whereas the empty-handed Jacob has to pay by work. This contrast between the relative ease for Isaac (who does not even need to travel) and the effort of Jacob further points to the motif of struggle in the life of Jacob.

It is also noteworthy that Laban does not waive this custom of offering a gift. Whereas in this whole narrative, custom and social circumstances work in his favour, for Jacob they are an obstacle - as they are indeed in his struggle with Esau.

daughter remaining in the family, thus keeping the family wealth together. Furthermore, even now might he be thinking about keeping Jacob indefinitely? His wording in v. 19 ('I will give *her* to you') leaves open the possibility of the future deception, and, in the light of later events, the narrator's mention of Leah in v. 16 can be seen as a warning bell.[21]

Nevertheless, to the enamoured Jacob all is well and the seven years are skipped over by the narrator,[22] the reference to 'a few days' (v. 20) pointing back to Rebekah's attempted reassurance (27:44).[23] At this point there is little doubt that our sympathies lie with this young man in love.

The contrasting of the sisters, one elder and one younger, reminds us of the contrast of Esau and Jacob, and it is significant that Jacob, the younger, should favour the younger of the sisters.

vv. 21-27: The true character of Laban is revealed as Jacob is deceived into marrying Leah and working seven more years. Jacob, forced by Laban's silence to act first, makes his demand in what seems quite a blunt way, especially in the final clause ('that I may go in to her').[24] Again, Laban insists on social convention and arranges the formal wedding occasion, something which he will again exploit to his advantage. The reference to the guests - the ominous sounding men of the area - reminds us of the shepherds at the well who showed no concern for the lonely stranger.[25] The actual deception of Jacob by Laban is brought out by the play between the different forms of the verb בוא (translated 'took' and 'went' in v. 23).

Throughout this deception are clear hints of Jacob's deception of Esau. One parallel is the setting of a meal, making the deception easier.[26] The

---

21 Fokkelman, *Narrative Art*, 127.

22 What Bar-Efrat describes as 'psychological time' (*Narrative Art in the Bible*, 160).

23 Hamilton, *The Book of Genesis: 18-50*, 260; Wenham, *Genesis 16-50*, 235; Alter, *Genesis*, 154.

24 Offended by any idea of sexual impatience, Rashi sees Jacob as being motivated by the concern to bear his twelve sons who would be bearers of the religious tradition - Rosenbaum and Silbermann eds, *Pentateuch*, 137-8; also Scherman and Zlotowitz, *Bereishis*, vol. 4, 1194ff.

25 See Sherwood (*'Had God Not Been on My Side'*, 97) on how this phrase brings in an element of threat (cf. Gen. 26:7, Judg. 19:16, Gen. 19:4.22). In this case, the men are useful to Laban in enforcing the local custom and making sure that Jacob accepts Leah.

26 There is also the hint that wine was part of this meal, with the idea of drinking implicit in the word משתה (שתה√) - Scherman and Zlotowitz, *Bereishis*, vol. 4, 273. See also Diamond, J. A., 'The Deception of Jacob: A New Perspective on an Ancient Solution to the Problem.' *VT* 34 (1984), 211-3, who points out the link with Lot's daughters (also referred to by the pairing בכרה and צעירה), who also deceived their father by making him drunk and having intercourse with him. (Also Hamilton, *The Book of Genesis: 18-50*, 262-3.)

darkness in v. 23 causes Jacob to mistake one sister for the other, just as his father's blindness caused him to mistake one son for the other. Then, as Jacob's eyes are opened in the daylight, just as his father 'saw' his mistake in chapter 27 and found there was nothing he could do, he finds that neither can he reverse what has been done. The wording of Jacob's accusation ('why have you deceived me' - √רמה) also links back to the earlier deception, and the irony is brought out most clearly in Laban's retort (v. 26), pointing to the customary precedence of the elder over the younger, with the word first-born as a reminder of the taking of Esau's birth-right.[27]

In v. 27 we learn the final cost to Jacob. The blunt way that Laban refers to Rachel ('the other' - גם-את-זאת) indicates his attitude to his daughters. Commentators point out the proscription against marrying two sisters in Lev. 18:18, and certainly this episode does not show such a situation in a favourable light.

vv. 28-30: What was eagerly anticipated by Jacob is now tempered by the deception of his uncle and the knowledge that he has to work seven more years. Thus the marriage is an anticlimax, and is narrated with restraint. Nevertheless, Rachel remains precious to him, emphasized by the redundant preposition ('gave to *him*') לו in v. 28b.[28] The final verse not only spells out this preference, but also prepares for the next scene where YHWH intervenes on behalf of the unfavoured one.

Conclusion

Jacob has got what he deserves. As commentators point out, the deceiver is deceived. Underneath the obvious irony we are left with the question of how to account for this reversal. It could be a simple narrative play, or it could be that we are meant to see some cause and effect between the two deceptions, and even the element of divine punishment. Gunkel denies any sense of this, seeing straightforward humour, so that any sense of Jacob being made a victim is overshadowed by the reader's knowledge that Jacob will eventually pay Laban back with interest.[29] At the other extreme,

---

27 'The nemesis is made all the more pungent by the fact that Jacob is caught in the same device he himself had once used. He pretended to be Esau in front of Isaac. Leah pretends to be Rachel next to Jacob,' Hamilton (*The Book of Genesis: 18-50*, 262).

Brueggemann (*Genesis*, 253) sees it quite differently as Laban voices the natural claim of primogeniture, now in conflict with God's will expressed by the blessing.

28 Omitted in some manuscripts.

29 Gunkel, *Genesis*, 319.

Fokkelman sees the clear motif of crime and punishment.[30]

Certainly it seems that there is an intended parallel with the earlier deception by Jacob, something which Gunkel neglects. However, the case of guilt and retribution is not at all clear-cut. We certainly feel that the tables are turned on Jacob, but to see this as a punishment probably goes too far. It is clear that Jacob's actions, perhaps partly by choice, partly by having no other option, are such that he will both succeed and suffer from such behaviour. This is Mann's reading: 'Jacob possesses that rare and dangerous combination of deceitfulness and cunning, a combination that both serves him well and is the source of unending anxiety.'[31] Mann also argues that the text is 'not interested so much in a doctrine of rewards and punishments as it is in a process of conversion that takes place over the course of Jacob's life, albeit through struggle and setbacks.'

In place of any idea of retribution is the absence of any divine perspective.[32] As is often the case with the Jacob story, we are left with more questions than answers.

Furthermore, any perspective is only complete in the light of the forthcoming birth of twelve sons, the founders of later Israel. In retrospect it could be claimed that the deception by Laban into marrying Leah is a necessary part of God's plan, since Leah is as much a chosen matriarch as Rachel.[33] Thus the Jacob story presents another example of the divine working through human deception.

A further element in the text is that of service and wages, which will be key words in the Haran phase of Jacob's life.[34] Westermann sees this from a sociological perspective with the introduction of social and economic conflict.[35] Without doubt the entrance of service and wages has soured the family relations in an irreparable way. As a result, uncle and nephew are estranged, sister is set against sister, and daughter resents father (31:15). Contra Gunkel, underlying the humour in this episode is the wider context

---

30   Fokkelman, *Narrative Art*, 130.

31   Mann, *The Book of the Torah*, 55-6.

32   A most striking contrast to this are the explicit theological judgements of cause and effect in the Books of Kings and Chronicles. There is hardly any hint of this in the Jacob story. As we shall see, rather than seeing in Laban an instrument of divine retribution, the only hint of explicit judgement regarding this episode will be in favour of Jacob against Laban.

33   For discussion on this: Scherman and Zlotowitz, *Bereishis*, vol. 4, 1195ff. Jacob's eventual act of burying Leah at a sacred site can be seen as a tacit acceptance of this (Gen 49:31).

34   Fokkelman, *Narrative Art*, 126.

35   Westermann, *Genesis 12-36*, 468.

of the tragedy of breakdown in family relationships caused by the greed of one man. Laban's gain is clear as he marries off his less attractive daughter to a relative and secures his hard work for another seven years; but this is at the clear expense of his daughters and nephew.

Jacob's Children (29:31-30:24)

Historical-Critical issues

The question of sources behind this section is difficult. Reasons given for seeing the text as the combination of different sources or elements include the use of both YHWH and Elohim, varying sentence structures, and possible doublets. The mandrake story also seems to stand out, as does the birth of Dinah. In addition the section as a whole stands out as there is no explicit reference to Laban, and Leah and Rachel come into the fore.

The use of the different terms for God has of course been cause for division between the E and J sources, with possible additions from P. However, much is unclear and von Rad comments on the 'extraordinary literary compositeness' of the text, where it is almost impossible to catalogue the small fragments.[36]

Westermann tries a different way by distinguishing different layers: an older layer is marked by the theme of rivalry between Leah and Rachel, consisting of 29:31-32 (the birth of Reuben), 30:1-6 (the heated exchange between Rachel and Jacob, and the birth of Dan), 30:14-18 (the story of the mandrakes), and 30:22-24 (the birth of Joseph, though with later additions).[37] A later writer expanded this to a genealogy of twelve (although, strictly speaking, this would necessarily include Dinah). This in itself can be questioned, since there is no obvious reason, for instance, for separating off the birth of Dan from the birth of Naphtali, Bilhah's second son; and it would seem more likely that an earlier narrative would have mirrored the giving of Bilhah to Jacob with that of Zilpah. Furthermore, it would seem just as likely that a narrator expanded the basic genealogy with the narrative sections. A further point is that Westermann's reconstruction cuts across the scenic development.[38] In short, although it is possible that the story was composed in two or more stages, these are difficult to trace in the text as it is.

---

36   von Rad, *Genesis*, 291.
37   Westermann, *Genesis 12-36*, 471-2.
38   So Wenham, *Genesis: 16-50*, 242.

On the other hand, Blum argues that we have here a well-constructed single unit.[39] He sees the consistent outworking of the theme of Leah's fertility being granted by God because she is 'hated', whilst Rachel remains barren. The etymologies stem from this. He also criticizes the division of texts into sources according to the use of the divine name.[40] Given the complexity of the text, we will assess Blum's arguments after the exegesis.

Exegesis

29:31-35: Leah's Earliest Children

v. 31 is the natural consequence of the previous statement that Jacob loved Rachel more than Leah, although the biblical idiom in v. 31 (שנואה - literally 'hated') is more colourful.[41] Now, the narrator takes us to Leah's own perspective. The theme of God opening the womb is familiar especially in the birth of important people, and in the vindication of those who suffer.[42] Familiar also is the language and idea of YHWH seeing and hearing and then intervening, and the final name, linking the birth of Judah with the praise of YHWH, forms a neat ending to what began with the description of Leah's distress and YHWH's intervention. Thus the thought is not far removed from the piety of Israel, particularly as expressed in the psalms.[43] Given this connection with the praise of Israel, together with the idea of YHWH's intervention, it is not surprising that the divine name should be used at this point as a link to later Israel.[44]

---

39   Blum, *Die Komposition der Vätergeschichte*, 111.

40   Blum, *Die Komposition der Vätergeschichte*, 107.

41   Some commentators (Keil-Delitzsch, *The Pentateuch*, 287; Dillmann, *Genesis*, 342) see the closing of Rachel's womb as a punishment on Jacob for favouring one wife over the other. The force of any punishment, however, is felt by Rachel more than Jacob.

42   cf. 1 Sam. 1:19-20.

43   So Westermann, *Genesis 12-36*, 473.

44   Keil-Delitzsch, *The Pentateuch*, 287-90, sees a deliberate contrast in the use of YHWH and Elohim: Leah has a clearer reliance on the faithfulness of YHWH, the covenant God. Rachel's concept of God is much lower: rather than looking to God, she blames Jacob for her lack of children and resorts to the earthly means of procuring children through her maid: 'For such a state of mind the term *Elohim*, God the sovereign ruler, was the only fitting expression,' (p. 289). However this distinction becomes forced in the case of the birth of Joseph, where both titles are used: in one derivation of the name Joseph, Elohim is used because Rachel is looking back at the past and the earthly means that had been used to obtain a child; in the second derivation she then remembers the promises of YHWH and prays for another son from his covenantal faithfulness (p. 291). By Delitzsch's later commentary (*A New Commentary on Genesis*, 173ff), this attempt has been abandoned in favour of a source critical reading. Our own reading attempts to steer a course between the two poles.

The name Reuben is associated with the verb ראה ('see') and the noun עני ('my affliction'). This fits in well with the context of Leah's distress, although the etymology itself is quite free.[45] The structure of this naming also stands out from all the others in that the giving of the name precedes the actual etymology.

The structure of the three other namings is the same, although there is some variation in the final clause.[46] The etymologies of Simeon and Levi are strongly related to the context, and that of Judah makes perfect sense in the context of the narrative.[47]

30:1-2 - the Heated Exchange between Jacob and Rachel

We now see the consequences of Laban's earlier deception as sisters are estranged from each other, and even the love between Jacob and Rachel is marred. Their exchange marks a stark contrast to their meeting at the well, and the idyllic picture represented there is now in ruins. Rachel in her frustration blames Jacob for her lack of sons, and Jacob becomes angry. His reply underlines the idea already mentioned that it is God who brings fertility, and shows the predicament of those caught up in the will of God where there is privation as well as blessing. Interestingly there is no recourse to prayer (cf. 25:21).[48]

vv. 3-8: Rachel's Surrogate Children

As a result of this, Rachel falls back on a common solution (cf. Sarai's use

---

Similarly, in Scherman and Zlotowitz *(Bereishis,* vol. 4, 1280) the view is supported that the specific use of the Divine Name emphasizes God as the dispenser of mercy, whereas the term Elohim refers to God as Judge and Ruler of Nature. Regarding the use of both titles with the birth of Joseph, Rashi is cited (p. 1311) to show how God as dispenser of justice now becomes God as attribute of mercy for Rachel.

45 A link with the noun בן ('son') would have been closer to the name. One plausible suggestion is that this would have been the original etymology, and that it has been suppressed to fit into the context of the story. The result as well is that whereas we might expect a note of joy at the birth of the first son, there is the dominant idea of affliction (עני).

46 The form קרא used for Levi is especially unusual, since with the birth of all the other sons of Jacob, the feminine form is used.

47 Note the alternative etymology in Gen. 49:8.

48 Note Rashi (Rosenbaum and Silbermann eds, *Pentateuch*, 139) who paraphrases Rachel's demand: 'Give me children - Did, then, not your father act so towards your mother? Did he not pray on her behalf?' Rashi explains Jacob's response to this to mean that since Jacob already has an heir (unlike Isaac when he prayed) it is from Rachel that the children have been withheld and not from him. Certainly, the matriarch's barrenness is focused much more on her own personal distress.

of Hagar in ch. 16), though one which we know from this earlier case is only second best. The synonyms אמה and שפחה (both translated 'maid') are used to describe Bilhah, words traditionally seen as criteria for source division, but perhaps just used for variation. Certainly there is no disturbance in the flow from v. 3 to v. 4.

The idea of bearing children on the knees of the mistress, whether or not reflecting a literal practice, seems to denote adoption of some sort.[49] Throughout these verses (as in vv. 1-2) the term Elohim is used. Two sons are born of Bilhah, and there is a slight variation in the naming formula.[50]

The etymologies are again linked to the wider narrative. In the case of Dan, Westermann argues that the final clause of Rachel's speech ('and has also heard...') is a secondary addition, intended to bring out the theological emphasis.[51] In the case of Naphtali, the reference to Rachel wrestling with her sister and prevailing (יכל - 32:29!) has wider allusions to Jacob's struggle with his brother and more graphically to Peniel. It again emphasizes the close affinity between Rachel and Jacob. The ambiguity of the word Elohim is particularly striking in this connection, indicating on one level the intensity of struggle ('mighty struggles'), but on a deeper level, how the fortunes of the two sisters are seen to reflect divine favour, and how their human struggle is the place where God's plan is worked out. It is fitting that Rachel's triumphant statement should finish the section, although we are left wondering whether Rachel is really as confident as she claims, given that she only has two (surrogate) sons compared to Leah's four sons.[52]

vv. 9-13: Leah's Surrogate Children

We now return to the perspective of Leah, as v. 9 forms a link with 29:35b. As opposed to the birth of Leah's own children there is no mention of God (and certainly not YHWH), and her own motivation (after all, she already has four of her own sons) comes to the fore. Consequently the namings are

---

49 Though compare Richter, H.-F., '"Auf den Knien eines andern gebären"? (Zur Deutung von Gen 30:3 und 50:23).' *ZAW* 91 (1979), 436-7.

50 The stronger על-כן is used for the first child (as with Levi and Judah) as opposed to the usual waw-consecutive clause.

51 Westermann, *Genesis 12-36*, 474.

52 This disparity between Rachel's claim and the reality is perhaps also due to the nature of the material here, since it may be that the writer is imposing this narrative link upon a list of names that is already established. Others see this disparity as evidence of the composite nature of the passage, since in an earlier version, perhaps the claim did match the reality (see also Gunkel, *Genesis*, 325).

more centred on herself and the sibling rivalry.

The naming of Gad is particularly difficult.[53] This textual difficulty may indicate how the writer has struggled to find a natural etymology. Certainly the form of this particular birth formula, containing a simple exclamation, is much shorter than the others and somewhat abrupt. The naming of Asher also has a one word exclamation, although this is followed by a longer and possibly secondary clause.

vv. 14-18 - the Selling of the Mandrakes

There is now an extended introduction to the naming of Issachar, as Leah gives to Rachel the fruit collected by her son Reuben in exchange for a night with Jacob. The tension is all the greater between the two sisters as this is the only narrated exchange. It seems that the fruit in question was considered an aphrodisiac, and, we may suspect, an aid to fertility,[54] and so behind the demand and giving of the fruit would lie a conflict about sexuality and fertility. The story also leads us to assume that Jacob is giving all his attention at night to Rachel.

Given this, we can appreciate the full force of Leah's accusation in v. 15. Equally revealing of her bitterness are her words to Jacob on his return home. The notion of selling or hiring is emphasized by the repetition of the verbal stem שכר (vv. 16.18), and Jacob himself is demeaned by being made an object of reward, to be bartered away. In reality, the exchange is something of a 'creative compromise', since both sisters gain something they need: Rachel, the possibility of fertility, and Leah, the opportunity to sleep with Jacob.[55] But it is a bitter and sorry compromise, which demeans all parties concerned.

v. 17 returns to the more standard birth and naming formula. The final etymology is odd in that it has no real basis in the tale just told but goes back to the giving of her maid to Jacob. Quite why God should regard this as something to be rewarded is also unclear. It could of course be that Leah's interpretation of the birth expresses more her own perspective.

This etymology is all the more unexpected since the story itself, with its repeated use of the verb שכר ('hire'), already furnishes an explanation. It would be wrong to call this a doublet since there is only one standard

---

53 The Qere form is בא גד.
54 Contra Jacob (*Das erste Buch der Tora*, 567-8).
55 So Fokkelman, *Narrative Art*, 137. Fokkelman also points to a parallel between this story and Esau selling his birth-right in exchange for the lentil stew. However this does not quite work as the roles are reversed - it is Rachel (the younger) who gives up her privilege (p. 140).

naming formula as such, but there is some inconsistency, perhaps because of a concern to preserve two rather different etymologies. Historically, it could be that vv. 14-18 were brought into the framework, in which case it would be more probable that the story already existed, since it is not unreasonable to suppose that something composed specifically for this purpose would have been made more consistent with the wider context.[56]

Nevertheless, this episode offers a snapshot into those years of conflict and rivalry, demonstrating not only what is true of the two sisters - their mutual jealousy as one has the need of fertility, the other of access to her husband - but also the way that Jacob's role is totally passive and he has become an object to be bartered, linking to the wider use of the motif of 'hiring' (שכר) in the Jacob-Laban story.[57]

vv. 19-20 Leah's Sixth Son, Zebulun

In this etymology, the name Zebulun is connected formally in the narrative with the verb זבל ('honour'), but there also is a looser connection with the verb and noun זבד ('dowry'/'gift').

The root זבד seems to sit awkwardly alongside the clearer etymology involving זבל, but Blum explains its inclusion by pointing to a structural connection between the namings of Issachar and Zebulun.[58] The verb זבד ('gift') sets up a contrast with שכר ('reward') in v. 18: Issachar is a reward, but the next son is not simply a reward but an additional 'gift'. Furthermore, he sees a chiasm in the naming of both of these sons of Leah:

Jacob hired by Leah (שכר) (v. 16)
Leah receives *God's* reward (שכר) (v. 18)
Leah receives *God's* gift (זבד) (v. 20)
Jacob will now live with Leah (זבל) (v. 20)[59]

---

56   Westermann (*Genesis: 12-36*, 476) sees the mandrake story as the more original and vv. 17-18 as a later interpretation - 'this is most inappropriate and is downright theologizing'.
57   Fokkelman also points to the name יששכר (Issachar) meaning 'man of wages' (שכר שיׁ): 'The name 'taints' the father: Jacob himself, we see now, is no longer anything but 'a man of wages'...It is by far the most important name in the whole Story of Jacob after that of Jacob himself,' (*Narrative Art*, 138).
58   Blum, *Die Komposition der Vätergeschichte*, 108-9.
59   Blum argues that זבל should be understood as meaning 'live' as opposed to the more usual understanding of 'honour'. He argues this from the traditional understanding of this word as found in the Targums and Ibn Ezra, and from other attested uses of the word in MT, which, he argues, all make more sense when translated in this traditional way.

The chiasm itself is far from obvious, although Blum does show a discernible progression from the idea of Issachar as reward to that of Zebulun as 'gift', over and above the reward.

v. 21: The birth of Dinah clearly stands out. Most obviously she is not one of the founders of the twelve tribes. In addition, there is no attempt to offer an etymology. The most plausible explanation is that the verse is added to the list in preparation for the later story of her rape. The effect of this is that when we come across her in chapter 34, Dinah is already introduced and closely tied to her brothers, especially her full brothers Simeon and Levi (v. 25).[60]

vv. 22-24: The Birth of Joseph

This final birth marks not just the end of this section but also the climax as Rachel finally bears Jacob a son. The fact that this son has been so eagerly awaited makes him all the more special. זכר ('remember') is commonly used to describe God coming to help after a time of waiting. Why God should remember Rachel now is not spelt out: perhaps so that Joseph is valued all the more as a gift from God, perhaps as an outworking of his favour, or perhaps there is the hint of a reward after Rachel allowed Leah access to her husband.[61] The etymology itself, seeing the child as a result of God's favour, would seem to exclude the idea that Rachel's new found fertility is a result of eating the mandrakes.[62]

Rachel responds with joy but also with the desire for another child, and so the passage looks forward to the birth of Benjamin. The significance of the birth of Joseph is emphasized by the fact that it comes closest of all to having two formal etymologies. Interestingly the verbs connected with the name have opposite meanings ('take away' and 'add'). The use of two terms for God may suggest two sources. However, other reasons for the variation should not be ruled out, such as poetic variation or the use of both

---

60   A question regarding ch. 34 is why Leah's other sons, Judah and especially Issachar and Zebulun (whose births are closer to her) are not as closely involved. This omission perhaps points to the different origins of ch. 34 and ch. 30.

61   So Fokkelman, *Narrative Art*, 140.

62   Coats (*Genesis*, 215) sees this statement as the work of the Yahwist, although he does not account for the use of the term Elohim in v. 22. Jacob (*Das erste Buch der Tora*, 597) also points out that Leah conceives even without the mandrakes, thus showing that it is not they that give fertility. Nevertheless, the lengths to which the narrator goes to tell about the mandrakes may leave room for a lingering suspicion that there is more than the final statement of v. 22 indicates.

names to bring the episode to a clear conclusion.[63]

Nevertheless, there are other arguments for literary growth. It is noticeable that the form of this naming diverges from all the others (except Reuben), in that it does not end with the name but with the formal etymology. Furthermore, if the final clause (...לאמר - 'and she named') were omitted, the form would match the others, giving the waw-consecutive (ותקרא) a resultative meaning ('and so she named...').

The effect of this final clause is that not only do we see the birth of Joseph as the fulfilment of Rachel's deepest desire, but we also see that fulfilment as incomplete until the birth of the twelfth son. The fact that Rachel's fulfilment will only be met as she dies makes her a tragic character indeed (as the naming of Benjamin indicates). Indeed, we can detect a hidden irony in Rachel's protest to Jacob that she will die if she has no children - she does have children, but dies in the process.[64] Even in this moment of joy and blessing at Joseph's birth lies the reminder of pain and death, as well as the lack of satisfaction.

Conclusion

Historical-Critical Summary

The above reading has suggested that Blum's view of the text being written from the outset as a single passage is false. At several points we have noted evidence of additions or development. How that development happened is difficult to assess: it could be that the names of the twelve were a given tradition, and that some of the etymologies predate this narrative. It could also be that the story of the mandrakes was introduced separately. It is even more difficult to look for the historical basis of the twelve tribes in relation to this passage as much discussion has relied on the hypothesis of the twelve tribe amphyctony in pre-monarchic 'Israel',[65] something now very much called into question.

---

63 Jacob (*Das erste Buch der Tora*, 600) sees a pattern in the use of divine names through the whole episode. The passage starts with the name YHWH. The change to Elohim occurs after Jacob's reply to Rachel where he rhetorically asks whether he is in the position of Elohim to grant fertility. Thereafter the name Elohim is associated with the struggle for fertility. Only when Rachel's shame has been lifted is the name YHWH used again, bringing the whole episode to a close, with the same term used at the end as at the beginning.

64 Hamilton, *The Book of Genesis*, 270. Alter (*Genesis*, 158) points out this irony in relation to 30:1, where Rebekah demands son*s* (plural), and it is precisely the birth of the second son which will bring about her death.

65 e.g. von Rad, *Genesis*, 296-7.

What is clear is that most of the etymologies in this passage are free and spring more from the context of the narrative than from the tribes, their social origins or the words themselves. This suggests that the etymologies were created or evolved as they found this new context. Nevertheless the fragmented nature of the passage has been overemphasized. For instance, there are no formal doublets, even if a second allusion sometimes sits alongside the formal etymology.[66]

It is also noticeable how this passage fits into the wider Jacob-Laban structure, as the births of Jacob's sons in Haran are all told together. This is then followed by the breeding of the flocks. This episodic style changes our focus from one place to another, as in this passage the subject of the flocks, Laban, and to an extent even Jacob are filtered out.

Nevertheless, behind this exclusive concentration are allusions to the wider context. Above all the conflict between the sisters presupposes the previous scene. Furthermore, there is the parallel to the conflict between Jacob and Esau, and the birth of Naphtali alludes not just to this but also to the struggle at Peniel.

Historically, it could be that the birth of these sons, who were the ancestors of the twelve tribes, is secondary to the Jacob-Laban story, and it could be that the narrator was building on a wider and common tradition of Jacob as the father of some or all of the tribal ancestors, whatever the particular circumstances in earlier traditions. However, the etymologies and allusions now make it very much part of the wider context.

A further question, raised by Coats, is what to make of the omission of any explicit reference to the promise tradition within the patriarchal story, given that the promise of posterity finds some fulfilment.[67] For Coats this shows that it is not the promise motif but that of family strife that is the main framework of this unit (as it is the whole Jacob plot).

---

66 A formal etymology would include a standard formula such as ותקרא את-שמו... ('and she called his name...'). An allusion is a word-play, where a verb or other word in the speech of either Leah or Rachel is similar or even of the same stem as part of the name given to the child. For any etymology, the actual etymological formula has to be linked to an allusion (thus שמון is linked with the allusion שמע). In some cases however, there are two different allusions (e.g. with Joseph), which may point to some development behind the text, and which some have wrongly called doublets. The most obvious such cases are Issachar and Joseph.

67 Coats, *Genesis*, 216. A similar issue will be the lack of any mention of Jacob's sons in the blessing of 35:11. This is not untypical, however, since Isaac is only promised a multitude of descendants after the birth of Jacob and Esau (26:3ff.24).

The Human and Divine

As with other parts of the Jacob narrative, the human and divine stand in a complex relationship with each other. Commentators unite in seeing the 'human' side of this passage, where jealousy provides motivation for the women. This is highlighted in Rachel's outburst to her husband, in the use of maidservants, and most especially in the mandrake episode. The impression is of a tense, triangular relationship, with no outside relief. Thus Rachel makes no recourse to prayer, receives no word of reassurance, and does not even find support from her husband.[68] For her, God is indeed absent. Furthermore, Jacob appears to make no attempt to make things better, and here we have an indication of a similar passivity leading to family strife at Shechem and indeed concerning Joseph.

The references to God are both an additional aspect and a contrast to this human side. They are additional in that references to God are predominantly through the words of the protagonists and coloured by their emotions. God's favour thus becomes a way of securing the favour of their husband over their sister.[69]

But some references go beyond this. Jacob himself reminds Rachel of the involvement of God in the events (30:2 - surely no consolation at all to Rachel in the circumstances), and the narrator refers to God seeing, hearing and remembering. Of particular note in this connection are the births of Leah's first four sons, where the motif of God's intervention on behalf of the underdog (29:31) is in evidence, and where the birth of Judah results in the exemplary response of praise, evoking the spirituality of the psalms. This is underlined by the use of the divine name in these verses, so that these verses in particular, present a type for the faith and worship of Israel.

This juxtaposition of the human and divine may be seen in diachronic terms,[70] but this observation in itself fails to do justice to the complexity of the relationship or to the text as it stands. For instance, some references to God are indeed part of the human side as noted above. Furthermore, even the most human aspects of this passage have parallels in the psalms, featuring as they often do, an equal amount of petition, desire for vindication over 'enemies', and praise and acknowledgement.

---

68   Alter, *Genesis*, 158.
69   'She [Rachel] pompously announces, that her cause has been undertaken by the Lord...
We see, then, that under the pretext of praising God, she rather does him wrong, by rendering him subservient to her desires.' - Calvin, *A Commentary on Genesis*, vol. 2, 143. Perhaps this overstates the case, where motives are more mixed and where there are expressions of real pain and hurt as well as triumph.
70   So Westermann, *Genesis 12-36*, 471-2.

From a theological perspective, Brueggemann's comments are nearer the mark:

> The narrative is a delicate balance. On the one hand, there are mandrakes and handmaidens and names of children which suggest the powers of fertility. There is a suggestion that births can be wrought by careful planning. But at the same time, there is the overriding theological affirmation: God is the only cause of new life.[71]

This balance of the human and divine is especially evident within the family, where the focus once more rests. In particular, Westermann highlights how the conflict between the women is rooted in their specific concerns: 'Whereas men were basically at strife over living space and means of subsistence, women clashed basically over position and status in the community.'[72] Westermann tries to see this against the background of a society where there was a conflict between a woman's function as a mother and recognition of her through personal liking. Certain caution needs to be exercised in any picture of society we imagine this passage to be reflecting, but the passage graphically shows the joys and hurts of women in a situation where their own personal standing is so tied up with motherhood. To what extent we can read a critique of this situation or a simple depiction of the way things were depends as much on our perspective as readers as on any intention of the passage.

On the other hand, we see how God is active in the family. One theological theme that emerges is that of God as judge, arbitrating between different parties and coming to the help of the person in need. This theme will become even stronger as the Jacob-Laban plot thickens. But behind this is also the realization that cases are rarely clear-cut, that the underdog can easily become the source of oppression, and that divine justice has to operate in a confused and complex web of mixed motives and situations.

Finally we see again how the divine plan is worked through human frailties, shortcomings and distress. As one commentator writes:

> The same casual observer may read the story of Rachel and Leah and smile as he recalls sibling rivalries and wifely jealousies that are the familiar fare of life and gossip...Of course they were jealous of one another. Of course, they tried to outdo the other...But to what purpose did they compete?[73]

---

71 Brueggemann, *Genesis*, 255.
72 Westermann, *Genesis 12-36*, 477.
73 Scherman and Zlotowitz, *Bereishis*, vol. 4, 1203-4.

Whatever the motives of Rachel and Leah, it is certainly true that their jealousy, and indeed the circumstances that forced them and Jacob into this unhappy situation, did further the divine plan, and in particular that the very emotions of the women and the resultant competition for as many sons as possible became the driving force which led to the birth of the twelve sons.[74]

Israel's Self-Understanding

The birth of the twelve sons clearly marks a turning-point in the Biblical narrative. In the words of Kunin, unlike the children of Abraham and Isaac, the children of Jacob are all 'inside'.[75] But as is generally proving to be the case in the Jacob story, the picture of Israel's beginnings that emerges is far from ideal or even complimentary. Without doubt the children born are meant to be identified as the ancestors of the twelve tribes, and once again these origins are seen in the context of struggle, rivalry and indeed, polygamy.[76] Although there is divine involvement in the birth of the children, there are also very human factors. Joseph seems to come out best, simply because he is the long awaited son of Jacob's loved wife, Rachel, and no doubt this helps to set the scene for the story of Joseph.

As a whole, this passage once again testifies to the realistic picture that Israel has of itself, and the way it sees God's involvement in its past: the presence of God is no guarantee of harmony.

---

74 Sherwood (*'Had God not Been on My Side'*, 139-40) points to the unresolved nature of the themes within this episode. The one theme is desire-fulfilment marked by Rachel's desire for sons (plural) and by Leah's desire to be loved by her husband. Neither of these desires is totally fulfilled. The other theme is conflict-resolution, which again is not resolved. It is perhaps this lack of resolution which makes this episode so uncomfortable, and there is a sense in which the matriarchs can be seen in tragic terms: caught up in their own sufferings with no prospect of resolution. For the reader of course, there is the bigger picture and the realization that these things may be happening 'for a higher purpose' and that there is some resolution outside of this episode.

75 'The key area of transformation between Abraham and Jacob is the movement from outside to inside. Abraham is the father of nations...while Jacob is the father of the nation' (Kunin, *The Logic of Incest*, 112, also p. 122).

76 So Calvin (*A Commentary on Genesis*, vol. 2, 133): 'Since Moses sets these crimes before the Israelites in the very commencement of their history, it is not for them to be inflated by the sense of their nobility.'

Jacob's Flocks (30:25-43)

Introduction

This is without question an extremely difficult passage because of the intricacies of the negotiated agreement between Jacob and Laban, the description of the animals and the breeding techniques employed. Needless to say this has given rise to discussion of sources and the composite nature of the passage.

The traditional source critical approach is taken by Gunkel who sees in the opening part (vv. 25-31a) repetitions which point to J and E sources.[77] These repetitions are: Jacob's request to leave (vv. 25.26a), the composite nature of Laban's speech shown by the repeated introduction to speech (ויאמר - 'and he said' - vv. 27.28),[78] Laban's question about what he should give to Jacob (vv. 28.31), and the repeated sentences of 26b and 29a. More telling is what seems to be evidence of two diverging agreements: v. 32 seems to contradict the previous assertion of Jacob that he will receive no payment, suggesting with vv. 33-34 an immediate payment. Thus vv. 32-34 are part of one agreement foreseeing immediate payment (Gunkel ascribes this to E). According to the Yahwistic version, Jacob does indeed receive nothing at this point (v. 31) and agrees to remain, but Laban will take the marked animals out, and any newly born which have the marks specified will belong to Jacob. This becomes the basis of the narrative.

Von Rad also finds 'factual obscurities', and in particular the two conflicting agreements.[79] However, he is also keen to show that 'one cannot on the whole doubt the way in which the narrative should be understood. Therefore even the statements which seem to presuppose another context are to be interpreted from the present understanding.'[80]

Westermann sees much more coherence in the text. Rejecting the presence of doublets or contradictory agreements, he sees the main source of difficulty in the description of the animals to be selected and in the breeding techniques. These he explains as glosses by later interpreters, trying to make sense of an old shepherd's story.[81]

On the other hand Blum sees no reason for questioning the original unity

---

77   Gunkel, *Genesis*, 327-9
78   The repeated verb at the start of v. 28 is not translated in NRSV.
79   von Rad, *Genesis*, 298.
80   von Rad, *Genesis*, 299.
81   Westermann, *Genesis 12-36*, 479-80.

of the text, arguing that it makes sense as it is, even though the subject matter is difficult to understand. Likewise Fokkelman tries to show that the passage makes perfect sense, though only after very hard and detailed work: 'This difficult text must 'mature' before we can explain the whole by means of the parts in a well-founded literary way.'[82]

Because historical-critical questions are bound up with the narrative logic of the passage which is also affected by the bargaining positions and possible ambiguity of the parties, we shall first attempt a reading of the text as it is.

Exegesis

vv. 25-34: the Agreement

vv. 25-30: The beginning of v. 25 marks the transition from the previous episode to the new. Jacob's reference to Canaan as 'my place' (מקומי) and 'my land' (ארצי) provides a link back to Bethel. Emphasis is placed on Jacob's service as the root עבד ('served'/'service') is used three times in v. 26 and again in v. 29. v. 26a is hardly a doublet (contra Gunkel) since Jacob's request now focuses on his wives and children, and the need for Laban to release his claim on them. It thus reminds us again of the advantage enjoyed by Laban because of social conventions at Jacob's expense.[83]

Laban's reply is indirect as he stalls for time and tries to divert Jacob from his purpose. His observation is an odd testimony to YHWH's blessing

---

82   Fokkelman, *Narrative Art in Genesis*, 144.

83   It is nowhere made explicit what social convention or law is in operation, or what justified claim Laban might have. This could either mean that such a law is presupposed by the narrator or that there is no clear-cut law or convention, in which case Laban is taking advantage of Jacob's weak bargaining position. Wenham (*Genesis: 16-50*, 254) points to the law of Ex. 21:3-6, but as he also points out, this law is only applicable if Jacob is deemed to be a slave, something which the text does not spell out. This points to a further unclarity in Jacob's situation. However, see also Morrison, M. A. ('The Jacob and Laban Narrative in the Light of Near Eastern Sources.' *BA* 46 (1983), 156-61), who points to illuminative parallels with Babylonian herding contracts. If such a comparison is valid, it would mean that Jacob could be seen as a herdsman attached to the family (but not enjoying the status of a family member), who enters an agreement to care for the flocks in return for some share in the profits. Certainly the way that the sons of Laban set a distinction between Jacob and themselves (31:1) makes such a definition of Jacob's status credible.

since the insight is gained through divination.[84] Nevertheless, the rather begrudging source of the testimony makes it all the more effective, and indeed the reference to 'increase' (פרץ - v. 30; also v. 43) may imply a fulfilment of the promise made by God at Bethel (28:14),[85] as may the reference to Laban enjoying YHWH's blessing through Jacob.[86] The offer reintroduces the theme of reward (שכר), which again is used as a hold on Jacob (assuming, that is, that Laban has in mind some reward for future work or a delayed payment).[87] Fokkelman makes an interesting point about the repetition of the phrase 'and he said' (ויאמר) at the beginning of v. 28: it marks Laban's pause as he thinks feverishly about how he can keep Jacob.[88] Then he comes up with the idea of making a wage offer (as he did earlier in a similar move).

The bartering has now begun. Although Jacob seems to have the advantage since the offer has been made to him, it is really Laban who has the power since he can simply refuse Jacob.[89] Thus Jacob is hesitant to show his hand for fear of being turned down and having his vulnerability exposed. Instead, he plays on the fact that he deserves good treatment and attempts to strengthen his bargaining hand by claiming the credit for

---

84 Compare the testimony of Balaam (Nu. 22-24). The unusual mention of the name YHWH in the mouth of Laban probably accounts for the preference for the term θεος (=Elohim) in LXX.

Jacob (*Das erste Buch der Tora*, 602): 'Er sagt יהוה, um sich bei Jakob angenehm zu machen, aber seine eigene religiöse Zweispaltigkeit kommt sogleich in den heidnischen נחשתי zum Ausdruck.' A better explanation for the unusual occurrence of the divine name is to emphasize that it is indeed YHWH, the God of Israel, whom even Laban has to recognize. The use of the name YHWH sharpens the polemic in a way that the more general term Elohim would not, reinforcing the polemic found in the outcome of the teraphim.

85 Hamilton, *The Book of Genesis: 18-50*, 279.284.

86 28:14b - ונברכו בך כל־משפחת האדמה ובזרעך.

87 It is also interesting that the narrator has not chosen to tell us first hand that Jacob's presence has led to blessing for Laban. The information is included here, because it explains Laban's motives in wanting to continue to exploit his nephew, but perhaps also, as indicated, because the source of the observation makes it all the more impressive.

88 Fokkelman, *Narrative Art*, 142-3.

89 Fokkelman reads the situation differently (*Narrative Art*, 143) in that Jacob has the advantage and by saying he is demanding nothing, he avoids the trap of last time and is putting the acquisition of wages into his own hands. Furthermore, he knows that despite what seem to be unfavourable terms, God will continue to bless him. Laban thus walks into a trap due to the modesty of Jacob's proposal. There may be something in this, but it assumes that Jacob did not really intend to leave straight away, whereas it would seem just as possible that Jacob's original intention of leaving is delayed by Laban, just as his intention of marrying Rachel was delayed.

Laban's good fortune.

vv. 31-34: Laban is giving nothing away but insists that Jacob declares a price. Jacob, knowing that he is in a weak position, appeals to Laban's greed, and so his demand is also an acceptance that he will stay. Nevertheless, such is the concealment of motives, that the reader does not know whether Jacob had intended all along to negotiate a new settlement allowing him to receive some reward for his work, or whether he had hoped that Laban would simply let him go.

The negotiation now intensifies. v. 31 could be seen as an opening posture by Jacob, saying that he is really demanding hardly anything, although his statement that Laban will give him nothing also proves to be literally true in what happens. The details are introduced in v. 32: by itself v. 32 seems to say that Jacob will take out the sheep, lambs and goats in question and keep them.[90] That would be the natural understanding of the phrase 'such shall be my wages' (והיה שכרי).[91] However a literal reading of v. 31 suggests a different meaning as the animals already marked are not to be included in Jacob's pay. This leaves an incongruity between v. 31 and v. 32. To the reader an impression of unclarity is created: is Jacob asking for the animals that are set apart at the outset? Is he leaving room for ambiguity? Or is it clear from the context that he does not expect to be paid with these?[92]

Another interpretation is to see the original offer (at least from Jacob's point of view) as being those animals set apart at the outset, but this reward being frustrated by Laban who removes them first. The difficulty of this reading is that it leaves the meaning of v. 31bα unclear, and it puts undue weight on the waw (usually translated 'and') at the beginning of v. 35,

---

90   שה is usually seen as sheep, although the first clause of v. 32 could be a general description of all the categories - so Westermann (*Genesis 12-36*, 478), who sees what follows as a gloss. Accordingly, Westermann translates כשבים with 'sheep' rather than 'lambs'. See also Fokkelman (*Narrative Art*, 145) who makes the same identification.

91   Blum (*Die Komposition der Vätergeschichte*, 114) tries to argue that the phrase in itself points to future payment. In support of this, he points to v. 31 and its claim that Jacob wants *nothing*, the word הסר which means 'take away', and the singular form of the verb היה, since a plural form would be more appropriate for referring to the specific animals taken out. This would mean that Jacob is suggesting that the coloured animals be taken away from the flock, but that such as these subsequently born would be his wages.

These arguments have some validity but are probably not enough in themselves to counter the overwhelming impression of the verse that Jacob is indeed referring to those specific animals. Here though, we must distinguish between the force of v. 32 in itself, and the wider context of which they are part.

92   See RSV, NRSV, NEB, REB and TEV translations.

treating it as an adversative clause (i.e. 'but...').

Jacob then offers to demonstrate his honesty (צדקה), that is his strict compliance with the agreement. This motif of proving innocence will become clearer as the encounter between Jacob and Laban comes to a conclusion. The word מחר ('later' in NRSV) can mean 'tomorrow', or, less typically, it can refer to a less specific time in the future.[93] Given the context it has the latter meaning here, though some have seen it as further evidence of the more immediate payment of Jacob. As well as the motif of innocence, that of stealing (גנב) will also reappear as Jacob will be accused of stealing Laban's teraphim.

A remarkable aspect of the passage is the list of the types of animals which qualify as Jacob's reward.[94] Unfortunately, it is difficult to know how the adjectives are distinguishable from each other. There are also variations in the lists, perhaps due to stylistic variation, glosses or a combination. In any event, the result is to add to the confusion in the mind of the reader.

As Fokkelman notes, Laban's response (v. 34) is just as vague as his agreement to allow Jacob to marry his daughter (29:19).[95] In Fokkelman's view this leaves room for changing the terms of the agreement (see 31:41).

vv. 35-43: Breeding Techniques

Jacob himself has offered to divide the animals, but Laban wants to make doubly sure. The description of the sheep taken out is different from the earlier one, with greater detail (the distinction between male and female goats), the new adjective עקד ('striped'), and the colour white (לבן). This detail perhaps reflects Laban's meticulous care to exclude any possible contender, and the colour white plays on his name.[96] The effort to place a large distance between the flocks is ironic, since the very distance enables Jacob to carry out his experiments undisturbed and then to escape

---

93 So *BDB*, 563 - see Ex. 13:14 as an example of the latter.
94 Terms used in the narrative are:
   v. 32 - every שה which is נקד and טלוא;
   among the lambs, every one חום;
   among the goats, every one טלוא and נקד.
   v. 33 - among the goats, as above (in reverse order);
   among the lambs, as above.
   v. 35 - among the he-goats (not before mentioned), העקדים, הטלאים;
   among the (female) goats, הטלאת ה קדות,
   and all (the goats?) with white (לבן!);
   and the lambs as above.
95 Fokkelman, *Narrative Art*, 144.
96 The name 'Laban' (לבן) means literally 'white'.

undetected. It is also worth noting that this is the first mention of any sons of Laban apart from the scene at the well. So far all the work has been done firstly by Laban's daughter Rachel, then by Jacob.

Jacob now sets about trying to influence the birth of the animals. Several stages are described. First of all, stakes are set up with exposed white streaks.[97] The details of the branches and of the watering-troughs seem repetitive and cumbersome, but the general meaning is clear. At this stage, Jacob is dealing with the צאן (normally 'flock'). Elsewhere this word is a general term covering the whole flock (vv. 36, 32). It is however unclear whether this stage includes the lambs/sheep (see below).

The next stage specifies the lambs or sheep (see earlier note). However the meaning is unclear. It seems that Jacob picks out the sheep or lambs, sets them facing the striped and black, and that these latter exercise a similar function to the peeled stakes in the earlier stage. It is not clear what is meant by the 'Laban's flock' (צאן לבן), since if these animals are striped and black, they could be counted as Jacob's, unless we are meant to understand those animals separated out by Laban at the outset. However, this does not make sense if they are three days' apart.

Fokkelman tries to make sense of it by suggesting that v. 40 is describing the process of dividing the coloured sheep from the others just as he does the goats. Thus הפריד ('separated') refers to Jacob's act of dividing the sheep (just as he has with the goats). He then puts the חום (that is, the sheep - see vv. 32, 33, 35, where the sheep are always חום) and the עקד (that is, the goats - v. 35) in the best position. This depends on giving פנים the meaning of the 'front' (of the flock - i.e. the best position) rather than the more obvious idea of facing opposite. This latter difficulty, as well as the lack of any earlier explicit mention of the division of the goats makes Fokkelman's reading problematic. In any case, Fokkelman admits that the text is difficult, putting this down to stylistic reasons. It still seems most likely that this stage is describing the placing of sheep opposite the marked goats, so that the latter influence the colour of the new-born sheep.

The next stage (v. 41) is more a refinement of what happened in vv. 37-38, as a distinction is made between the better breeding stock (the vigorous). Jacob's concern is now with the quality of his stock as well as the quantity.

---

97 Can the use of the word לוז (30:37), used only here in the Bible for almond, be a cryptic nod in the direction of Bethel, formerly Luz, and the promises made (28:19)? - Sherwood, *'Had God Not Been on My Side'*, 230.

Conclusion

In terms of literary-historical considerations, the above reading suggests mixed conclusions. There is little cause for finding doublets in the opening dialogue, and certainly nothing to point to two parallel accounts. Repetitions pointed out by Gunkel (the request to leave, the composite nature of Laban's speech, the question as to Jacob's reward, the assertion of Jacob about his service) are all part of the bargaining positions adopted, with both Jacob and Laban trying to force the other's hand.

A comparison of vv. 31 and 32 is different, since, in itself, the latter suggests that the payment is immediate, whereas v. 31 and the subsequent developments make it clear that this is impossible. It would seem that the best solution is one along the lines of von Rad where the synchronic reading is clear in seeing the payment in the future rather than immediate, but where the original meaning may have been different. It is difficult to go much further than this, particularly as the whole of the narrative presupposes the information given in v. 32 regarding the distinction between different types of animal. One solution might be to see v. 32 as an original description of immediate payment, but then qualified by later additions to the story which delay this payment and assimilate the breeding tricks employed by Jacob.

The description of Jacob's action also presents difficulties, and although attempts can be made to find an underlying unity and logic, they are unconvincing in the detail. The complication is also compounded by the different ways in which the animals are described. Whereas we can point to the general confusing effect of this, reflecting a confusion of Jacob and Laban's motives and intentions, Westermann's suggestion of expanding and explanatory glosses seems to make sense.

Regarding the original context of such a story, although there is much to reveal an interest in the economic and social aspects of the life of a herdsman, it is not possible to say with any degree of certainty whether this was originally a 'herdsman's narrative'.[98]

Nevertheless, underneath these difficulties, clear themes emerge. The picture of Jacob is consistent with the wider portrayal, and other motifs in this episode resonate with those found elsewhere. Thus there is a parallel between the rather blunt picture of animals breeding, itself an example of the fertility that blesses Jacob 'wherever he turns' (30:30), and the crude struggle between Jacob's wives. This impression from this second episode further colours the impression of the first. Furthermore, the piling up of descriptions of different sorts of animals and the vigour of the animals

---

98   Contra Westermann, *Genesis 12-36*, 484.

belonging to Jacob add to the impression given elsewhere of his own strength and enthusiasm. This is highlighted by the contrast of v. 42, reinforcing the contrast felt more generally of the sloth of Laban and his sons with the vigour of Jacob and his household, not to mention his cunning. We are left to wonder at the exact nature of the tricks employed which to the modern reader appear more like magic than science, a distinction perhaps false to the ancient reader. In this way we can also see some reflection of the episode with the mandrakes.

Strictly speaking Jacob is not cheating or using deception in the way that Laban did earlier, or in the way he himself did against his father, but there is nevertheless the sense of a reversal, as Laban gets his come-uppance. The impression of confusion in method and motive also pervades the passage, leaving the way open for an alternative interpretation of the events.[99]

For the moment, though, apart from a hint of Laban getting his come-uppance, there is no explanation, least of all, in theological terms: the divine has retreated into obscurity, and Jacob seizes the situation for himself, employing all means to advance his cause. Admittedly, Laban's confession (v. 27) introduces the divine perspective, but this is lost in the confusion. Indeed, the reference to God is unusual on the lips of Laban (30:27): 'This is one of the strangest confessions of Yahweh and his blessing in the Old Testament, a confession which even Laban had arrived at by the dark process of his superstition!'[100] Nevertheless, the last word on the episode has not been said, as becomes clear.

Jacob's Decision to Flee and the Final Parting (31:1-32:1)

Introduction

There is much to suggest historical development in this passage: differing perspectives which often follow each other closely (such as the reason for Jacob fleeing), the greatly differing picture of previous events, and, in the case of the treaty, unevenness in the text and repetitions. Questions have

---

99 Jacob (*Das erste Buch der Tora*, 607) makes the point that the narrator never explicitly spells out that the animals give birth as a result of seeing the stakes. The action can be seen as a demonstrative gesture made to indicate the occurrence of a divine miracle. He also notes that even Laban never accuses Jacob of using tricks.

Alter (*Genesis*, 165) cites an interesting idea that the peeled rods are used by Jacob as a diversion, a gesture to popular belief - and no doubt Laban's superstition - whilst Jacob is actually relying on the much sounder principle of selective breeding.

100 von Rad, *Genesis*, 300.

also been raised because of geographical descriptions.

Gunkel again finds evidence of J and E in the passage: large parts are ascribed mostly to E (vv. 4-16, vv. 17-25 and v. 43) because of the term Elohim, communication through dreams and the interdependence of these units.[101] However, these units also contain traces of J.

Gunkel also detects two versions of the treaty: one is a family agreement, the other a national boundary agreement; in one case, a column is erected, in the other, a pile of stones; two place names are given: Mizpah and Gilead; there are two sacrificial meals (vv. 46b, 54); two appeals to God (vv. 49f, 51f); two divine names: the 'Fear of Isaac' (v. 53b) and 'the God of Abraham and the God of Nahor' (v. 53a).

In addition, Gunkel points out that the journey undertaken by Jacob and his family cannot possibly be from Haran (as recounted in 27:43, 28:10, 29:4 - all J texts according to Gunkel) since the distance to the mountains of Gilead is too great for ten days. References to the journey length suggest that E must have considered the home of Laban to be beyond the immediate East Jordan region.

It should however be noted that the source critical approach which Gunkel accepts, does not match with his view of the story evolving from a secular to a 'religious' story, since both sources contain aspects of both.[102] It is for instance odd that the account of E found here, which in Gunkel's view is trying to put forward a more religiously and ethically 'acceptable' Jacob, where Laban has changed Jacob's wages and God has clearly intervened, is not found anywhere in E's actual version of the event in chapter 30.[103] Furthermore, three reasons are given in the narrative for

---

101 Gunkel, *Genesis*, 331ff.

102 There is of course no textual basis for this assumption. It depends on the view expressed by Gunkel in several places that the ethical perspective in Israel's religion was a relative late-comer. It also assumes that stories such as these were 'secular' and the interests of the later writers became more 'religious'.

103 The question of how much of E can be found in ch. 30:25-43 is unclear among source critics (see below on von Rad). From v. 37, most is ascribed to J (so Gunkel, *Genesis*, 336), but at least for Gunkel there are also fragments of E, which add to the technical descriptions, but offer a no less 'secular' perspective on the events.

There is also a slight contradiction in Gunkel's judgement on E's ethical stance. In writing about E in ch. 30, he sees that the writers, 'especially E', emphasize Jacob's honesty by depicting the action not as deception but as maintaining 'every appearance of righteousness' (p. 328). However, on commenting on Jacob's speech to his wives in ch. 31, Gunkel sees this as an example of E's 'excuse attempts', which are often to be found 'everywhere piety feels bound to material which originates in morally or religiously undeveloped times' (p. 332). Thus in ch. 31 E no longer wholeheartedly endorses the action taken in ch.30, despite Gunkel's earlier comment that E in ch. 30 was showing that the

Jacob's decision to flee as we shall see, but only two sources are posited. There is therefore a contradiction between the documentary approach and the traditio-historical approach. A solution to this means rejecting one in favour of the other, or strictly modifying them both.

Von Rad avoids some of the problems of Gunkel by eliminating any elements of E from the earlier account.[104] However, he does not make it clear whether E followed J's version to any extent. Again he sees the hand of E in Jacob's words to his wives: 'This amazing change from the Yahwistic narrative, especially the moral purification...apparently corresponds to the refined demands of a more sensitive group of readers.'[105] In the Elohist's hands Jacob is 'without moral offence'. E therefore saw the earlier events differently.

In contrast, Westermann sees the narrator as the Yahwist.[106] There are expansions in vv. 4-16, giving a theologizing thrust similar to the theological expansion of the birth of Jacob's sons and in the treaty. Regarding the blatant difference between the presentation of events in chapter 30 and Jacob's version here, Westermann sees an explanation in the setting and intent of Jacob's address to his wives. Thus Westermann rejects a diachronic solution to the difference between the two accounts and argues for seeing two perspectives on the same event, particularly seeing the interest of chapter 31 in the idea of the legal confrontation (ריב). It should of course be noted that his conception of the Yahwist as the basic narrative structure is so totally different here from that of traditional source criticism that it can be questioned to what extent his use of the term is meaningful.[107]

Blum agrees with the view that chapter 31 represents a later interpretation of the events of chapter 30.[108] However, its origin was never independent of the previous passage, although he believes that there are remnants of an earlier account in chapter 31. This passage was conceived as a corrective addition, whose purpose is to change the emphasis to God's action and to Laban's continued unfair treatment of Jacob. He also looks closely at 31:13 which refers explicitly to 28:10ff (Bethel) and which is

---

action was not blameworthy.

It would of course have been easier for Gunkel if he saw no traces of E in the first passage. What the difficulties above also show are the dangers in trying to see particular ethical or religious nuances as dependent on an evolutionary progression, or as denoting particular authorship.

104 von Rad, *Genesis*, 305.

105 von Rad, *Genesis*, 307.

106 Westermann, *Genesis 12-36*, 490.

107 See Westermann's overall conclusion, *Genesis: 12-36*, 571-2.

108 Blum, *Die Komposition der Vätergeschichte*, 118ff.

both a compositional element in the wider Jacob narrative and anchored in its present context, especially by v. 16b where the women refer back to it. Thus this verse is part of a layer which is later than the basic Jacob-Laban story. Regarding the unity of the passage itself, he does see some complexity but is not confident of being able to distinguish different layers of tradition and redaction.[109] Regarding the final treaty, Blum again sees repeated elements but does not go on to posit two accounts of different origins. The family agreement is more linked to the narrative context, and so is original to the story, whereas the border treaty (an independent tradition) has been drawn into the larger context.[110]

Fokkelman also sees the difficulty of reading chapters 30 and 31 together.[111] Ruling out historical-critical questions, he has to decide whether Jacob is telling the truth in chapter 31 or whether he is lying, using the idea of Providence to justify his own means. For Fokkelman it is unthinkable that even Jacob would go so far and he concludes:

> In this speech the narrator presents a Jacob who is the pious and grateful interpreter of his own history and who, pointing away from himself, confesses that God is the only decisive factor in his life...Jacob is the keen observer and genuine believer and grateful proclaimer of God's help; his interpretation is profound and authoritative.[112]

From the assumption that this is the authoritative version, Fokkelman reconstructs the earlier events: Laban and Jacob agreed that Jacob should have all the 'abnormal' animals bred from the 'normal', and the latter used his breeding methods to assure successful results. Laban took advantage of the different types of markings to continually reinterpret the terms of the agreement. But then Providence intervened and adapted the breeding to Laban's new conditions. The first account stresses the simple acquisition of wealth and Jacob's part in it; the second gives the more complete view.

Before looking at the passage, some points need to be drawn out from the above:

• The above survey has shown the obvious problem of relating Jacob's

---

109 Blum singles out vv. 19-21 which disturb the flow. Furthermore, like Gunkel, he sees a tension in the geographical locations. The river, referring to the Euphrates, is part of the D-redaction, also found in 35:1ff where the stolen teraphim are interpreted as gods 'from beyond the river' (thus alluding to the Dtr. passage in Josh. 24).

110 Blum, *Die Komposition der Vätergeschichte*, 140; agreeing with Westermann, *Genesis 12-36*, 499.

111 Fokkelman, *Narrative Art*, 151ff.

112 Fokkelman, *Narrative Art*, 162.

account of the previous episode to the narrator's account in chapter 30.

- This is not just a question of determining sources or different historical backgrounds: it is above all a question of reading the text as it is. The real problem is not how to explain away the difference in the accounts but to read them side by side.
- Only then can we consider whether a diachronic solution fits the criteria. In deciding on what sort of historical-critical pattern -if any -is most appropriate, we need to ask what does most justice to the text as it is.
- Clearly the final treaty is a distinct unit, even though there is no clean break in the text.

Exegesis

vv. 1-3: These verses set out the reasons for Jacob's decision to leave. There is a curious mixture of reasons, but a structure is clearly discernible: first, Jacob hears (שמע), then he sees (ראה), and then YHWH speaks (אמר). Thus each stage is complementary. There is also a progression of reasons which become more compelling: firstly, Jacob hears the words of Laban's sons, then he sees Laban himself, and then, the most compelling reason of all, YHWH speaks directly. Thus there is no justification for seeing unnecessary repetition.

The reference to Laban's 'face' (פנים) emphasizes the directness with which Jacob sees his uncle, and it also anticipates a motif that will be picked up later (e.g. 32:21, 32:30 - MT, 33:10).[113] v. 3 clearly gives the clinching reason in this progression, and alludes to the Bethel experience, the last time that YHWH spoke to Jacob: the long period of silence is ended and things begin to come to place.[114]

vv. 4-13: As is usual with Jacob, obstacles have to be overcome before his goal is achieved, and we are faced with the question of how he can get away from Laban, who seems to have a total hold over Jacob.

Throughout the following passage we need to bear in mind the different audiences that are involved. On the level of the narrative, Jacob is speaking and seeking to justify himself first before his wives, and then before Laban; but on a second level, he is explaining himself before the reader. The conclusions of his testimonies will be parallelled by conclusions drawn by

---

113 Literally: 'Jacob saw Laban's face...' - v. 2.
114 Parallels to ch. 28 are the designation YHWH, the theme of returning to the land - first promised, now commanded, the assurance of being 'with you' (עמך). It is also noticeable that the promise of posterity has begun to see fruition. For an explicit link, see v. 13.

the reader.

Jacob first decides that before he can leave he must secure the cooperation of his wives. We are expressly told that he sends for them. This preface to his speech emphasizes the fact that he is working in the fields, that is, that he is dedicated in his work.[115] It may also suggest a symbolic distance that has come between him and his wives, or simply that he is more comfortable away from their mutual jealousy. A further reason may be to ensure greater secrecy away from Laban.

Jacob now states his case. From now until the final agreement between Jacob and Laban this legal aspect will dominate. At various points Jacob and Laban put their cases, and the other human characters watch on and, with us, are invited to make a judgement. This theme is most explicit with Jacob's final onslaught from v. 36, where the verb ויָּרֶב ('confront') appears. This in fact describes the whole of the proceedings, as we are judges in a legal confrontation (רִיב).

In this first round, Jacob begins by spelling out the immediate reasons for wanting to leave (v. 5). He first refers back to v. 2. It is more likely that the reference to God's presence with Jacob refers not to v. 3 but to God's more general intervention as described in what follows.[116] Then Jacob appeals to his wives to agree with him from their own experience, since, claims Jacob, they have seen his hard work. The rare pronoun וְאַתֵּנָה ('you' - v. 6) has an emphatic effect, emphasizing the role of the wives.[117]

However Jacob's real grievance follows with v. 7: Laban has cheated and changed his nephew's payment ten times ('ten' perhaps a concrete way of saying many times), and God has been present in the situation on Jacob's behalf. It is unclear what effect this claim would have on Jacob's wives at this stage, as it is unclear whether the clause 'You yourselves know...' might include this part as well. However to the reader the effect is dramatic. Both claims of Jacob - the manipulation of wages and the intervention of God - seem to contradict flatly the narrator's version of events in chapter 30. In case we think that Jacob is talking about a stage in the dispute not covered by chapter 30, v. 8 with its reference to the different types of marked animals previously mentioned, makes it clear that two versions of one and the same thing are found in the mouth of Jacob and in chapter 30,

---

115 Alter, *Genesis*, 167.
116 In favour of this reading is the imprecise description of this presence, and also the syntactical function of the waw, which attached to the noun disrupts the flow of the sentence and so is best translated 'but', meaning that the clause ('God has been with me') is not sequential but contrastive to Laban's cheating.
117 Westermann, *Genesis 12-36*, 488.

and the reference to God in v. 9 is a complete contrast to the view previously given that the cause of the particular births was Jacob's own scheming.

Jacob then heightens this discordance by appealing to revelation from God in the form of a dream. In this dream, not only does Jacob see the animals, he also hears the words of the angel. The reader is even less sure of what to make of the dream. First there is the rather blunt, if not grotesque, vision of the animals mating. It could be that Jacob is just describing things as they were, or that he is lying, but to lie on such a matter is no small thing. v. 13 refers explicitly back to the Bethel experience. The reference to the anointing of the pillar reminds us of the oath to return to the shrine.

Before going on, we need to pause and let the full force of this sink in. We are left wondering whether Jacob is telling the truth or whether he is lying, or whether the truth is somewhere between the two. At this stage it is impossible to tell. If he were telling the truth, that would leave in question the report of chapter 30. This should not be played down, and although Fokkelman may have a point in seeing room for this later reading, especially in 30:34, he tends to play down the difficulty of the reader. After all, are we not more likely to trust the narrator than Jacob, and if the dream is genuine, why is it not described directly by the narrator but only secondarily through Jacob at this later stage? As a result we experience even more bewilderment than already felt after trying to make sense of chapter 30 on its own! If Jacob were lying, this would not be totally out of character judging from his past deceptions, but could even he stoop so low and use God in this way? In the context of the Torah the reader knows full well that Jacob would be breaking the third commandment. The reference to the dream seems to increase the stakes since we are left with Jacob either truthfully recounting a dream from God, or parodying divine revelation in a rather grotesque way. The reference to Bethel reinforces and intensifies the issue, as Jacob is all but swearing by his most sacred experience.

vv. 14-16: Rachel and Leah seem to accept Jacob's version of events, and certainly agree to leave. At last, the sisters, divided through strife, find a point of agreement.[118] Their real concern and motivation is the way Laban has mistreated them. Thus, in terms of coming to a judgement between Laban and Jacob, their response might add a further piece of evidence against Laban, but does not really help us to decide on the truth of Jacob's

---

118 Coats, *Genesis*, 218.

case.

vv. 17-21: The verb קוּם ('arose') in vv. 17 and 21 forms an inclusio. Whereas the first clause (...וַיָּקָם - 'and he arose') is a stereotypical way of describing the start of a long and important journey, the following words highlight what is distinctive about Jacob's position: he has camels, sons, wives, cattle, livestock of his own. The reference to his father Isaac is perhaps odd, since the emphasis later is on his encounter with Esau, and Isaac's role is minimal (35:27ff). It could be argued that this is an insertion from P,[119] but its effect is to stress that Jacob's return is not just to the land of Canaan, but also to his family. A reconciliation with Isaac would also entail some coming to terms with Esau. Perhaps, above all, it refers to the oath made by Jacob at Bethel (28:21) about a return to his father's house. v. 19 explains how Jacob could get away with the deception, and underlines the irony mentioned earlier in Laban's excessive caution in separating the herds.

In the Hebrew idiom, the stealing of the teraphim by Rachel is parallelled by the stealing by Jacob of Laban's 'heart' (לֵב - i.e. deception). The former act prepares for the later confrontation. We are nowhere told why Rachel steals the gods. Perhaps it is an attempt by Rachel to compensate herself for the injustice done to her,[120] or she believes that they will secure some blessing for herself or some advantage for Jacob.[121] Alternatively she might simply be reluctant to part with these familiar objects as she goes to a strange land.[122] Importantly, though, this act also shows that she is acting

---

119 This is assuming that 35:27ff is part of the priestly source or redaction.

120 Fokkelman, *Narrative Art*, 164, and Westermann, *Genesis 12-36*, 493. Note also the parallel with the Israelites' despoiling of the Egyptians (Ex. 12:31-36 - see Coats, *Genesis*, 218) - again, there is no explanation for why it should happen.

121 Speiser and others, bringing to bear Nuzi parallels (*Genesis*, 250-1). Speiser sees behind the text the idea that teraphim denote legal ownership of an estate. Hence to take the teraphim is to effectively make a claim on the property. However, the validity of such parallels has been questioned (e.g. Greenberg, M., 'Another Look at Rachel's Theft of the Teraphim', *JBL* 81 (1962), 239-48); and as Speiser admits (p. 251) such a custom would be lost on the later Biblical writer. If this were so, his parallel does not really help us in making sense of the action as depicted in the text. To some extent, this objection also applies to the argument of K. Spanier ('Rachel's Theft of the Teraphim: Her Struggle for Family Primacy.' *VT* 42 (1992), 404-12) that in stealing the teraphim, Rachel is trying to secure a role for Joseph as chief heir after Jacob.

122 Greenberg, 'Another Look at Rachel's Theft of the Teraphim', 246.

most like Jacob.[123] Jacob's corresponding act of deception against Laban shows that even in this chapter the writer is not giving us a Jacob without any moral offence.

vv. 22-24: The wording in the dream, that Laban should refrain from saying anything 'good or bad' (מטוב עד-רע), literally means that Laban should say nothing, which does not fit the context where Laban is not afraid to speak to Jacob. Von Rad suggests that we understand the phrase as meaning that Laban is not to influence the events.[124] It could be that Laban is not to use his superior power, and so has to restrict himself to the legitimate means of proving his case. This is indeed the tack that Laban takes. A parallel with chapter 24 is interesting in that the same words are in the mouth of Laban (v. 50). Here, Laban and Bethuel see the hand of YHWH in the events leading to the meeting of Abraham's servant with Rebekah. In both cases therefore Laban is forced to recognize the work of God and to refrain from interfering.

vv. 25-30: Laban's first accusation is that Jacob has deceived him (the phrase refers back to the narrator's conclusion in v. 20). The deception, claims Laban, is that he has stolen his daughters as if by the sword, and, more realistically, without due formality. He claims that his concern would have been to send off Jacob and his daughters and grandchildren with due festivity. We know that this would have been unlikely, and also that the daughters have agreed to leave, and in these exaggerated claims we see how unsubstantial Laban's case really is. Nevertheless, underneath are hints of an aggrieved father. In v. 29 Laban draws attention to his strength and potential to harm but admits that he cannot use this force.[125]

---

123 For Fuchs, E. ('"For I have the Way of Women": Deception, Gender, and Ideology in Biblical Narrative.', *Semeia* 42 (1988), 68-83) there are important differences between the way that the parallel acts of Jacob and Rachel are portrayed. She comments that the narrator pulls out all the stops to exonerate Jacob's action, but that Rachel is depicted as arbitrary since there is no description of motive, no passing of judgement or closure to the incident. This failure to 'problematize' her behaviour or to understand it means that the moral ambiguity around Rachel's act is not resolved. For Fuchs this is part of the way women are generally depicted, but also by contrasting Rachel with Jacob, Jacob is seen in a better light. Also, we are able to see Laban mocked without Jacob playing an active role in what might be seen as a vindictive action.

124 von Rad, *Genesis*, 308.

125 For a reading of the legal aspect of this episode, see Mabee, C., 'Jacob and Laban: The Structure of Judicial Proceedings (Genesis xxx1 25-42)', *VT* 30 (1980), 192-207. Mabee argues that at this point Laban has the authority to 'do harm' (by, for instance, taking the daughters back with him) if Jacob is shown to have done wrong.

Even now, Laban grudgingly accepts that Jacob should want to return home (once again, a reference to Jacob's father, this time less direct), so he falls back onto the more concrete and seemingly better grounded accusation: Jacob has stolen the gods. Significantly, the objects are called 'gods' (אלהים) in the mouth of Laban alone.

vv. 31-32: Jacob's defence. Jacob begins by dealing with the first accusation: he does not so much deny that he has acted wrongly as plead extenuating circumstances.[126] Furthermore we know that the wives themselves have fully consented to go with Jacob. But then he moves to the second accusation. Cleverly, Jacob turns the tables around by forcing Laban to prove his case, confident that he has not stolen the teraphim.[127] Here he repeats the word 'gods' (אלהים), although the pronominal suffix ('your') gives it a sarcastic force: they are only gods in the sense that Laban affords them that status, and as to the real value of Laban's 'gods', their final position will graphically expose that! The writer explicitly lets us know that Jacob did not know about Rachel's act.[128] This helps to further establish Jacob's innocence and also adds dramatic irony to the tension since the reader knows what Jacob does not.

vv. 33-35: Tension increases as Rachel is last to be searched, but the situation is saved by her prompt action. Because we already know about this (v. 34a), the picture of Laban groping for these objects is made to appear more comic. Note the verb 'felt' (וימשש), used also in the picture of Isaac touching Jacob (27:12, 23), reinforcing the parallel of Jacob's deception of his father and Rachel's deception of her father. There is also the irony of reversal in that Laban is now deceived by the daughter who he himself has in a way deceived.[129] However the parallel here is much less serious and more farcical, and we cannot help but grin at Rachel's words. Her mode of

---

126 Mabee, 'Jacob and Laban: The Structure of Judicial Proceedings', 199.
127 Thus Laban is forced into the role of plaintiff rather than judge (Mabee, 'Jacob and Laban: The Structure of Judicial Proceedings', 196).
128 Note the observation that, although Rachel escapes any execution of Jacob's declaration of v. 32, she does not long survive this episode (Rashi - Rosenbaum and Silbermann eds, *Pentateuch*, 150, and Ibn Ezra - Strickman and Silver eds, *Ibn Ezra's Commentary*, 303). Such a reading reminds us of Jacob's rashness in making such a declaration. Y. Zakovitch ('Through the Looking Glass: Reflections/Inversions of Genesis Stories in the Bible.' *BI* 1 (1993), 139-52) sees an ironic reflection of this episode in the accusation later levelled against Benjamin of stealing Joseph's goblet (ch. 44) - the sin of the mother is reaped on her son.
129 Jacob, *Das erste Buch der Tora*, 620.

address ('my lord') is ironically set against the situation where she shows no respect for her father's treasured objects. Furthermore, the sitting of a woman upon objects during menstruation renders them unclean (Lev. 15:20).[130] We thereby see their true worth, and Laban's attachment to them is ridiculed.

As well as providing a way of ridiculing Laban and also the faith placed in what Israel saw as idols, the episode gives Jacob the opportunity to vent his anger.

vv. 36-42: The mood changes from buffoonery to anger. Jacob's anger is not just at Laban's false accusation (although that is a convenient target) but at the whole of his treatment. Now that Laban has been made to look a fool with his groping around after worthless objects, he has lost any psychological hold over his nephew, and Jacob feels no barrier in expressing himself. Suddenly Laban is cut down to size and Jacob releases the tension that has built up over the years.

As with Laban, Jacob's accusation is in the form of questions. He begins with Laban's 'false' accusation and the humiliation of being subjected to a search, but then moves onto more substantial matters. He points to the care he has shown to Laban's flocks, his honesty in not taking any for food, the difficult working conditions and Laban's exacting demands.

Jacob then moves to more familiar ground for the reader. He recalls having to serve fourteen years for the two daughters, and a further six (the first mention of the duration) for the flock. After this, he repeats the accusation made before his wives, which we had reason to question, namely that his wages have been changed ten times, and he further points to the intervention of God as further proof of his innocence.

The reference to God stands out because of the names to describe him. The phrase 'the God of my father' (אלהי אבי) is the simplest of the designations and is therefore often seen as the original phrase, later expanded by the references to Abraham and Isaac.[131] In this context it stresses the personal nature of Jacob's God, and perhaps the promise of blessing passed on by Jacob's father. The meaning of פחד 'of Isaac' is not certain but most commentators follow the suggestion 'fear' or 'dread'.[132] As Gunkel remarks, if this is the meaning, its inclusion here is deliberate, since God has caused Laban to fear, and so protected Jacob.[133] On the other hand,

---

130 von Rad, *Genesis*, 310.
131 So Westermann, *Genesis 12-36*, 497.
132 Westermann, *Genesis 12-36*, 497.
133 Gunkel, *Genesis*, 338.

a case has been made for understanding the word פחד as 'thigh', itself a euphemism for strength or procreative power.[134]

Westermann points to the wider social perspective of Jacob's accusation within Israel. Throughout the tradition of the Torah and the prophets it is a serious crime for the employer to deprive the employee of wages. By contrast, God does not stand by but intervenes on behalf of the weaker; and Westermann sees in the (original) phrase 'If the God of my father had not been with me...' echoes of Ps. 124:1.

v. 43: By now we are made to feel that the version of events given by Jacob to his wives is not fabricated. This is implied if not proven by Laban's response, which makes no attempt to deny what Jacob has just said. Instead, the response is rather half-hearted and hollow. Laban's rhetorical question about whether he would really do any harm to his own family (implying that he could by rights) is really a face-saving ploy: in the circumstances, he recognizes that it is time to let Jacob go, and he makes the best of the situation by proposing a treaty.[135]

We can now return to the question of Jacob's innocence. The reader's judgement is shifted gently as the action and dispute progress. At first, there is complete surprise as we hear Jacob's explanation to his wives. Then our attitude to Jacob is gradually softened. First, he wins over his wives, although we noted that this was not difficult given their own grievance. Next we see for ourselves that God intervenes against Laban in a dream, perhaps adding credence to Jacob's claim to have had a dream himself. Then we hear Laban's unfounded charges against Jacob, and finally we see no attempt by Laban to deny Jacob's version of events. Instead he looks for a compromise in the form of a treaty.

This leaves the question of the previous chapter. Hamilton suggests that in this chapter Jacob realizes in retrospect that it was not his tricks which

---

134 Koch, K. ('*Pahad jisaq* - eine Gottesbezeichnung?', in Albertz, R. et al., *Werden und Wirken des Alten Testament* (Festschrift für Claus Westermann zum 70. Geburtstag), Göttingen, 1980, 106-15) who also argues that it is not a term for God, but that Jacob is referring to the procreative power of his father which he believes has accompanied him. This view is supported by Malul, M., 'More on *pahad Yishaq* (Genesis xxi 42.53) and the Oath by the Thigh.' *VT* 35 (1985), 192-200; also Puech, E., '"La crainte d'Isaac" en Gen 31:42 et 53.' *VT* 34 (1984), 356-61.

135 By doing this he acknowledges a change in relationship as Jacob is now an equal (Mabee, 'Jacob and Laban: The Structure of Judicial Proceedings', 194).

brought prosperity but God's intervention.[136] Nevertheless the force of Jacob's version of events in chapter 31 is not simply to deny the efficacy of the methods used before, instead his silence about them seems to be a denial that he ever tried them in the first place. An alternative is to see this chapter offering a different perspective of the same events, not so much denying the cunning methods shown by Jacob as giving another explanation.[137] In particular the emphasis has shifted from the human, with detailed interest in Jacob's skill, to the divine, with the intervention of God as the key factor. We have before us two starkly different accounts of the same event where any mention of the divine is absent from chapter 30, and any mention of human methods absent from chapter 31.

However, this does not quite go far enough in doing justice to the disquiet of the reader. Already in chapter 30 the reader felt confused by the description of events, now we are even more so, and we are made to wonder whether the narrator is playing tricks. Perhaps all we can say for the moment is that this unclarity points to the complex task of discerning God's part in human affairs. In the wider context, Jacob's innocence is a relative state. If he is innocent, it is not because of his exemplary behaviour, and we are still a little suspicious that we have not quite had the whole truth. However, Jacob is innocent in the sense that he has been more the object than the subject of exploitation. Thus the impression felt by chapter 30 should not be left behind. The Jacob who is pronounced innocent here is the same Jacob who has used scheming methods. We are still left, therefore, with a feeling of uncertainty, and on a deeper level, we have lost confidence in the ability or at least the desire of the narrator to give us an impartial and definitive account of how things are.

Regarding traditio-historical development, the plain difference between chapters 30 and 31 seems to demand some sort of conclusion, probably

---

136 Hamilton, *The Book of Genesis: 18-50*, 288. Also Kidner, F. D., *Genesis*, London: Tyndale Press, 1967, 163. On ch. 30 itself, Hamilton writes,

> How does Jacob manage to succeed?...Jacob's rods function much as do Rachel's mandrakes. It is not the mandrakes that produce fertility, and it is not Jacob's white rods that produce the right kind of offspring for Jacob - although perhaps that is what Jacob wanted Laban to think.

If this is indeed the case, Hamilton still has to account for the version in the previous chapter told by the narrator, which, under normal circumstances, we would expect to be the most reliable.

137 From a redaction-critical perspective, Levin argues that chapter 31 is a 'Theodizeebearbeitung' of the story, added by a later redactor (*Der Jahwist*, 242).

along the lines of Blum who sees a corrective interest. Even so, even assuming that chapter 30 does present an earlier account, there is no surviving evidence of that version of events having its own ending. Instead, there is only one version of the outcome of the Jacob and Laban story, and in itself chapter 31 shows no trace of an earlier strand or of any unevenness. More importantly, a traditio-historical or supplementary model cannot be used to 'solve' the problem by explaining away the paradox. Nor must we set the Jacob of chapter 31 against the Jacob of chapter 30 as von Rad does, since even if the approaches came from different places, the final version forces us to read them as one.[138]

vv. 44-32:1 (MT): The prompting for the treaty comes from Laban who now recognizes his weakness in the face of Jacob. As just mentioned, it also witnesses to his ongoing claim over his family's state.

The masculine form of the verb היה ('let it be' - v. 44b) is a little incongruous, disagreeing with the feminine ברית ('treaty'), and some have also argued that only a visible object can act as a witness, and that the treaty, far from being a witness, is what a witness should point to.[139]

vv. 45 and 46 describe two acts of Jacob to provide some concrete symbol. For the first, no explanation is given. Although the stone may act as a sign of an agreement with Laban, which is how Laban sees it in v. 51, to Jacob it is a visible testimony to God's protection promised at Bethel, and to the partial fulfilment of promises made there. The unexpected reference to 'bread' (לחם - v. 54; cf. 28:20) may underline this.

v. 46 presents its own difficulties. It seems to be a doublet with the previous verse, although it should be noted that the function of this heap of stones is much more related to the treaty. Some follow the old Latin versions in treating Laban as the subject here, an impression reinforced by the reference to 'kinsfolk' (אחיו - cf. v. 23). The reference to a meal seems preemptory at this stage, as the meal described at the end seems more natural to the context. Another reading of this last clause is to see it as describing the heap as the place where the meal would take place, without necessarily claiming that it took place at this stage.

---

138 See for instance, von Rad's comment: 'One must remember that here the blameless Jacob, the Jacob of the Elohist, is speaking, the Jacob who was repeatedly wronged by Laban, whose honor has now been stained and who looks back with righteous indignation.' (*Genesis*, 310).
139 Westermann, *Genesis 12-36*, 498, also Wenham, *Genesis: 16-50*, 279. The masculine form could simply be referring to the whole event of setting up the stone (so Delitzsch, *A New Commentary on Genesis*, 196).

The naming of the place described in vv. 47 and 48 is also difficult. v. 48 has the longer etymological statement, whereas v. 47 is more succinct with no accompanying speech. It also shows both parties giving the name in their respective languages, indicating a cultural separation. Since v. 48 is followed immediately by the continued speech of Laban with no further introduction, it is more likely that v. 47 was included at a later stage. The name 'Mizpah' (המצפה, meaning 'watchpost'), also given by Laban, finally hints at the terms of the treaty. First of all, Laban proposes terms regarding the family, with a guarantee of Jacob's good treatment of his wives, and with YHWH acting as all-seeing witness. No indication is given of Jacob's attitude to this as he seems to go along with the terms. Indeed, after the previous events, it would seem far from likely that he is going to want to take any more wives.

In addition to this agreement on the level of the family, Laban introduces a national-political perspective, with the guarantee of borders and a non-aggression pact. This is a reminder to the reader that the story of Jacob is not just the story of a family but also of a nation.

After this there is one more invocation of the divine as witness, although this time the god of each of the parties is invoked since the obligation is mutual. The phrase 'the God of their fathers' (or 'gods...') seems to be an explanatory clause. Then Jacob gives his assent, by calling on the פחד ('Fear') of Isaac. Having done this, he seals the treaty with the customary solemn meal.

The next morning, this unhappy episode in Jacob's life is brought to a close as Laban takes his leave. It is more true to say that Laban and Jacob part with a truce rather than fully reconciled, and the omission of any final embrace or word between the two is noticeable compared with the warmth of their first meeting. The optimism at the well when we might have assumed that God's blessing would make things easy for Jacob is long forgotten.

Historical-Critical Conclusion on the Treaty

Regarding historical-critical questions, we have seen that there are several repetitions in the passage. Von Rad is typical in seeing two recensions. The doublets he sees as follows: in v. 45 a landmark is erected as a sign of the covenant, in v. 46 a heap of stones; v. 46 and v. 54 both tell of meals; and the treaty has two meanings - the treatment of Laban's daughters (v. 50), and the boundary (v. 51).

However even this does not account for all the difficulties mentioned above.[140] Furthermore, there is no evidence for these versions corresponding to the wider J and E sources, and von Rad assumes the border treaty is J simply because it seems older.

Evidently there has been some historical development within the passage, although it is difficult to trace. Regarding the two terms of the treaty, these in themselves are not doublets since it is reasonable to conceive of a treaty with two clauses. However, given the overall unevenness of the passage, it is highly probable that these two elements have been brought together. The family agreement is the logical conclusion to the Jacob-Laban episode, whereas the border agreement has the appearance of an independent tradition joined to the story.[141]

v. 45 also stands out. However instead of seeing it as part of an earlier source, it is better to see its inclusion as strengthening the link to Bethel where Jacob also takes a stone (אבן), and sets it up as a watchpost (מצבה) (28:18). Thus the redactor depicts Jacob as independently using this occasion to witness to the faithfulness of YHWH and perhaps to recall the vow he made at that stage. As well as forming a link to Bethel, there is also a reminder of the opening well scene, itself containing hints of the Bethel scene with its reference to the stone at the well. That gave the false hope that things would go easily for Jacob with God's help. However, only now, after these years of hardship and deception, can Jacob feel that the promise at Bethel is any nearer to being fulfilled.

Conclusion to the Jacob-Laban Story

Literary and Historical-Critical Summary

The Jacob-Laban story shows what is often characteristic of Hebrew narrative: on the one hand, it forms a fairly self-contained story, with a simple unilinear plot involving a few main characters. Given this, it has rightly been called by the German term 'Novelle':[142] the hero arrives in a foreign land penniless and without family, enters into a struggle of cunning and counter-cunning with his protagonist, and through his own resourcefulness and the blessing of God, comes away with a large family

---

140 For instance, regarding the earlier comments on the verb היה in v. 44b.
141 Westermann, *Genesis 12-36*, 499; Blum, *Die Komposition der Vätergeschichte*, 140.
142 So Gunkel, *Genesis*, 316; Coats, *Genesis*, 222.

and wealth.[143] Each episode represents a logical step in this plot. Added to this is what Coats describes as the deep psychological probing of character and relationship.[144]

On the other hand, the Novelle is strongly episodic and contains a wide variety of genre to the extent that it could almost be called a collection of smaller stories. The opening scene is an idyllic scene, whose familiarity leads us to expect an early and easy outcome. Then there is the scene of deception by Laban where we are confronted with the darker side of interhuman relations. This is followed by a genealogical tale, where the two main protagonists of the wider Novelle are hardly mentioned, and where interest shifts to the women in the story. Next comes a tale of shepherd's tricks with the technical and rather crude description of breeding methods. After this, the tone becomes that of a legal dispute where the hero is vindicated, and finally there is the complex and formal description of a treaty bringing a conclusion to the Novelle. There is also the simple narrative of the opening scene contrasted with the obscure description of the shepherd tricks, which leaves the reader baffled, followed by a scene offering a completely different version of the same events.

Furthermore, although each episode within the larger Novelle is distinctive, the episodes play off against each other. For instance, the idyllic scene of the opening contrasts starkly with what follows, leading us into a false expectation. Then the blunt episode with the birth of the sons and the conflict between the two sisters can be read separately, but it suggestively offers a comparison with the crude breeding of the flocks as well as with the conflict between uncle and nephew.

What has been said of the literary features within the Novelle is even more true of the way the story relates to the wider Jacob narrative. As outlined above, the story contains its own plot, understandable on its own. Indeed one could imagine this story being told this way. However, its fullest significance is only appreciated when we spot certain implicit contrasts.

---

143 cf. the description of Sherwood (*'Had God Not Been on My Side'*, 275-6) of the last episode as a grand finale:

> All the characters that have played roles in the previous episodes - Jacob and Laban, Rachel and Leah, the maids, Jacob's children, the 'brothers' (= 'the men of the place'?), Jacob's retainers, and his (formerly Laban's) flocks, and God, of course, who in this episode communicates with Jacob and Laban - return to the stage for a final act which features a daring escape, a secret theft, a chase scene, a frenzied search in which the heroine's life hangs in the balance, a trial scene, a treaty, and a parting of ways.

144 Coats, *Genesis*, 222.

Gunkel misses this by recognizing a story of deception and counter-deception, but by not admitting the obvious parallel with the Jacob-Esau relationship, so that when Jacob is first deceived by Laban, we are invited to see that the 'deceiver is deceived'. We have also seen the influence of the Bethel incident, once explicit, at other times pervasive, and the incompleteness of the narrative of the births as we still await the birth of Benjamin. In addition, the relationship between Rachel and Leah suggestively reflects the relationship between Jacob and Esau (see especially 29:26), and there are obvious links to the patriarchal family in Laban's relatedness to Rebekah and reminiscences of chapter 24.

On a literary level, this interplay of the self-contained Novelle and the wider Jacob story, as well as the variety of material contained within one simple story line, reflects the wider aspect of biblical narrative, where at each stage we deal with individuals and their stories piecemeal, each with a plot and integrity of its own. But then each is part of a whole, each story part of the main story, and the complex web of intertextuality invites the reader to see everything together. On a wider horizon, individual episodes and the cycle as a whole are linked explicitly and implicitly to the life story of Jacob before and after his years in Haran. Wider still, links are made with the earlier generation through Laban at one end, and the story of Jacob's twelve sons at the other end. This then links into the wider patriarchal story, itself part of the story of Israel, underlined by national allusions within the text itself. These very many levels of connection between particular events and the wider story of Israel witness to a tendency within Biblical narrative to create an overall uniting perspective, without smoothing over distinctive features.[145]

Secondarily, this has *literary-historical* implications. As well as the obvious problem of doing justice to both synchronic and diachronic approaches, another danger when looking at the Jacob narrative is of going too far in one of two directions within the diachronic approach itself: arguably, source criticism fails to do justice to the distinctiveness of each part of the patriarchal story by cutting across the obvious stages in the story itself; but the danger of form criticism is of not doing justice to the overarching links.[146] One such mistake made by Gunkel, mentioned above, is his failure to see parallels with the Jacob-Esau plot. This is because of his own view of the independence of the two stories from each other.

---

145 On this aspect of biblical narrative, Alter, *The World of Biblical Literature*, 78-79.
146 This is one of the main criticisms that de Pury brings against the consensus approach established by Gunkel (*Promesse Divine*).

Commentators such as Blum have tried to find a middle way by seeing the main work on the literary level, allowing for a greater overarching unity because of the strong redactorial work and by playing down oral tradition. This avoids the false divisions of source criticism. At the other end of the historical-critical time scale, de Pury finds an overarching unity in positing a pre-Yahwistic oral Jacob cycle, with few parts ever having a separate existence.[147] However, against these approaches, as well as against those who want to rule out any historical development behind the text, little justice is done to the distinctiveness of different episodes, to difficulties in reading the text, and to the practical insights that readings by Gunkel and von Rad can bring. In comparison, some more synchronic 'literary' readings in particular can seem dull, squeezing all ambiguity out of the text.

Reading the parts of the Jacob-Laban story, there is strong evidence of a creative hand that has written the Novelle, and that has made this Novelle part of the wider story. On the other hand, parts of the story have a distinctive background or voice. To some extent, this may simply be due to different genres employed by the narrator at different points. However, in some cases we have seen evidence of the narrator introducing a new perspective over an older narrative, for instance in the way that chapter 31 offers a different picture of the preceding events, and also in different layers of application in the final treaty. Regarding the birth of Jacob's sons, it is conceivable that the figure of Jacob was known and identified as the father of the ancestors of the twelve tribes as well as being known as a relative of Laban, but the precise relation between these two traditions did not reach final form (although told alongside each other?) until the creation of what we might call the Jacob-Laban Novelle.

As for the historical relation of this Novelle to the Jacob-Esau story, could it not equally be the case that they were once both traditions about Jacob, growing up together, assuming elements from each other and exercising a mutual influence, until the final form which links them formally? This process may be called canonical in the sense that they were assumed to be part of a wider story, that the momentum was towards a greater interdependence which found final form in the canonical text, and that these stories were recognized as something worth preserving and developing.

Of course, all this is speculative and begs questions about the setting for

---

147 de Pury makes an exception for the story of the birth of Jacob's sons - *Promesse Divine*, vol. 2, 524.

the telling of such stories,[148] and also about the relation between oral and written.[149] But it seems from reading the Jacob-Laban story, especially as part of the wider Jacob story, that a new historical-critical paradigm must be found that does justice to the overall unity without quashing the distinctiveness of each part and possible development within each part. Such an approach must also be aware of its own limitations and lack of 'assured results' and be seen as the handmaid of a better reading of the text as it is.

Mention should also be made of the question about the original geographical location of the story. There is a case for arguing that the narrative was once about a Laban figure from Aram. For instance, this would account for the difficulty perceived by some in harmonizing Laban's location in Haran in Mesopotamia with the relatively short journey to the land east of the Jordan and the emphasis on Gilead. Blum argues for a 'Haran-redaction' which is part of the same level as the Abraham tradition of Haran.[150] The reference to the 'people of the east' (בני קדם) is the most convincing, as he argues that this name normally refers to the Palestinian grazing land at the edge of the deserts of Syria and Arabia (Judg. 6:3, Jer. 49:28, Ezek. 25:4). Although this view may be correct, the paucity of material warns us against investing too much into this point of view, especially as the relation of the final treaty, which stresses the location of Gilead and is used by Blum as evidence, to the bulk of the Jacob-Laban material is unclear.

Narrative Perspective: Individual, National, Sociological

As Gunkel writes, this is above all else a story about individuals.[151] It is the story of deceit and counter-deceit between two shepherds, and about how the underdog comes out on top. No doubt we are meant to see all characters involved as definite people of the past. Furthermore Jacob and Laban are encountered outside this story, and certainly in the case of Jacob, we are meant to see this as one episode in his life.

But the reader is also aware that these are stories about Israel. This is particularly brought out in the birth of the sons who represent the later

---

148 There is also the question about geographical locations of different traditions, and the extent to which these could be judged to have once been separate.
149 The issue of oral tradition is especially open to debate - Whybray, R. N., *The Making of the Pentateuch*, Sheffield: JSOT Supp 53, 1987, 138-85; Kirkpatrick, P. G., *The Old Testament and Folklore Study*, Sheffield: JSOT Supp 62, 1988.
150 Blum, *Die Komposition der Vätergeschichte*, 164ff.
151 Gunkel, *Genesis*, 315.

tribes. It also comes to the fore with the treaty and its border agreement. Nevertheless, it is also noticeable that the tale of the sons' birth is highly influenced by its narrative context, with the etymologies relating to the situation of the two sisters. The identification of Laban with Aram is less clear and depends on the above discussion regarding the original geographical location of the tradition.

Sociological Perspective

In their different ways, Westermann and Fokkelman show how this is not just the story of individuals but also about the family unit, the economy of service and reward, social conventions, and legal procedures. On the whole, these elements prove to be of mixed value. There is no idealized view of the family, even in the understanding of Israel's own origins. Instead we see what happens when deceit poisons family relations. Not only is nephew set against uncle, but also daughter against father and sister against sister. In particular, we see the negative side of the introduction of service (עבד) and reward (שכר). By introducing this, Laban secures a hold over Jacob, and what seems to be a favour to Jacob becomes a burden. The lowest point is reached where Jacob is 'sold' to Leah by Rachel for some mandrakes. We also see how Laban exploits his social position to his own advantage, using customs (such as not giving the younger daughter in marriage before the elder) as a screen for his deception. To the Jacob who has flouted convention (in deceiving his father, and at the opening well scene where he takes matters into his own hands in uncovering the well), he finds that convention has not let him go that easily.

But the social fabric also has its positive sides as we see that only an externally ratified treaty can guarantee peace, and Jacob finds justice through the legal procedure (ריב), to which Laban (thanks also to divine intervention) has to submit. In the end, therefore, right prevails.

In addition, given the wider context of the Torah, we can see a concern relating to how Jacob is treated. Around Jacob's situation are clustered issues such as the treatment of the foreigner,[152] but also, paradoxically, of the member of the same family group,[153] and also the issue of service and exploitation.[154] In addition, in the marriage of the two sisters we see the difficulties brought about by polygamy, although this is countered by the fact that the beginnings of Israel are found in just such a marriage. In

---

152 E.g. Dt. 10:18-19.
153 E.g. Dt. 15:12-14 - Sherwood *'Had God Not Been on My Side'*, 219.
154 E.g. Dt. 24:14-15.

relation to chapter 27 we were able to reflect on the extent to which Jacob's dilemma problematized life without the Torah, whilst also recognizing that all the ambiguities of faith are not necessarily solved once the Torah is given. In this chapter, set in a far off country with customs clearly different from his own, Jacob is exploited and finds no protection except from his God and his own guile and hard work. Whereas a connection can be drawn with Israel's experience in exile, a connection can also be drawn to the way the foreigner and the vulnerable are treated in Israel, and how the Torah provides a safeguard for such people.

A further perspective is that of women in such a society. We see in Rachel a resourceful shepherdess, capable of outwitting her uncle and showing sarcasm at the same time. But we see also the despair of two daughters when treated by their father as objects to be traded. Then we see how their happiness becomes dependant on the number of children that they can give to Jacob. Indeed the episode of the birth of the sons has a claustrophobic effect, where all interest, and all the fortunes of the women are restricted to the small confines of the family. Bitterness takes over, and Jacob no doubt finds refuge in the fields with his sheep! In their own ways, Leah and Rachel (not to mention their maids!) command our sympathy in their struggles, and Rachel, who will die at her moment of fulfilment, has the marks of a tragic heroine.

Nevertheless, this note of bitterness and hurt is relieved by a vein of humour running through the narrative.[155] The humour is emphasized in the depiction of the lazy shepherds at the beginning, the bargaining, Laban's groping around. As well as providing relief in this long chapter of Jacob's struggles, the humour also brings a note of sarcasm and polemic. This also relates to the depiction of superstition and magic: the use of the mandrakes, Laban's reference to his divination, Jacob's shepherding tricks, the stolen teraphim. We are often not quite sure how seriously to take these elements, but they stand in sharp contrast to the several references to the intervention of YHWH.

The Presence and Absence of God

One of the key issues in our reading has been the absence of God for much of the events. In the wider context, after the blessing of Jacob and the dream at Bethel, one expects to find the clear hand of YHWH controlling Jacob's destiny. The opening episode gives hints that YHWH's promise at Bethel will find easy fulfilment. The reader familiar with the parallel well scene in

---

155 So Brueggemann, *Genesis*, 20ff.

chapter 24 knows how YHWH clearly guided Abraham's servant (in that case it could not be plainer!), and we are led to expect the same for Jacob. Indeed the passage confirms this impression, although even at this stage there is no mention of God. But these hopes of God's guidance are dashed, as in the ensuing deception and counter-deception, God seems totally absent. For instance, we are not told how to relate the deception by Laban to Jacob's earlier deception of Esau and Isaac. Laban's ironic statement (29:26) indicates some connection (contra Gunkel), but is there the principle of divine retribution in operation (Fokkelman), or some other natural law of retribution? Or is it just an example of how someone who lives by his own wits sometimes comes out on top, sometimes at the bottom? As well as recognizing an irony on the level of the narrative, our own interpretation comes closest to the last of these options. It seems that Jacob's own way of dealing has now backfired,[156] and there is a sense of reversal, but perhaps also the hint of justice at work. There may also be a sense of Jacob being chastened through this, although there is certainly no dramatic change in the way he behaves (ch. 30).

The birth of the sons presents this paradox of the human and divine in a concentrated form. As already mentioned, we are not always sure how seriously to take the claims of the women that God is siding with one then the other, but in the case of the birth of Leah's first sons and the birth of Joseph, one feels that God has indeed shown his favour, and so it is no coincidence that in these cases the divine name is found on the mothers' lips. As Westermann has shown also, the thoughts of the women are not far from the spirituality of the psalms.[157] However Westermann does not go far enough in one respect, since this passage, as already stated, reflects the psalms in their humanness - the expression of raw emotion - as much as in their confession of YHWH's saving intervention.

This episode also prepares us for another theme that emerges immediately afterwards, which is that of God as judge. At first, it seems that Jacob is getting what he deserves after his deception of Esau and Isaac, but the theme of reversal at the expense of Jacob is subsumed, and a new reversal operates between Jacob and Laban once we have seen how Laban's action affects not just Jacob but also his two daughters.

It has already been seen that from chapter 31 the divine becomes a lot more visible. As with the name of God on the lips of the women, we are not

---

156 So Mann, *The Book of the Torah*, 59: 'What a different Jacob this is from the one who left Canaan, the victim of his own dishonesty and pride.'
157 Westermann, *Genesis 12-36*, 477.

sure at first how sincere Jacob is being in his recall of the dream. However there is no doubt from the start that YHWH has come back onto the scene as he commands Jacob to return. The mention of the land 'of your fathers' (31:3) reminds Jacob of the promise and blessing and brings him back into the mainstream of the history of God and this chosen family. We have not dismissed a diachronic solution to the problem of the differing perspective of chapter 31, but it seems that it is not as easy as that. This is not only because the writer left the earlier account of chapter 30 intact, but there is a feeling that by itself chapter 31 is incomplete. It is as though the writer wants us to see the same events through the perspective of both chapters. In one case, it is Jacob's cunning and skill that brings about success, in the other it is God's blessing. Perhaps, in the end, we are meant to see the two aspects as being two sides to the same coin: just as God worked through the deception of Isaac by Jacob, so here, God works through Jacob's very nature, the divine through the human. This seems to be consistent with much of the Jacob narrative where Jacob's efforts and strength are the means by which he experiences God's blessing. One feels that there is great mystery here which cannot be resolved easily, certainly not by a simple recourse to historical-critical solutions.[158]

This also leads us to the tricky question of Jacob's innocence. As mentioned above, innocence is perhaps best seen as a relative term, where the innocent party is the one who has been more wronged against, but this fails to do full justice to the discordance between chapters 30 and 31. Perhaps all that we can say is that the implementation of justice is a complex task, and that we are reminded that there is no one, objective way of seeing things.

In the end though God is clearly at work, not just in providing the momentum for Jacob to leave (again, interestingly alongside more natural considerations), but also in warning Laban. Finally, this is recognized by Jacob himself in the way he interprets the treaty. As mentioned, 31:45, which in the simple terms of marking the treaty seems redundant, is Jacob's way of remembering the appearance at Bethel. Furthermore we come across an abundance of divine terms at the end, following the lack of any in the opening scene of the Novelle or in most of the following. Both 31:42 and the invocation of the 'Fear' (פחד) of Isaac followed by the solemn sacrifice are a form of confession of the God who, in the end, has come to the help of Jacob.[159]

---

158 Likewise attempts to harmonize the incongruity do not really do justice to the question.
159 Thus also anticipating the fulfilment of the vow made at 28:20-21.

The above mentioned polemic directed at superstitious elements, and especially the episode of the teraphim are a contrast to this, which although threatening to ruin the situation for Jacob, end up being a ridiculing comment upon Laban's misplaced faith in these objects. In the end, the reader can agree with Jacob that, despite the struggle and seeming absence of God, YHWH has brought this long episode of Jacob's life to a conclusion. Laban's begrudging testimonies to the work of YHWH only serve to highlight this.[160] We are left asking why it had to be so difficult, but that is also a question posed by the psalmist and the wisdom tradition of Job and Ecclesiastes, not to mention by faith itself.[161]

The above comments attempt to show how the divine and the human are interwoven in the Jacob-Laban story. This contrasts with Coats, who sees divine intervention as a theme introduced rather clumsily to resolve the narrative tension set up by the conflict between Jacob and Laban.[162] This is typical of a view which sees the divine-human contrast in diachronical terms, where one is superimposed over the other and is seen as foreign to the story. So, for Coats, the introduction of the divine into the story is a weakness, in comparison, for instance, with what he sees as the more skilfully constructed Joseph novella where there is no equivalent resort to a *deus ex machina* solution.

However, it is difficult to imagine the story without the theme of the divine as described above, especially as there is no evidence of any other resolution than that given. Furthermore, the whole question of what is central depends on one's own decision about the main theme. For Coats, the theme of the Jacob story is that of family strife without reconciliation. Because of this definition, which limits the interest to the 'human' side, anything else is judged to be secondary, especially any reference to the divine. By contrast, I have argued that the divine-human contrast is key to the Jacob story. The motif of family strife is no doubt part of this, but full justice is done only by acknowledging interest in the human and the divine together.

---

160 Gen.30:27, 31:29 - cf. Nu. 23:8.
161 See Turner, L. A., *Announcements of Plot in Genesis*, Sheffield: JSOT Supp 96 1990, 121-2. Turner points to the irony in the idea of service in relation to Jacob, since his long period of service stands in contradiction to the words of the oracle at his birth and in Isaac's blessing, both of which indicated that Jacob would be on the receiving end of service. The expression of this irony is heightened in the 'hiring' out of Jacob to Leah in exchange for mandrakes, and then in Jacob's statement at 30:26. For Turner this is part of the complex relationship between 'announcements of plot' found at key points in the narrative and the actual plot itself.
162 Coats, *Genesis*, 222.

Chapter 6

The Struggle for Survival:
Jacob and Esau Part 2
(32:2-33:20)

Introduction

Having resolved the conflict with his uncle, Jacob has to face his brother Esau. The tension of this next episode builds up to the final face to face encounter. However, this build up is interspersed with three distinctive episodes: the encounter with the angels at Mahanaim (vv. 2-3), Jacob's prayer (vv. 10-13) and the encounter at Peniel (vv. 23-33), the latter being the most extended and significant.[1]

Thus this section can be divided as follows:

vv. 2-3: encounter at Mahanaim
vv. 4-9: Jacob despatches messengers
vv. 10-13: Jacob's prayer
vv. 14-22: Jacob despatches more messengers
vv. 23-33: Jacob's encounter at Peniel
33:1-17: the final encounter with Esau.

The final verses (vv. 18-20) attach rather loosely onto this episode.
It is evident from the structure that a divine-human contrast is in operation, with the stages in the encounter between the brothers balanced by the encounter between Jacob and God or God's emissaries.[2]

---

1 The versification given for ch. 32 is that of the Hebrew Text (MT), which differs from English translations by one verse - e.g. 32:2 (MT) = 32:1 (ET).

2 It is mainly because of this contrast that we are considering 32:2-3 with the following verses rather than the previous, in spite of the traditional Hebrew setting which sees v. 4 (וישלח) as the beginning of a new section.

A Reading of Chapters 32-33

Jacob's Encounter at Mahanaim (32:2-3)

This odd episode is passed over as soon as it is introduced. As it stands it is hardly a passage in its own right, but rather a notice. Despite its peculiarity there are clear overtones of Bethel (28:10ff): 'met him' (פגע ב), 'angels of God' (מלאכי אלהים),[3] the pairing of 'went' (הלך) and 'way' (דרך) (28:20; 32:2), and the similar images of the heavenly host (cf. 28:17b). Both passages also culminate in an etiology. Furthermore, the placing of the two passages seems to be deliberate, one at Jacob's departure from the Promised Land on the way to Haran, the other at his departure from Haran to the Promised Land.

The significance of this brief incident is not clear. On the one hand reminders of Bethel suggest an encouragement to Jacob, recalling God's promises made there and indicating his ongoing presence.[4] On the other hand, the word 'camp' (מחנים), though not necessarily a military term, often carries that implication and the context of conflict with Esau raises that possibility. Another parallel in this connection is Josh. 5:13-15, where the phrase 'army of YHWH' (צבא-יהוה) perhaps points to the same motif of the army of angel hosts. In this way these verses contribute to the increasing tension by hinting at a possible conflict, and their very ambiguity reflects Jacob's uncertainty.

Regarding the prehistory of this passage, despite the strong links with the episode at Bethel, Blum's suggestion that this incident was perhaps formed from nothing by an editor seems to overstate the case.[5] It would seem more likely that the narrator has incorporated a tradition about the place Mahanaim, albeit whilst shaping it. This better explains the abruptness of the passage and the lack of any explicit connection to Jacob's situation. On the other hand, the implicit connection to Jacob's division of possessions into two camps (מחנים) does suggest why it should be incorporated into this context. Regarding the origins of such a note or any original form, that must remain unclear.

---

3 Whilst the expression מלאכי האלהים is frequent in the Bible, מלאכי אלהים is peculiar to 28:12 and 32:2 - Hamilton (*The Book of Genesis: 18-50*, 317).
4 Houtmann, C., 'Jacob at Mahanaim. Some Remarks on Genesis xxxii 2-3.' *VT* 28 (1978), 37-44. Jacob (*Das erste Buch der Tora*, 628) sees the angels as the 'Engel der Heimat' which ascended at Bethel as Jacob left the promised land, and which now descend again to offer further protection.
5 Blum, *Die Komposition der Vätergeschichte*, 141.

Jacob Despatches Messengers (32:4-9)

The focus now shifts to the human: Jacob sends messengers to try to pacify Esau and to find out his intentions.[6] In Hebrew, the ambiguity of the word מלאכים, which can denote both human and divine messengers (i.e. angels), adds to the contrast of the divine and human in this chapter.[7] These verses contain a classic message formula ('thus says'/כה אמר + originator of message), as well as a classic setting for such a formula. The speech contains several clauses, starting with the simple narrative clause ('and he commanded them' - v. 5), followed by Jacob's words to the messengers ('thus you will say to my lord...'),[8] followed by the message formula ('thus says your servant Jacob'), and finally the actual message ('with Laban...'). This piling up of clauses before Jacob's message emphasizes the fact that at this point Jacob is not seeing Esau face to face but is hiding behind his messengers. Furthermore the lack of direct contact between the brothers keeps Jacob ignorant of Esau's thoughts as Jacob, with the reader, is left to guess at Esau's intentions. The long list of Jacob's acquisitions (v. 6) also seems to put a distance between Jacob and his brother as Jacob tries to distract Esau's attention from himself and the past, and a final distancing factor between the two brothers is the way Jacob defines their relationship as 'lord' and 'servant'. There is also a clear irony here on which we will comment later.

The reply of the messengers conceals Esau's intentions, and the final clause ('and four hundred men are with him') is indeed ominous, hinting at Isaac's words that Esau would live by the sword (27:40). As a result Jacob takes precautions by dividing the party.[9] v. 7 contains a rare description of feeling, emphasizing even more the dread that Jacob feels.

---

6 *Pace* Rashi (Rosenbaum and Silbermann eds, *Pentateuch*, 155), who sees these messengers as the angels that have just encountered Jacob.

7 Houtmann ('Jacob at Mahanaim', 42) sees this sudden switch from the divine to the human meaning of the word מלאכים as incongruous, betraying a historical tension. Whilst there may be historical development, the switch from one meaning of the term to the other also heightens contrast of the divine and the human.

8 Another suggested translation is: 'Thus shall you say, "To my lord Esau, thus says your servant Jacob..."' - e.g. Alter, *Genesis*, 178.

9 This is often seen as a military precaution. In the Midrash the point is made that Jacob employs all the methods to be used in such situations: gifts, battle and prayer (see especially in Leibowitz, *Studies in Berishit*, 359ff). This contrast of methods very much encapsulates how Jacob takes recourse to both human ingenuity and divine help (so Mann, *The Book of the Torah*, 59-60).

Jacob's Prayer (32:10-13)

In desperation Jacob turns to God in prayer. The heart of the prayer is a request for help (v. 12) as Jacob not only admits his fear but also, by implication, his need of God. However the prayer is far from a simple plea for help as it is framed at the beginning by a reminder of promises made to Jacob, and, at the end, of the promises originally made to Abraham. The result of all this, as well as depicting Jacob admitting his reliance on God, is to test the specific promise of God made in chapter 28 and the wider promise made to Abraham. In this way, Jacob is pointing to the faithfulness of God rather than to his own worthiness. Indeed, v. 11, if not a confession of guilt in a full or formal sense, at least implies some sense that his conduct has not been fully exemplary.[10]

Regarding the origins of the prayer, it is frequently ascribed to J or to a redactor (note the term 'YHWH'), and in particular it has been seen as a creation of the Yahwist, intended to bring a theological meaning to the episode.[11] Blum likewise sees the prayer as the work of a redactor, although he ascribes it to an exilic or post-exilic Deuteronomic stage.[12] This is based on the pattern of self-abasement, request, recollection of past revelation (cf. 2 Sam. 7:18ff - reckoned to be also Deuteronomic), the plural form חסדים ('steadfast love') which is peculiar to exilic or post-exilic literature, a similarity with 1 Ki. 3:5ff, and the phrase 'this Jordan' (הירדן הזה) which stands out from the context, but which is found in the Deuteronomic conquest tradition. Westermann, however, claims to find a simple plea (v. 12) behind the final form, with expansions at vv. 10 and 13, forming links with the tradition of the patriarchal promises, and v. 11 to the Jacob-Esau

---

10   Elliger, 'Der Jakobskampf am Jabbok', 18. However Elliger also makes the point that the prayer should be read more as a theological statement from the writer, than a psychological exploration of Jacob's thoughts. Leibowitz (*Studies in Bereshit*, 364), sees Jacob re-appraising his conduct through prayer. As a result of this change of mind, Jacob sends the gifts, having realized how much God has given him.

By contrast, Brueggemann (*Genesis*, 265): 'In this brief prayer, Jacob is deferential. But at the same time, he intends to hold God firmly to his promise of 'good'.'

11   E.g. Elliger ('Der Jakobskampf am Jabbok', 19-20), who describes the prayer as a 'programmatische Äußerung des jahwistichen Schriftstellers'. Likewise de Pury (*Promesse Divine*, vol. 1, 102) sees the prayer as expressing the kerygma of the Yahwist that divine blessing operates over and against the unworthiness of the patriarch. For de Pury, this is the theological theme that the Yahwist has imposed on the Jacob cycle.

12   Blum, *Die Komposition der Vätergeschichte*, 152ff. Similarly, Schreiner, J., 'Das Gebet Jakobs (Gen. 32, 10-13)' in Görg, M., ed., *Die Väter Israels: Beiträge zur Theologie der Patriarchenüberlieferungen im Alten Testaments*, Stuttgart: Verlag Katholisches Bibelwerk, 1989, 287-303.

story as a whole.[13] Thus the prayer itself shows different layers of development.

Overall, the prayer does seem to stand out from its context which suggests a different origin from the surrounding verses. Regarding Westermann's argument that part of the prayer at least is original, this carries some weight, and it could be that the prayer itself has undergone some development (this is particularly possible with v. 13). However, it is difficult to be certain, since there are certainly different levels of reference in the prayer, but there is also a united structure, with the beginning and the end broadening the scope to the wider patriarchal story. More importantly, it is also correct to see this prayer as bringing out the theological emphases of faithfulness to the patriarchal promises and of the unworthiness of the patriarch vis-à-vis divine grace, although whether we are to see this is a specific 'kerygma' of the Yahwist or any other figure is unclear.

Jacob Despatches More Messengers (32:14-22)

Having divided his group into two camps Jacob decides to take the further, more drastic precaution of sending a series of gifts in the hope of gradually mollifying his brother.[14] As with the earlier detailed instructions to the messengers (vv. 5-6), these precautions and the long inventory of the gift emphasizes the buffer that Jacob is setting between himself and his brother, and the delay in having to see him 'face to face' (פנים-אל-פנים - 32:31).

As the plot develops, we shall see that the word 'face' (פנים) does indeed play a crucial role. Besides the literal meaning of 'face', the word forms the heart of the place name 'Peniel' (literally 'face of God/El'). Furthermore, when combined with the word 'cover' (כפר), the word takes on the meaning of 'appease' (v. 14). This motif will itself become very important in Jacob's meeting with Esau.

An interesting parallel to v. 21 is Prov. 16:14: 'A king's wrath is a messenger of death, and a wise man will appease it (יכפרנה).'[15] A further

---

13 Westermann, *Genesis 12-36*, 508.
14 Note the alliteration between מחנים ('camps') and מנחה ('gift'). Hamilton also adds the word חן ('favour') - *The Book of Genesis: 18-50*, 345.
15 A parallel incident is the meeting between David and Abigail, on behalf of her husband Nabal (1 Sam. 25) where gifts are used as an appeasement - so Hamilton (*The Book of Genesis: 18-50*, 325), who also points out the 400 men described in each case. The most significant difference is that of perspective: in Genesis, the story is told from the perspective of Jacob, the non-aggressive party whilst the motives of Esau remain hidden; in the other case, the story is told mainly from the perspective of David, whose violent intentions are quite clear, although also from Abigail who acts as an intermediary. In this latter incident the expression of remorse is much more explicit, at least from Abigail. Thus

resonance of the word 'appease' is that of the cultic language of atonement.[16]

There may be some doubt about Jacob's motive at this point. Is he simply using the presents as a bribe, or are they a genuine expression of contrition? For the moment it is not possible to tell, and the action happens so quickly that there is no time to stop and think about motives.

Peniel (32:23-33)

From the earlier treatment of this passage, it is clear that its scope reaches well beyond the immediate context of the Jacob story, drawing on the self-understanding of Israel and reflections both about the nature of divine self-revelation and human striving. But it is also clear that the passage is understood as a major turning-point for Jacob himself. As indicated, this leads to the question as to how much things really do change for Jacob, both in relation to the events around him and his own character.

One further possibility is that this encounter is in some way an answer to Jacob's earlier prayer.[17] Whether or not we are to see the episode as a specific answer to prayer, there is some justification for seeing the earlier prayer as casting further light on this passage. For instance, de Pury sees the same hand that shaped the prayer evident in the reshaping of the Peniel story.[18] In the case of the Peniel incident, the emphasis has shifted from the hero's valiant defeat of a local god to the sparing of his life by God himself, and so both passages point to the theme of divine grace over Jacob's endeavour: God remains faithful to Jacob, and Jacob receives the fruits of his blessing, but it is despite and not because of his deceptions.

The Meeting of the Brothers (33:1-20)

Chapter 33 describes the meeting and reconciliation of the two brothers. As such it seems to bring to a neat resolution the problems caused by the deception. This in turn brings a conclusion to the Jacob-Esau plot and the question of primacy raised in the opening oracle. However, we shall see that beneath this simple story line lie certain ironies and reservations, and as with the rest of the Jacob narrative, there is a clear relation between the divine - and in particular the Peniel experience - and the human, in the family reconciliation.

---

the Genesis episode has a greater sense of suspense, ambiguity and also irony.
16   Wenham, *Genesis 16-50*, 292.
17   So, for instance, Elliger 'Der Jakobskampf am Jabbok', 26.
18   de Pury, *Promesse Divine*, vol. 1, 100ff.

Jacob's Approach (33:1-11)

The anticipated drama of the meeting of the two brothers has been interrupted by the unanticipated drama of the meeting of Jacob with the solitary figure. Now, all of a sudden, the former encounter is resumed, leaving the reader no time to pause and weigh up motives of either character: whether Esau is bent on harm, or the significance of the changed order in Jacob's procession as he now proceeds at the head.[19]

What is striking about this scene is its underlying irony. This is especially clear when the depictions of Esau and Jacob in this scene are read alongside those in chapter 27 and the birth-scene oracle. On the one hand, Esau seems to behave much more magnanimously than expected towards the brother whom he had sworn to kill (27:41), on the other hand Jacob plays out the role which, according to the oracle given to Rebekah and the blessings by Isaac, properly belongs to Esau: it is Jacob and his family who bow down to Esau - cf. 27:29, also 25:23, with 33:3, 6-7.[20] There is then the ironic use of the word ברכה (v. 11), where the narrator is playing on the ambiguous meaning of this word which can mean 'gift', as מנחה (v. 10), but which also has the meaning of 'blessing' and is so central to chapter 27.

Those who take note of this irony, interpret it in several ways: Jacob is merely pretending to be subservient in order to save his own skin;[21] his action is totally sincere, especially after the life-transforming experience of Peniel;[22] the irony is not so much concerned with Jacob's character but with the shortcomings of the theme of blessing - either in the way it is used politically to back up imperialistic claims[23] or in the way it brings division in family relations.[24] Similarly, Turner sees the discord between the oracle and blessing on the one hand and the episode here as part of a wider discord where oracles and other narrative announcements of divine will often fail to find fulfilment in the Genesis narrative.[25]

Whereas Jacob's motives might not be totally pure, Gunkel's reading seems unwarranted. In particular his interpretation of v. 10 is unsatisfactory,

---

19 This change in the order of the procession is underlined by the emphatic pronoun which disrupts the syntax (והוא - v. 3).
20 This irony is reinforced by the way that the brothers address each other: Jacob calls his brother 'my lord' and refers to himself as 'your servant', whereas Esau calls Jacob 'my brother' - so Hamilton (*The Book of Genesis: 18-50*, 345).
21 Gunkel, *Genesis*, 354.
22 Fokkelman, *Narrative Art*, 223ff.
23 Blum, *Die Komposition der Vätergeschichte*, 147.
24 Westermann, *Genesis*, 366.
25 Turner, *Announcements of Plot in Genesis*, 115-41, 175-83.

since he takes no account of any reference to the Peniel incident, seeing in
the verse an example of Jacob's flattery as he compares Esau with God. On
the contrary, it would seem that Jacob's act is a token of admitting his
wrong towards his brother - although this is never actually spoken out - and
the gift is meant to be a restitution of the stolen blessing.[26] Furthermore, it
is not Esau but Jacob who suffers from the irony in the passage. Esau comes
out in a much more favourable light, and the irony directed at Jacob tends
to prevent us from seeing in him a model, even of repentance. This seems
to tell against Fokkelman who sees Jacob's acts after Peniel as exemplary.
Just as the picture of Jacob before Peniel is probably not so totally negative
as Fokkelman suggests, neither is it as shining as he now portrays.
However, this question will be resolved only as we look at the nature of the
reconciliation.

Westermann, Blum and Turner all see the full irony of the incident: for
Blum, chapter 33 is a deliberate questioning of the attitude to blessing and
to Esau shown in chapter 27. He sees this most clearly against the different
historical and political backgrounds of the two passages: chapter 27 is an
earlier text written in the Judean South around the time of David, reflecting
the 'imperialistic triumphalism' of the time, particularly with regard to the
Edomites. Chapter 33, written from the perspective of the northern
kingdom, challenges what were perceived as the imperialistic and
centralizing tendencies of Judah and the legitimization of its claims through
the theological theme of blessing. This challenge is made by putting Esau
in a better light and throwing the theme of blessing into question, showing
that it is really a 'mixed blessing'.

Westermann also sees a questioning of the theme of blessing and a
pointing to its potential divisiveness by contrasting the word 'blessing'
(ברכה), which Jacob is now ready to give back to Esau from whom he stole
it, with the word חנן (meaning 'favour' or 'grace' - v. 5b and v. 11).
Furthermore, the latter word חנן also has the meaning of divine forgiveness,
and so Jacob's use of the term carries an implicit acknowledgement of
fault.[27] The blessing was the start of the conflict, itself leading to the
conflict with Laban and threatening to lead to war between the two
brothers. Now that Jacob has experienced God's favour (חנן), he is
prepared to relinquish the troublesome blessing. He goes on:

---

26 Likewise, Bar-Efrat (*Narrative Art*, 67) sees Jacob's deliberate use of the address 'my
lord' as an admission of guilt (cf. Aaron's address to Moses in Ex. 32:22).
27 Wenham (*Genesis 16-50*, 299) supports this, and also gives the further interpretation
that by avoiding the word ברכה ('gift'/'blessing') at this stage, Jacob is steering clear of
the earlier cause of dispute.

The Yahwist uses this theological element further to point to the transition from the patriarchal story to the story of the people (from Jacob to the 'sons of Jacob'): the patriarchal story, determined by blessing, passes over into the story of the people determined by God's gracious, saving action...he points out to his contemporary listeners, state dwellers, that they should never forget the other alternative, rising above political conflicts, of coming to a resolution by reconciliation.[28]

Turner rejects any prime appeal to the history of Israel and Edom, as for him the meaning is contained within the narrative itself. His argument is part of a wider thesis about how human and other factors get in the way of the unfolding of the divine plan. The reader is often surprised to find things do not turn out as they should.

Certainly Westermann's reading is worth taking seriously, and it shows a strong theological interest. We might be wary of too forceful an opposition of 'blessing' (ברכה) with 'favour'/'grace' (חן), but Westermann's reading gains further plausibility in that Jacob is keen to use the former term (ברכה) when it comes to his 'gift' to Esau in v. 11 where the two terms form a particularly marked contrast. Blum's interpretation relies on a close identification of theological themes with specific national political ends. This contrasts with the open-ended nature of the narrative itself which escapes such precise interpretation.[29] However, as with Westermann, Blum's approach also points to an ambiguous treatment of blessing in this chapter. Finally, Turner avoids dangers of going further than the text warrants in opposing different contexts and in resolving narrative problems by simplistic historical references, and so he allows us to make sense of the text as it is. Nevertheless, some consideration of how themes in the text resonate with the circumstances of Israel is also valid, given the clear references to Israel - as indeed to Edom - in the Jacob story.

Reconciliation and Parting (33:12-17)

On the face of it, as Esau reluctantly receives Jacob's gift (ברכה), there seems to be a full reconciliation, but there are still some doubts as we look at the text more closely. Jacob refuses Esau's suggestion that they travel on together. To be sure, the reason he gives is plausible (v. 13), but the decline

---

28 Westermann, *Genesis 12-36*, 530.

29 A similar theological point, but which does not rely so heavily on a particular historical reconstruction is that of Brueggemann: 'The positive presence of Esau warns against claiming too much for the elect one, as though the whole company of God has been committed to him,' (*Genesis*, 210).

is an anti-climax after what seemed to be a full reconciliation. Esau is still keen to show some sign of solidarity, so he offers to let some men accompany Jacob. This time Jacob is unable to find a reason for declining, but still firmly refuses to agree. Furthermore although Jacob states his intention to go to Seir (v. 14), we never read of him doing so (cf. v. 17).

There are two opposing ways of understanding this. One is to read Jacob's motives at face value, judging his reasons for declining Esau's offers to be reasonable and well-founded. We could also point out that it is quite appropriate that Jacob does not go to Seir since the two brothers now represent two peoples. Or it could be argued that the passage simply neglects to tell us of any visit to Seir, or that it has been omitted by some redactor - in any case, to make something of Jacob's failure to go to Seir is to read too much into the text.

The approach of Fokkelman falls into this category.[30] Fokkelman is clear that Jacob's actions to Esau are completely open after Peniel. On seeing Esau, Jacob places himself at the front of the group, rather than hiding behind, and his subservient actions are to be seen as an admission of past guilt and a ready counter-act to the blessing he has received. It is however impossible to the Israelite reader that Jacob who represents Israel should now live with Esau (Edom). Instead the two are to live as peaceable neighbours. For Fokkelman, therefore, Jacob is now a new man, purified by the Peniel experience, with a new name and identity, and the events of chapter 33 bear this out.

An alternative is to perceive an ongoing ambivalence in Jacob's motives. There is no question of the goodwill of Esau. Indeed, his goodwill and unrestrained enthusiasm serve to highlight the cautious measuredness on Jacob's part.[31] Thus we sense that Jacob still does not trust his brother when Esau offers to accompany him to Seir, and that maybe his concern is not reconciliation but survival.

This interpretation is followed by Coats: 'Reconciliation should apparently be symbolized by physical community. What good is reconciliation if the brothers do not live together?'[32] Furthermore, Jacob misleads his brother by letting him believe in a future reunion, and then by

---

30 Fokkelman, *Narrative Art*, 228-30.
31 Significantly, Jacob still refers to his brother as 'my lord' (אדני) and himself as his 'servant' (עבד) in v. 14 (Jacob, *Das erste Buch der Tora*, 647). Surely Jacob's subservience is wearing thin by now.
32 Coats, G. W., 'Strife without reconciliation: a narrative theme in the Jacob traditions.' In ed. Albertz, R., etc., *Werden und Wirken des Alten Testaments* (Festschrift für Claus Westermann zum 70. Geburtstag), Göttingen, 103, and *Genesis*, 227.

going to Succoth.[33] This separation marks a permanent division.

Contra Fokkelman, the omission of a reference to Jacob going to Seir is noticeable, and the fact that Jacob has explicitly told Esau that he will rejoin him there suggests that he does not fully trust his brother, or that he wants to maintain a distance from him. On the level of the story between two brothers, this is far from a perfect solution. However, we should not underestimate the danger from which Jacob has escaped and the change in Esau's feelings from chapter 27. To say that there is 'strife without reconciliation' in particular fails to do justice to this turn-about.[34] Finally, there is no recognition by Coats of the note at 35:29, where the brothers are together for the burial of Isaac.[35]

The final verse (v. 17), perhaps incorporating a traditional etiological element about Succoth, underlines that Jacob is now settled in the promised land, but also that he does not go on to his brother as promised.

33:10 -The Reconciliation of the Brothers and Peniel

We have seen that both in the Peniel incident and in the preceding verses (especially 32:21) the word 'face' (פנים) or its construct are strongly attested. This continues in 33:1 and especially 33:10 which seems to be a clear reference to 32:21 (MT):

33:10   כי ..ראיתי פניך כראת פני אלהים   ותרצני

(literally): 'For I have seen your face like seeing the face of God and you have accepted me.'

32:31   כי   ראיתי אלהים פנים אל-פנים   ות צל נפשי

'For I have seen God face to face, and my life is preserved.'

This indicates a further parallel between Esau and God, at least as far as Jacob is concerned. In terms of 33:10, this is because Esau poses the same dangers. The final verbs are different, one denoting acceptance, the other survival. However, in context, Jacob's survival depends on his being accepted by his brother, something explicitly brought out in Jacob's prayer

---

33   In Rabbinic interpretation it is claimed that Jacob is going as far as he can in keeping to the truth and that, indeed, the reference to a journey to Seir can be understood as a messianic prediction that one of his descendants would enter in triumph over Edom, (Scherman and Zlotowitz, *Bereishis*, 1388.1460; Rashi in Rosenbaum and Silbermann eds, *Pentateuch*, 163).

34   Turner prefers the phrase 'separation within reconciliation' (*Announcements of Plot in Genesis*, 133).

35   No doubt because this is seen as a Priestly text.

before his encounter at Peniel where again the verb 'preserve' (נצל) is used (32:12), but this time with reference to Esau.[36]

There is obviously a parallel between both of Jacob's escapes from death, and between the graciousness of God and the graciousness of Esau towards Jacob. This parallel between the two does not necessarily mean a causal connection, but there is at least a hint that what happened at Peniel has somehow made a difference. Peniel has clearly marked a change, although it is difficult to say how much this change relates to Jacob's character as opposed to the circumstances around him (contra Fokkelman), given an ongoing ambivalence in Jacob's attitude to his brother.

For the Israelite reader there is the further recognition that Jacob and Esau are now nations, each living in their own place. The atmosphere in their relations is no longer one of intimate fraternity which can easily turn to hostility, but of a respectful distance which needs to be preserved.[37]

Finally the point should be made that, irrespective of how much Jacob might have changed, Esau certainly has, although no reason is given for this. Is it because God has changed Esau's heart? It does not seem to be because of Jacob's ploys. It might be argued that the depiction of Esau in this chapter is inconsistent with that of Esau in the earlier episodes. However the tension of this episode only works because we assume from chapter 27 that Esau is bent on revenge. Furthermore, one might wonder whether Esau's all too ready acceptance of Jacob is just as much an indication of an impulsive character living for the immediate as were his fit of rage in chapter 27 and his dismissive attitude to the birthright in chapter 25. This might account for Jacob's ongoing reticence towards his brother, knowing how easily his mood might swing back.

The Move to Shechem and Jacob's Final Testimony (33:18-20)

Although v. 17 is often treated along with v. 18, it would seem better to see v. 17 as corresponding to v. 16. It seems odd that, having settled in one place, Jacob now moves on. There is no mention of how long Jacob was at Succoth, nor as to why he should move. The most obvious function of these

---

36 So Fokkelman, *Narrative Art*, 227.

37 Dicou, B., points to the parallel movement by Esau away from the promised land with his family and herds after Jacob has entered (cf. 36:6 and 31:17-18). As Dicou points out, Gen. 36 is the only place where this movement is applied to a nation or family other than Israel. This marks the transition from family to nation, where Israel's settling in the promised land means that Esau and his family have to leave (*Edom, Israel's Brother and Antagonist: The Role of Edom in Biblical Prophecy and Story*, Sheffield: JSOT Supp 169, 1994, 130-1).

verses is to serve as a bridge to the next chapter. As such, the new journey inaugurated by v. 18 emphasizes that Jacob's journeys are not over, nor are his conflicts, and there is still unfinished business.

Whether שלם is a place-name ('Shalem') or an adverb ('safely' - NRSV), overtones of 'peace', 'in safety', 'intact' are still suggested by the word.[38] Thus there is a further allusion to the oath given by Jacob at Bethel regarding a safe return (28:21).[39]

v. 19 shows another aspect of settlement: commerce with the local population and the buying of land. As well as pointing to a later settling in the land, there is also a narrative link back to the tradition of Abraham buying land (Gen. 23 - see also Josh. 24:32).

The final verse provides fitting testimony to God's leading of Jacob. Much discussion of this verse centres on the traditio-historical origin of the phrase אל אלהי ישראל ('El, the God of Israel'), and the identity of 'Israel' here.[40] Whatever the case, in the canonical context, a distinction between Jacob and Israel is too rigid - Jacob clearly has received the name of Israel and so he also serves as a type for Israel. As it is, the setting up of the altar and accompanying confession is motivated not by the specific locality but by the situation: Jacob has returned safely to the promised land, and credits this to his God. In the wider context, the verse surely has a polemic intent, emphasizing that the cult of Jacob/Israel is the legitimate heir to the cult of El. This polemic is driven home by referring to El in a way which would

---

38   Ehrlich (*Randglossen zur Hebräischen Bibel*, 172) suggests 'friedlich gesinnt' as the best translation, making a comparison with 34:21 where the same adjective is used to indicate the peaceful attitude of Jacob's family. The mention here of Jacob's peaceful intention, states Ehrlich, will make the rape of Dinah all the more despicable. Also Alter, *Genesis*, 187. Similarly Ibn Ezra, sees the word as adjectival, denoting 'intact' or 'safely' (Strickman and Silver eds, *Ibn Ezra's Commentary*, 324).

39   Seebass, *Der Erzvater Israel*, 26. Hamilton (*The Book of Genesis: 18-50*, 349-50) sees other connections with the first Bethel incident: the unusual use of the word נצב for the setting up of an altar corresponds to the double use of this verb in ch. 28, and the naming of the altar is a fulfilment of the vow made at Bethel (28:20-21). This latter point however does not account for God's command at 35:1, which is a more obvious fulfilment of the earlier vow.

On the use of the word נצב, see concluding historical-critical remarks. Alternatively, Leibowitz (*Studies in Bereshit*, 388-393) cites the Rabbinic interpretation that a verb associated with the erection of a pillar with its connotations of pre-Israelite worship is deliberately used alongside the word altar associated with the Mosaic worship of sacrifice. This is to indicate the transition to a new type of worship. Interestingly, this interpretation is not that distant from a literary-historical judgement that a later Israelite writer is editing out of the passage any pre-Israelite worship. Both interpretations see the text as evidence of a development in religious practice.

40   e.g. Westermann, *Genesis 12-36*, 529.

not be achieved if the altar referred to YHWH. On the other hand, of course, this epithet assumes that the God of Israel can be identified with the Canaanite El, and so there is some link between the religion of Jacob and that of a wider El cult.[41]

Conclusion

Historical-Critical Summary

Our reading of chapters 32 and 33 has revealed a variety of passages and genres. The basic development is that of the anticipation and actual meeting of the two brothers. This forms a continuous development, though divided into scenic episodes by other passages. This development is narrated with no hint of historical tension, and is best seen as written as a deliberate close to the Jacob-Esau plot. Regarding its relation to chapter 27, the passage has a very different character. Most striking is the depiction of Esau, and also, in relation to the oracle of chapter 25, the respective behaviour of Jacob and Esau. Clearly the writer has this earlier depiction in mind, and is writing with deliberate irony. Also lacking are the folkloric motifs of the opening episodes. In these verses the only traditional elements are the association of Esau with Seir, and 33:17-20.

Within this unilinear development, the three episodes show varying historical-critical results. Regarding the central episode at Peniel, the earlier investigations confirmed the impression that this passage has its own origins, independent of the wider context, and that it has undergone a complex development.[42]

The scene of Mahanaim is much more fleeting which would seem to suggest that it was only ever a fluid oral tradition or saying about the place of Mahanaim, or that it has been severely curtailed to fit into the context. Echoes of the Bethel incident suggest a reworking of the tradition, an impression confirmed by its placement on Jacob's return to the Promised Land.

The prayer (32:10-13) is much more dependent on the wider Jacob story, a factor which tells against it ever having an independent existence. Given

---

41   An interesting translation of v. 20b is found in the LXX: και επεκαλεσατο τον θεον 'Ισραηλ ('and he called upon the God of Israel'). This would indeed fit the context, but makes no sense of the pronoun לו, and the translation could be seen as an attempt to avoid associating the god 'El' with the God of Israel.

42   See above, p. 89.

the way that the prayer does stand out, it may seem best to see it as an addition by a redactor or writer, although differing levels of reference within the prayer may suggest supplementary additions, with v. 12 being the heart of the prayer.

In addition to these three episodes, the closing verses (33:18-20) stand out. In a sense the whole Jacob-Esau plot ends at v. 17. Even Fokkelman hints that a diachronic perspective better illuminates the text here:

> However much the conclusion 33:16-20 may integrate the return to Canaan into the whole of the Story of Jacob, it consists of three or four rather stray travel-notes. Now that the tensions have disappeared and the conflict in Jacob's life has come to an end, the narrator loosens his grip.[43]

The question of the origins of the name El-Elohe-Israel is not easy to resolve because it depends so much on the wider religio-historical development in early Israel and the development towards a tribal entity of 'Israel'. Clearly the name reveals a concern to understand the religion of 'Israel' both in contrast to surrounding religious allegiances, but also by recognizing a continuity or connection as Israel's God is equated with El. There is also the possibility that the passage once told of the erecting of a pillar (מצבה) since the verb associated with altar is normally בנה ('build') or עשה ('make'), whereas נצב ('erect') matches a pillar (מצבה).[44]

However, much more fruitful, is to give full weight to the word 'Israel' - something surely required when reading the passage from a canonical perspective - and to relate this short note to the wider context where it functions as a clear testimony from Jacob and an equation of the character's religious practice with that of Israel.

The Divine-Human Contrast in the Structure of Chapters 32 and 33

The structure of these chapters reflects a clear divine-human contrast. To argue that a later divine perspective has been superimposed over the tension of the human drama is to miss the point. Indeed, the episodes referring to divine presence only heighten the tension by delaying the encounter and by increasing its significance. Furthermore the motifs of 'camp' (מחנים), 'angels'/'messengers' (מלאכים) and 'face' (פנים) in the action resonate with the scenes at Mahanaim and Penuel. Finally, the building of the altar represents Jacob's response of praise and testimony to the God who has

---

43   Fokkelman, *Narrative Art*, 230-1.
44   So, e.g., Westermann, *Genesis 12-36*, 529.

protected him.

On one level, we have seen how recourse to divine help and human resource is combined in the character of Jacob. Just as in his stay at Haran he uses human tricks whilst also seeing God's hand in his blessing, so here he both makes practical preparations to mollify his brother and to defend himself and his party, whilst also turning to God in prayer.

However, behind this structure of contrasts in the chapter lies the deeper, theological point that for Jacob, divine and human relationships are inextricably related. Human messengers operate alongside divine messengers, and most important of all, Esau is as God to Jacob. This is the significance of Jacob first of all concealing himself from Esau, and then seeing Esau face to face and surviving. At first, Jacob puts a barrier between himself and Esau, then after he has seen God face to face and lived, he has to see his brother face to face. Just as God confronts Jacob, so Esau sweeps aside the envoys and gifts and rushes towards his brother. This is all made explicit in 33:10 which clearly refers back to 32:31.

Quite why Esau should be like God to Jacob is not spelt out: perhaps there is the sense that Jacob is very much in Esau's hands. But there is also the theme of reconciliation and acceptance: an open relationship with God includes an open relationship with one's kin, involving reconciliation and forgiveness. As Brueggemann writes: 'In the *holy God*, there is something of the *estranged brother*. And in the *forgiving brother*, there is something of the *blessing God*.'[45] Thus Jacob's approach to Esau is expressed in theologically rich language: 'I may appease [אכפרה פניו] him with the present...and afterwards I shall see his face [פניו]; perhaps he will accept me [ישא פניו]' (32:21). We saw earlier the parallel with Prov. 16:14, but the resonance goes deeper and touches the cultic language of atonement (e.g. Lev. 16:32).[46] In this sense, Jacob's gift to Esau operates as a peace offering or sacrifice of appeasement. Although Esau is not at all concerned

---

45   Brueggemann, *Genesis*, 273.

46   It may be argued that it is invalid to read a cultic or Priestly use of the term כפר into a reconciliation on a human level (as used in Prov. 16:14 and also, for instance, Ex. 21:30). However, it is also true that the term is used in pre-Priestly Pentateuchal texts to denote reconciliation with God, even if the theology behind the term might not be so developed (Janowski, B., *Sühne als Heilsgeschichte: Studien zur Sühnetheologie der Priesterschrift und der Wurzel KPR im Alten Orient und im Alten Testament*, WMANT 55, 1982, Neukirchen-Vluyn: Neukirchener Verlag, 103-14). See also Schenker, A., '*Koper* et expiation', *Bib* 63 (1982), 32.

Furthermore, with reference to Gen. 33, the link between human and divine reconciliation is made in the text itself (v. 10) - a factor often overlooked in considering the use of the term.

with such a gesture, it is somehow necessary for Jacob that such an offering is made and accepted as a mark of reconciliation. Given this, it is surprising that the reconciliation does not result in an intimate living together: that this does not happen perhaps reflects a realism from a national perspective that these two peoples cannot live close together, but also it hints at an ongoing reluctance on Jacob's part -the old Jacob lingers on despite Peniel.

Thus in this episode, behind the dialectic structure of the divine-human, the divine and the human are also closely connected, as Jacob's relationship with God and his relationship with Esau impinge on each other. Furthermore, the episode confirms the impression given more generally in the Jacob story: that underneath the very human activities and struggles, the divine plan is unfolding. The more explicit encounters with the divine serve to underline this.

Chapter 7

Bethel Revisited
(34:1-35:29)

We have already seen that the plot of the Jacob story comes to a pause with the resolution of the conflict with Esau. Certainly the narrative changes, with a looser plot, decreased tension and the sense of tying up loose ends. These involve relations with the indigenous population, unfinished business at Bethel, the birth of Jacob's twelfth son, and news of Isaac, with Jacob and Esau meeting again, to bring the story of the 'descendants of Isaac' (תולדת יצחק) to a formal end.

Jacob and the Shechemites (ch. 34)

This passage raises many complex questions relating to the passage in itself, independent of any part it plays in the Jacob story. Much of this shall be avoided here, especially the knotty question of prehistory.

There is also the question of how much this passage can be regarded as properly belonging to the story of Jacob.[1] In favour of this, it is observable that the incident serves as a counter-point to the story of Isaac at Gerar, inserted within the Jacob material, which also recounts troubled relations with the indigenous population. It is also noticeable that Jacob acts very much as a background figure, with his sons being the main players.[2] Nevertheless, all the characters - at least on the 'Israelite' side - are part of the wider Jacob story, and the story does fit into the wider plot, however awkwardly and uniquely.

Regarding our ongoing study, the main concern here is of the very

---

1 E.g. Ryle (*The Book of Genesis*, 331) points out that the Jacob family, having been at the mercy of Esau's four hundred men, is now able to sack a major town; also Dinah is now a young woman. Dillmann (*Die Genesis*, 368), noting that this is the first indication of strife between Jacob and his sons, argues that the story belongs more properly to the תלדות יעקב ('the descendants of Jacob' - ch. 37ff).

2 A parallel may be drawn here to the story of the birth of his sons, where again Jacob is the background figure.

'human' or 'secular' nature of the passage. This is not just because of the absence of direct intervention from God (apart from the later reference of 35:5), but also the unsavoury nature of the material and the morally ambivalent action of the sons.

Chapter 34 as Israelite Scripture

Whilst it is true that the patriarchal narratives are Israelite scripture, they describe a 'patriarchal', pre-Mosaic age, which although organically related to later 'Yahwistic' faith, shows certain distinctive traits. However, there are often indications of a later 'Israelite' or 'Yahwistic' perspective. This passage in particular seems heavily influenced by such a perspective. It is not unique in showing patriarchs dealing with the people of the land, or even coming into conflict, but here the conflict is that much sharper and seen in different terms. This is especially clear when compared with chapter 26 where Isaac encounters the Philistine king.

Noticeable 'Israelite' elements are:

- terminology - in particular, the depiction of the sexual act. The word 'defile' (טמא), used three times (vv. 5, 13, 27), is striking because it is the first use of the verbal root in the Pentateuch, and it is mostly used in Leviticus and the legal parts of Numbers, as well as, to a lesser degree, in Ezekiel. Thus a key term associated with the purity laws has been made central to the concerns of this narrative. Another such term is 'outrage' (נבלה) in v. 7, which again appears nowhere else in the patriarchal narratives.[3]
- The word 'Israel' to depict not Jacob, but his family as a collective whole. In particular the phrase 'in Israel' (בישראל) is striking, as it sees 'Israel' as a collective entity (Dt. 22:21, Josh. 7:15, Judg. 20:6,10,13.6). Dt. 22:21 is particularly noteworthy because of the combination of the terms 'outrage' and 'in Israel'.
- Circumcision as a way of marking the family as distinctive. Unlike at Gen. 17:11 it is not seen in the theological context of covenant but more as a cultural or ethnic mark.
- The issue of intermarriage as described in Joshua and Judges, as well as Ezra and Nehemiah. It is of course true that the theme of marrying within the clan is part of the patriarchal narratives, but here the theme seems

---

3 Dt. 22:21; Jos. 7:15; Judg. 19:23,24, 20:6,10; 1 Sam. 25:25; 2 Sam. 13:12; Job 42:8; Is. 9:17, 32:6; Jer. 29:23.

more generalized (see esp. vv. 9-10). Again, there is the omission of any
explicit theological perspective.
* The episode does not result in any compromise or agreement (unlike, for
  instance, 26:30-31). Instead there is the fear of war. This is unlike the
  generally pervasive note of what Wenham describes as 'ecumenical
  bonhomie'.[4]

The overall effect is to see the story less as a 'patriarchal' and more as an
'Israelite' incident, especially as Jacob plays a weaker role. However it also
shows that the story has a deeper dimension than the simple story of rape
and revenge, as the interests of Israel are reflected back into the story of the
patriarchs. So far, it is to be noted that these interests focus on questions of
ethnicity and social relations rather than explicit theological issues.
Nevertheless, the narrative can take us to a further dimension.

Chapter 34 as Torah

Our approach throughout has been to see how a canonical perspective is
appropriate to the Jacob story. One outworking of this is to see each episode
not just as part of the wider story of Jacob, but of the Torah with its overall
concern to be a book of guidance and instruction. Furthermore, in view of
the above-mentioned distinctive terminology, references to the 'Torah' are
intrinsic to the material itself. Thus any talk of the 'secular' nature of this
passage needs to take account of this other dimension.

Blum is particularly useful at this point as he points to two laws alluded
to in the passage:[5]

*i) Laws Governing Sexual Relations (Ex. 22:15ff and especially Dt.
22:28ff)*[6]

We have already noted the similarity of terminology between this passage
and Dt. 22, but there is also a similar case study. Here the law prescribes
that if a man has sexual intercourse with a virgin, he is to pay a price and
marry her. Blum also points to parallels with the story of Amnon and Tamar
(2 Sam. 13 - cf. especially 2 Sam. 13:12 and Gen. 34:7). In both cases, he
argues, the emphasis is not so much on the sexual act itself as on the proper

---

4 Wenham, 'The Religion of the Patriarchs' 184.
5 Blum, *Die Komposition der Vätergeschichte*, 210ff.
6 Blum calls these 'laws of rape' (*Die Komposition der Vätergeschichte*, 211) but for
reasons which will become clear below, this may be misleading - see Blum's own comment
on Ex. 22, p. 212.

or improper conduct afterwards. What is striking is that Shechem is prepared to more than fulfill the obligations which the Torah was to lay down (unlike the Israelite Amnon! - cf. also 2 Sam. 13:15 and Gen. 34:3). Indeed the narrator is far from depicting Shechem (or his father) in stereo-typical terms as there seems to be an attempt to understand his feelings and the perspective of the Canaanites as they consider the proposals. Thus v. 3 in particular is striking in depicting Hamar in a sympathetic light as he falls in love with Dinah, and the final phrase 'he spoke tenderly to her' (literally 'to her heart' - על-לב) may imply a degree of reciprocity of attachment.[7] Furthermore, no account is taken of the feelings of Dinah in the story: her motives for going out in the first place, what she felt about Hamar, and the fact that her brothers 'take' her at the end does not indicate how she might feel about the matter.[8] It has even been argued from a careful examination of the terms used and references in Deuteronomy, that the humiliation indicated by the verb ענה (v. 2) is not so much rape as illicit sex, occurring outside marriage or outside the clan.[9]

In this light, the reaction of Jacob's sons is exaggerated and inappropriate. This may even be reflected in the language used in the passage. Alter sees the plural verb form of v. 27 ('they had defiled' - טמאו) as an example of free indirect discourse, whereby the language of the narrative reflects the speech or thought of the brothers as they no doubt justified to themselves the killing of all the male inhabitants.[10] However, there may be a similar ambivalence in some of the earlier language (in particular v. 7b).

According to this reading, we may indeed be invited to agree with Jacob's conclusion, even if Jacob's motives for condemning his sons seems more based on the desire for survival than on a genuine revulsion at their cruelty.[11] In addition, Blum sees a reference to this reading of the story in Gen. 49:5-7, where the curse uttered on Simeon and Levi is read as a

---

7 See esp. Fewell, D. N. and Gunn, D. M., 'Tipping the Balance: Sternberg's Reader and the Rape of Dinah.' *JBL* 110 (1991), 193-211.

8 Fewell and Gunn, 'Tipping the Balance', 210, argue that from Dinah's point of view, the best solution would have been for her to marry Shechem, but that the brothers forcibly take her, and, in so doing, are acting only in the interests of their own honour.

9 Bechtel, L. M., 'What if Dinah is not raped? (Genesis 34)' *JSOT* 62 (1994), 19-36. The verb ענה is translated by the phrase 'by force' in NRSV (v. 2).

10 Alter, *Genesis*, 194.

11 So Brueggemann (*Genesis*, 278): 'Jacob is the seasoned voice of maturity. He has lived a long time...Now he rebukes such a childish religion which will endanger its own life rather than face realities...His response is not one of great faith, but of clear-headed pragmatism.'

judgement on this incident.

Regarding the relevance of Dt. 22:28ff, it might of course be argued that because Shechem is not an Israelite, the laws of the Torah cannot be applied to him,[12] but as Blum argues, the use of the phrase 'in Israel' puts the episode into the context of Israelite law.[13] Furthermore, the parallel with 2 Sam. 13 would seem to justify this approach.[14]

ii) The Proscription of Intermarriage

Note especially the correspondence between Hamar's offer and Dt. 7:3:

והתחתנו אתנו   בנתיכם תתנו-לנו   ואת-בנתינו תקחו לכם Gen 34:9
'Make marriages with us; give your daughters to us, and take our daughters for yourselves.'

ולא תתחתן בם   בתך לא-תתן לבנו   ובתי לא תקח לבנך Dt 7:3
'Do not make marriages with them, do not give your daughters to their sons, and do not take their daughters for your sons.'

Westermann sees this as the main thrust of the final form of the passage.[15] Because of clear echoes of Dt. 7:2-3, he thinks this story may be a later midrash, written at the time of the exile, when intermarriage had become a particular temptation: 'a narrative exemplifying the execution of a command of the Torah. Zeal for the law was the motivating drive.'

Blum also argues that the appearance of foreign gods in chapter 35 corresponds to the link made in Deuteronomy between intermarriage and the turning to false gods.[16] This contributes to a reading which is more sympathetic to the sons of Jacob, even if there is a recognition of the harshness of their action.

In his detailed reading of this passage, Sternberg is aware of this

---

12 So Sternberg, M., 'Biblical Poetics and Sexual Politics: From Reading to Counter-Reading.' *JBL* 111 (1992), 482.

13 Blum, *Die Komposition der Vätergeschichte*, 213. It should also be noted that the phrase וכן לא-יעשה ('for such a thing is not done') is a stereo-typical legal term (so Westermann, *Genesis 12-36*, 538), which suggests that we are dealing with a question of the application of Israelite law.

14 For an investigation of how these passages might be linked, see Freedman, D. N., 'Dinah and Shechem, Tamar and Amnon', 485-95 in ed. Huddleston, J. R., *Divine Commitment and Human Obligation: Selected Writings of David Noel Freedman*, vol. 1, Grand Rapids/Cambridge UK: Eerdmans, 1997.

15 Westermann, *Genesis 12-36*, 544.

16 Blum, *Die Komposition der Vätergeschichte*, 221.

ambivalence, but sees the narrator loading the evidence in favour of the brothers.[17] For instance, he argues that the opening description of Shechem's action (v. 2) creates maximum sympathy for Jacob's sons, although his reaction in v. 3 adds to a more complex depiction of his motives. Sternberg also sets Jacob's inactivity in contrast to his sons' readiness to defend family honour and purity in such a way that Jacob is seen to be cowardly and purely interested in self-survival. Regarding the reasonableness of Hamar's offer, this can be seen as the soft-spoken web of deceit of the negotiator.

Furthermore, the crucial point for Sternberg is that Dinah is being held by Shechem all the time.[18] This factor is only revealed by the author during the description of bloodshed and carnage (v. 26) in order to put the action of the brothers in a better light: they had no alternative than to enter into negotiations and then use violence to extricate their sister. In particular, for Sternberg, the narrator is keen to distinguish between the idealistic motives of Dinah's two full brothers, Simeon and Levi - only here singled out - from the other brothers. This is achieved not only by leaving the information about Dinah's captivity until now, but also by making explicit that they alone are the full brothers of Dinah (v. 25).

By normal standards, we would judge the act of murdering every male as more worthy of condemnation than the subsequent act of pillaging. However in the context of this narrative, argues Sternberg, the reverse is true since the two brothers are simply interested in rescuing their sister and maintaining family honour, whilst the motives of the other brothers move from idealism to material gain in the orgy of plunder. Finally, Jacob's protest at the end is the pathetic appeal of the self-interested: 'the voice of egocentricity and self-preservation finds itself opposed by the voice of idealism'.[19]

We are therefore left with two contradictory readings. For Blum, as for others, the answer is to explain the tension in diachronic terms. An earlier narrative giving a positive view of Shechem and a negative view of Jacob's sons has been overwritten by a Deuteronomic redaction showing the sons of Jacob exercising the correct attitude to threats of assimilation and intermarriage. Interestingly, Sternberg's reading is not as far away from this as might be imagined, as his concept of the narrator altering what would be our natural judgement by narrative touches is akin to that of the redactor

17 Sternberg, M., *The Poetics of Biblical Narrative: Ideological Literature and the Drama of Reading*, Bloomington: Indiana University Press, 1985, 445-75.
18 Also Alter, *Genesis*, 193.
19 Sternberg, *The Poetics of Biblical Narrative*, 474.

reshaping an earlier text.

In terms of the diachronic judgement, the above view may have some plausibility as far as it goes, but it does not help us to make sense of the text as it is in its entirety. Furthermore, as often in such cases, we are left with the question of why a redactor - whether Deuteronomistic or whatever - allowed certain elements to stand in such a way as to create an ambiguity: why allow a portrayal of Shechem which is not completely negative? Why allow the ironic statement to stand that the sons acted as their father had done earlier in his life, 'with deceit' (במרמה - v. 13 - cf. 27:35)? Why not make the later theological perspective clearer? And finally, why not have the patriarch Jacob congratulating his sons rather than criticizing them?

Sternberg attempts to do better justice to the complexity of the text by arguing that the narrator is concerned not to paint a black and white picture, in recognition of the complexity of the issues. Even so, argues Sternberg, the narrator's 'rhetorical maneuvers throughout, the final set of oppositions, and above all, his gaining the last word - and what a last word! - to Simeon and Levi, leave no doubt where his sympathy lies.'[20]

Nevertheless one wonders whether Sternberg does justice to both sides of the case. Part of his argument is that although Biblical narrative reveals ambivalences and ambiguities, the story is told in such a way that it is clear to the 'competent' reader what the overall meaning is. On the one hand, one might question whether this does enough justice to the context of the reader as much as the narrative,[21] but on the other hand, one might argue that the voice of the 'narrator' is much less easy to discern. For instance, there is the obvious gap in failing to address Dinah's viewpoint. It might be true that she was forcibly withheld by Shechem, but it might equally be true that she had chosen not to return - assuming that she had not returned to Jacob before the negotiations. There is also the suggestiveness of the opening phrase that Dinah 'went forth' to see the daughters of the land, and there may be some question of whether she was really raped: of itself, the verb 'take' (לקח -translated 'seize' in NRSV) need not imply violent force, and there is no account of struggle or protest (see Dt. 22:23-24).[22]

---

20   Sternberg, *The Poetics of Biblical Narrative*, 475.

21   So Segal, N. ('Review of *The Poetics of Biblical Narrative*, by M. Sternberg', *VT* 38 (1988), 243-9) who points out that Sternberg takes no account of post-structuralist and reader-response theories. For Sternberg it is self-evident that the reader is comfortable or agrees with what he calls the 'ideology' of the narrator.

22   Bechtel, 'What if Dinah is not Raped? (Genesis 34)', 25-28. Also Carmichael, C. M., *Women, Law, and the Genesis Traditions*, Edinburgh: Edinburgh University Press, 1979, 28.

Sternberg claims that the positive portrayal of Shechem in v. 3 does not fully cancel out the negative portrayal of v. 2, but is this really the case, especially as the opposite reaction from Shechem would have been expected? This impression is reinforced if there is indeed in v. 3bβ a hint that his affections were received with at least some sympathy by Dinah. Sternberg also admits that the phrase 'with deceit' (במרמה - v. 13) tells against the brothers, but argues that the narrator balances this with the last part of v. 13 and by not spelling out at this stage how they are acting in deceit.[23] We should also bear in mind the vocabulary used by the narrator to describe the 'defilement' 'within Israel', and the scandal of crime committed in the first place, which would lean in favour of Sternberg's reading. On the other hand, since such explicit language is so rare in Genesis, one might wonder how much it is coloured by the extreme views of the sons and or is simply borrowed by the narrator to represent one point of view (thus being an example of indirect free discourse). Finally, why, according to Sternberg, should the narrator make his task so complicated by wanting to point to the complexity of the issue whilst also steering the reader to a final sympathy for Simeon and Levi? Given all the possibilities open to the narrator, he seems to have painted himself into a corner. One feels that Sternberg's reading itself contains the truth, but not the whole truth.

Thus it would seem that this passage contains two standpoints, which are left unreconciled. This is summed up in the final statements by Jacob on the one hand and Simeon and Levi on the other, with both claiming a validity.

Conclusion

We have seen that this story has more than one dimension. On one level is the very human story of love, rape or illicit sex, deceit, revenge, murder, family strife. On another level, there is a continuing tendency to see in the main characters embodiments of nations: just as Jacob becomes Israel in chapter 32, and Esau in Seir and Jacob in Canaan put us in mind of Edom and Israel, so here Shechem seems to embody the people of Canaan, and the Jacob family is 'Israel'. Likewise the passage has a distinctly ethnic tone. The difference is that Israel is embodied by the sons of Jacob rather than by Jacob alone. This latter point is part of a more general idea that Jacob and the ideas associated with him (and, we may add, with Isaac and Abraham) are giving way to his twelve sons who here seem to reflect, at least in part, later Israel. Westermann writes: 'When the sons reject their father's rebuke

---

23 Sternberg, *The Poetics of Biblical Narrative*, 458-59.

(34:31) this sounds the end of the patriarchal period when war and killing of enemies were avoided.'[24] In other words, the passing from the patriarchal age to the age of Israel is thematized in the shift from one generation to another. In this chapter, this is seen especially in relations with the surrounding peoples.

However the development is not straightforward, since we have seen above that there is no clear acceptance of one perspective or rejection of the other. Indeed, we have seen how two laws in the Torah come into conflict. Furthermore, the open attitude to foreigners associated with the patriarchs is not lost in the fully-fledged Yahwistic faith.[25] Thus we can see how this passage raises or reflects questions about the proper attitude of Israel towards other peoples.[26] This brings us to the theological dimension as we see how questions of national identity and integrity relate to the covenant relationship of the Torah. Thus in this episode, dimensions of family and nation, human and divine are intermingled.

Jacob and God (35:1-15)

Thematically, vv. 1-15 are consistent in marking a shift back to Jacob's explicit relationship with God. However, within these verses, there is a clear break between v. 8 and v. 9, where a new episode begins ('God appeared to Jacob again' - וירא אלהים...עוד).

35:1-8

This passage describes the command from God to go to Bethel and build an

---

24   Westermann, *Genesis 12-36*, 545.
25   As testified in laws in Dt. relating to the stranger (e.g. Dt. 10:19); also the books of Ruth, Jonah, parts of Trito-Isaiah (e.g. Is. 56:4ff).
26   Herbert (*Genesis 12-50*, London: SCM, 1962, 112):

> The purpose of this story in the Book of Genesis is not merely to report an incident of Israel's ancient past. First it is pointing to the perils consequent upon the adoption of the Canaanite way of life...But it is also concerned to condemn the kind of deceit and violence which all too often characterized the settlement of nomadic tribes in Canaan. It is the will of God that Israel should retain its integrity; but this must be in God's ways and not through arrogance and violence that disregards moral considerations.

Whilst acknowledging the tension which the text reflects, Herbert's judgement is perhaps too clear-cut for a passage which refuses to give a clear authorial voice.

altar (v. 1), Jacob's command to the household, the process of preparation (ridding of foreign gods, changing of clothes), the journey and arrival (vv. 5-6), and the building of the altar and naming of the place El-Bethel (v. 7), followed by a death notice (v. 8). Thus internally the passage seems coherent, although v. 8 seems to fit rather loosely to the structure.

There are certain connections with other parts of the Jacob story. v. 1 refers clearly to chapter 28 and the dream of Jacob, and the name Bethel is presupposed in God's initial command. Thus this passage is seen as fulfilling an obligation based on God's appearance at Bethel.[27] The reference to foreign gods most likely refers to the gods stolen from Laban, and v. 3 may refer to the plea for help before Jacob meets his brother again (32:10ff) or to the vow in 28:20-22. This passage therefore forms an inclusio with chapter 28, and serves to bring us back to the promise given by God and to the vow made by Jacob.[28]

However, the fulfilment of the vow does not correspond exactly to the vow itself, both in terms of the religious acts described here and the lack of any mention of tithe (28:22). This suggests a certain independence between the two passages, and that, beyond the schema of vow-fulfilment, there are other interests.[29]

These other interests are shown especially in the religious activity of Jacob. The following elements stand out:

- the verb 'go up' (עלה) to describe Jacob's movement -v. 1 and especially v. 3 where the phrase 'let us go up to Bethel' (נעלה בית-אל) sounds like the call to go on a pilgrimage. The verb is often used in connection with going to Jerusalem (Jer. 31:6, Ps. 24:3, Ps. 122:4).[30]
- The phrase 'The God who answered me in my day of trial' (v. 3), seen by Westermann as the language of the psalms, who points to Ps. 120:1

---

27 Ibn Ezra (Strickman and Silver eds, *Ibn Ezra's Commentary*, 332) makes another connection with ch. 28 by translating אלהים (v. 7) with the word 'angels'. He justifies this by pointing to the unusual use of the plural verb form (נגלו).

28 Brueggemann (*Genesis*, 280-3) also sees a connection with the previous incident, in that the purification commanded by Jacob is in response to the defilement described in ch. 34 (especially vv. 5.13. Also the plunder of v. 29). For Brueggemann, the action described here is a ritual of renunciation and reclothing, a symbolic distancing from the gods and influences of the Canaanite culture.

29 See Richter, 'Das Gelübde als theologische Rahmung der Jakobsüberlieferung', 21-52, who sees an independent tradition behind this story, but that the story has now been adapted by the Elohist's vow-fulfilment schema.

30 As with Jerusalem, the journey to Bethel is also a literal ascent - Ryle, *The Book of Genesis*, 336.

which begins the pilgrimage psalms.[31]

* The command of Jacob to dispose of the foreign gods. There is a similar demand made by Joshua (Jos. 24:14), again executed at Shechem.
* The command of Jacob to his family to purify themselves and to change their clothes.

Also significant is the description of the 'terror from God' (חתת אלהים) experienced by the neighbouring towns, corresponding to the response of the Canaanites in the conquest tradition -see Ex. 23:27 although the word חתת ('terror') is admittably a hapax legomenon.

All these elements lend to the passage a clear 'Yahwistic' mood, making it quite unique in the patriarchal narratives. It seems that the writer is wanting to show in this episode of Jacob's life an example of obedience to God and its result on surrounding peoples.[32] Thus there is a typological interest.[33] The avoidance of the name YHWH here helps to maintain some distinction between the patriarchal and Mosaic eras, but the long chronological gap between the two ages seems to have narrowed immensely for a moment.

Furthermore, it could be that the typology is meant to go further in drawing a parallel between Jacob and the later Israelites, who, having escaped from Egypt, receive the commands at Sinai, including rites of purification, and who then, as long as they are faithful to YHWH, experience protection from the peoples of Canaan. In this case, Jacob is 'delivered' from the threat of destruction, commanded to make the appropriate response, and having done so, is protected from the Canaanites.

Finally, a comparison of these verses to chapter 34 is interesting since both reflect the interests of later readers, and Deuteronomic traces have been discerned in both passages. On the other hand, in chapter 34 interest is 'Israelite' in a broadly ethnic sense, whereas interest here is 'Yahwistic' in a much more religious sense.

35:9-15

Internally, this passage seems to flow with no breaks or inconsistencies. The only possible additions seen by scholars are v. 10, where the giving of the

---

31   Westermann, *Genesis 12-36*, 550.
32   The word YHWH is never used in the passage (see following comment), but the tone of the passage is nevertheless 'Yahwistic' in the wider sense described here.
33   Jacob, *Das erste Buch der Tora*, 660: 'Was Jakob jetzt tut, ist eine Wallfahrt, das Vorbild aller späteren.'

name 'Israel' is without firm etiological basis, the repetition of the phrase 'the place where he had spoken with him' (a possible dittography), and the setting up of a cultic stone (v. 14), although this is based on an assumption about what would and would not be acceptable to the (Priestly) writer.

However, most interest has been focused on the relation of this passage to passages elsewhere. On the one hand, there is a clear continuity and consistency with two passages in particular:

- the appearance of God to Abraham in chapter 17, which also includes the divine self-revelation as El Shaddai, the giving of a new name, promises of nations and land, the verb 'be fruitful' (פרה), and the 'ascension' of God (17:22, 35:13). In both episodes this is followed by a cultic response - in one case, the theologically weighty circumcision, directly commanded by God, in the other, the (problematic?) setting up of a stone.
- The blessing given by Isaac to Jacob before he flees to Paddam Aram (28:3-5). The name El Shaddai is used again; also found are the blessing, the stem פרה ('be fruitful'), the land promised to Abraham (though ch. 35 adds the name of Isaac), and the promise of becoming a 'company of nations' (קהל גוים/עמים). The mention of Paddam Aram again (35:9) seems to form another deliberate link.

Despite minor differences between these passages, it is highly likely that they come from the same hand, and the common view of these passages as part of a Priestly source or redaction seems justified.

On the other hand, this passage has an unclear relationship to Gen. 28:10-22, 32:23-33 and 35:1-8, since once again the place Bethel is named, and once again Jacob is given the name Israel. It seems that this passage contains genuine repetition and may be described as a doublet.[34] However, it remains to be seen whether this doublet should be seen as a replacement of the earlier episodes or a correction or complement to them, although the ultimate resolution to that question is part of the wider debate about whether P should be regarded as a once separate source or as a redactional strata.

Bethel

The fact that three passages tell of the importance of Bethel to Jacob demonstrates the centrality of the place in the Jacob tradition, and it is not

---

34 'Eine der wenigen 'echten' Dubletten in der Genesis' - Blum, *Die Komposition der Vätergeschichte*, 267.

unreasonable to suppose that the figure of Jacob was linked to this place of pilgrimage at an early stage of the tradition. Furthermore, differences in style and a precise lack in correspondence in the three passages clearly suggest that the passages were not all written by the same writer.

Regarding ch. 35:9ff, the main emphasis is even more on the promise and less on the presence of God than is the case in chapter 28. Indeed the etiological element seems weak and secondary to the purposes of the passage. In particular, v. 15 does not bear the marks of an etiology as there is little correspondence between the name Bethel itself and the clause 'the place where he had spoken with him' (במקום אשר-דבר אתו). Although one might simply see this as reflecting the sparseness or restraint of P, von Rad's view does most justice to the passage:

> Thus our section limits itself to that which God revealed to Jacob by summarizing in essence what is theologically important from ch28:10ff and ch32:23ff, the promise of land and the change of name.[35]

We shall comment on this later on, as it is quite an important point and obviously relates also to the giving of the name Israel. It would seem then that P summarizes or restates the older passage in order to emphasize certain points.

Blum also sees this, albeit in a more negative way. For him, P is concerned to 'correct' aspects of the Bethel story.[36] In particular, in chapter 28 the central idea is that God is present, and indeed lives, at the place - hence the term 'house of God' (בית אלהים), whereas P 'corrects' this (mis)understanding by making it clear that this is the place where God speaks and, having spoken, leaves (v. 13). He also argues that in P the stone is no longer a cultic stone but a memorial stone. This is emphasized by three new elements: the appositional 'pillar of stone' (מצבה אבן) which prevents an understanding of the column in a technical cultic sense; the phrase 'the place where God has spoken with him', which interprets the column as a memorial stone (and emphasizes it as the place where God speaks); and the problematic 'pouring of oil' becomes a libation offering rather than the consecration of a stone.

It is certainly true that P wants to emphasize the fact that God speaks, but

---

35   von Rad, *Genesis*, 338-9.
36   Blum, *Die Komposition der Vätergeschichte*, 263-70. Also Gross ('Jakob, der Mann des Segens.' 342): P is forced by the strong connection of Jacob with Bethel to mention the place but tries to lessen its significance: 'Für P ist Bethel nicht ein Ort dauernder göttlicher Gegenwart, sondern der Schauplatz einer einmaligen Gottesoffenbarung.'

this aspect is also present in the earlier account. Furthermore the passage does describe God appearing (v. 9) as well as speaking, and in describing God as 'going up', the passage is implying that God has been somehow present at the place, even if not permanently. Regarding the libation offering, it is questionable whether such an offering would really be much more acceptable to a writer bent on eliminating any cultic acts before Sinai than would the act of consecrating a stone. Finally the explicit mention of a stone in v. 14 is best seen positively as a link to chapter 28 where Jacob uses a stone for sleep and then as a pillar.

An aspect which Blum neglects are the words spoken to Jacob - for the giving of the name see below, but the blessing of v. 11 and v. 12 are also important. The name El Shaddai reminds us of the appearance of God to Abraham (ch. 17 - see above), and so emphasizes the persistence of the promise, and it also reminds us of the blessing given to Jacob by his father (28:3). This repetition is especially forceful when seen in the wider context of the (non-Priestly) narrative as it serves as a confirmation of the blessing, since it is God himself who now speaks. Just as the first Bethel appearance was a confirmation for Jacob before he arrived at Paddam Aram, so this appearance is a confirmation now he has returned. It is important in reminding us that Jacob and his descendants are still to see the promise in its totality fulfilled, and so it keeps the reader looking forward. In particular the command to be fruitful is now more direct (v. 11) and reminds us of the command in Gen. 1. It is as though Jacob, safely returned as promised (28:15), is now ready not just to see the survival of his family, but to see the beginning of the fulfilment of the promise of many descendants. It has been pointed out that this command would make more sense before the birth of any of Jacob's sons,[37] and in a strictly chronological account this may be so, but the command has in mind not just the birth of twelve sons, but their expansion into a people. It is indeed 'Israel' that is addressed.

Before considering the reference to Israel, we should briefly consider how this passage follows from 35:1-8. The element of repetition is obvious, and again suggests that P be best taken in the final narrative as a concluding summary of Jacob and Bethel. But it is also important to note that P adds certain aspects to the previous verses. Whereas vv. 1-7 tend to see Jacob as a type of the later Israel in his paradigmatic response to God and his resulting protection, P stresses that Jacob is still a figure of promise, even if, as with the previous verses, the distance between the patriarchal age of promise and the Yahwistic age of fulfilment is getting very short. The

---

37   von Rad, *Genesis*, 339.

difference between the two ages is also emphasized by the name El Shaddai, which is picked up at Ex. 6. Again there is also the shift in emphasis from concern for the mere survival of Jacob and his family to their expansion.

To summarize so far, in relation to chapter 28, P moves from the etiological aspect of the Bethel tradition to bring out other aspects: Bethel is significant as the place where God speaks as much as the place where God appears, and any idea of God 'residing' here is played down. The contents of the speech relate to God's renewed promise to Abraham, a confirmation of the patriarchal blessing, and a more immediate reference to the promise of many descendants with the related shift from the idea of the survival of the clan, so central to patriarchal story so far.

The Name 'Israel'

The giving of the name 'Israel' is even less grounded in the passage etiologically than is the name Bethel. This need not mean that it is a secondary addition to the Priestly passage,[38] but again may indicate that it is a deliberate complement to the earlier Peniel story, since in the final form of the narrative, it serves as a confirmation of the name given at Peniel.[39] Here, the giving of the name is much less shrouded in mystery and darkness, so that there is no doubt about who has blessed Jacob. Furthermore, the emphasis is now on the simple giving of the name, as a gift and not as something which might seem to be extracted from God. In this passage, Jacob's part is much more receptive and God takes the initiative and acts freely.

35:9-15 as a Summary Conclusion to Jacob's life

To return to von Rad's comment that P here summarizes what is theologically important in the Jacob narrative, it is clear that the Bethel and

---

38   Neither is there any etymology in the Priestly account of the giving of the divine name in Ex. 6.

39   As argued in reference to 32:29 (above, p. 85) this is close to the idea in some Jewish commentary that it is not until ch. 35 that Jacob receives the name Israel, whereas at Peniel he is told that he would, subsequently, be called Israel (see also Jacob, *Das erste Buch der Tora*, 664). As argued earlier, this distinction is overstated and not sufficiently grounded in the text, but nevertheless, at Peniel there is the sense that only when the situation with Esau has been resolved, will he be able to truly say that he has prevailed in his struggles. In that sense the outcome of the Peniel incident (a new name and an escape from danger) still looks forward, whereas now that Jacob has safely returned to Bethel, there is a sense of resolution.

Peniel encounters were important, and P has chosen to restate the important aspects of them here. From a traditional source critical perspective this fits with his idea of P as a once independent treatment of the earlier patriarchal narrative, but the approach taken above has suggested at several points that P can be seen here as a redactional framework.

In this light, the repetition of Bethel and the name Israel is a reaffirmation of the importance of these incidents in the life of Jacob (as well as offering a new perspective on them) and not just a 'correction' of them as Blum asserts. Thus this passage, although ostensibly represented as a new incident in the story of Jacob, is best understood as a pause, as we look back on Jacob's life, and the important points are rearticulated in a concise way, adding to the Jacob narrative another perspective.

However, not only does this incident look back, but having consolidated what has been achieved in Jacob's life, it looks forward. To quote von Rad again:

> A primary concern of our text is to show that the promise to Abraham was renewed completely to Jacob. Indeed it is now expanded by the creative command 'be fruitful and multiply'! Abraham's seed branches out for the first time in Jacob...[40]

The Relation of vv. 9-15 to vv. 1-8

We have seen that vv. 1-8 and 9-15 are very different passages. On the one hand, they both depict an encounter with God, showing strong links with later Israel. In the first passage this is through a depiction of Jacob's actions and his relationship with surrounding towns in a strongly 'Yahwistic' way, with a strong paradigmatic overtone. In the second passage, the theological theme of promise is highlighted as well as the name 'Israel'. Here the emphasis is less on Jacob's religious actions and more on the work of God.

Although the introduction of v. 9 allows for a sequential reading of these two passages, the full force of vv. 9-15 is to be felt as a retrospective summary of the whole of Jacob's experience with God, where the themes of promise and the name 'Israel' are restated without any ambiguity and with full clarity: as von Rad puts it, the subject here is *'Deus revelatus'* rather than the *'Deus absconditus'* of so much of the Jacob story.[41] This in

---

40   von Rad, *Genesis*, 339.
41   von Rad, *Genesis*, 338. Also: Keil (*The Pentateuch*, 316-7):

> God appeared to him [Jacob] again there [at Bethel]...as He had appeared to him 30 years before on his journey thither, - though it was then in a dream, now by

214 Thou Traveller Unknown

many ways, serves as a final comment on the complex relationship of the human and divine: as the Priestly writer makes it clear that through Jacob's life, it is the sovereign act of God which is the decisive factor, not just in determining the course of Jacob's life, but reaching to his countless descendants.

The human story of Jacob is not over: the following verses, although somewhat disparate, touch on the important theme of land, reminding us that Jacob's relationship with God does not just affect his relationship with other people but also with the land of Canaan (see also 33:18-20) - it is here that Deborah and Rachel are buried, it is here that Jacob travels and spends most of his life, it is the home of the twelve sons, especially of Benjamin. These verses also complete the family story: the drama of Benjamin's birth and Rachel's death, the serene death of Isaac and solemn reunion of his two sons, and then the story of Jacob carries over into the story of his sons.

Conclusion to Chapters 34 and 35

Historical-Critical Summary

It has been clear that there is a marked change in the narrative following the resolution of the conflict between Jacob and Esau. This can be seen in different ways. From the point of view of the narrative, the plot is not as tightly knit, and despite the problems in chapter 34, the tension has relaxed. Each incident also seems more complete in itself. From the literary-historical point of view, this is probably because of the nature of the material, where varied material has been brought together and worked into the overall pattern. From a literary point of view, the narrator is happy for each part of the whole to preserve its own distinctive voice within the broad sweep of the plot. The plot itself is much looser once the tension between Jacob and Esau has been resolved.

Jacob and God

Despite the diversity of material an overall impression emerges of a change in Jacob. On one level, this change relates to how he is depicted, as he seems more and more to embody Israel both in his conflicts and in his religious expression. It is more difficult to judge how Jacob's character

---

daylight in a visible form...The gloom of that day of fear had now brightened into the clear daylight of salvation.

might have changed, particularly in the light of Peniel. Certainly, a new character is not consistently worked through all the material. On the one hand, he does seem to have mellowed, and there are no longer any of the great deceptions, and in chapter 35 there is a closer sense of obeying God and receiving his blessing and promise, without any of the past struggles. However, some of this may be for the reason that Jacob's blessing and survival are now secure. If anything we are given the impression that Jacob is simply getting older.

Certainly, any changes never overtake the old Jacob, and the fact that his sons, in chapter 34 and later, act in ways similar to the younger Jacob shows that God's grace does not overcome nature. It is for instance interesting that Jacob still keeps his old name (unlike Abram). It would have been much more consistent to change all references to Israel. We can only make intelligent guesses why this did not happen: there remains a slight ambiguity over who or what is Israel - Jacob himself, or the family of Jacob; the narrator is keen to show that Jacob is still in the patriarchal age of promise; Jacob never ceases to be an individual in his own right, and to use the name Israel exclusively would undermine his individuality in a way that the name Abraham did not for Abram; to consistently use the name Israel now would give the impression that it is only the post-Peniel Jacob who represents Israel, whereas the truth seems more that it is precisely in that paradox of grace working with (and against) flawed human nature and striving that Jacob represents Israel.[42] It is therefore natural that although Jacob might gradually mellow in his old age as he experiences the grace of God and renewed promises and assurances, the process of change is never complete or permanently overwhelming, and he can never rest in the assurance that his strivings have ceased - something that remains true to the end of his life.

Finally, the return to Bethel is a clear testimony to the divine in the Jacob story. It both marks Jacob's response of gratitude to the God who has been with him (35:1-8), and God's unambiguous and unsolicited promise and ongoing blessing (35:9-15). These episodes, each in their own way, work retrospectively by looking back over Jacob's life and making it clear that God has been involved; on the other hand, they both look forward, by pointing to the religious practice of Israel and especially by restating the patriarchal promise and the blessing and accompanying commission.

---

42   'The name Israel denoted a spiritual state determined by faith; and in Jacob's life the natural state, determined by flesh and blood, still continued to stand side by side with this.' - Keil-Delitzsch (*The Pentateuch*, 306-7 -repeated in Delitzsch, *A New Commentary on Genesis*, 214-5).

Conclusion

Historical-Critical Conclusion

As remarked in the introduction the Jacob story forms a substantial unity around the theme of flight and return.[1] This involves the Jacob-Esau plot, sandwiched around the Jacob-Laban plot. Into this structure significant episodes have been placed retelling encounters with the divine: as Jacob flees from Esau on his way to Laban, and as he is about to confront Esau on his return. We have seen how both these episodes reflect older traditions, with pre-Yahwistic roots, but are now adapted and part of the Jacob story, throwing a theological perspective over the wider plot. This perspective is also introduced at the very beginning of the story by the oracle and accompanying verses, constructed as an opening to the Jacob story, and the whole story is brought to a conclusion as Jacob returns to Bethel to fulfill his earlier vow. As he does this, so he receives confirmation of his blessing and new name. Nevertheless, we have also argued for a theological interest in the bulk of the narrative material as there are hints and also clear indications of the presence of God at several points. Furthermore, because of expectations raised by such points of revelation, the very absence of God in so much of the story is itself a theological issue, adding to the complex picture of how God is present in the life of Jacob. For this reason, to argue that a theological perspective has been superimposed over the human story misses the point.

Regarding more general observations, from the different conclusions reached, and given the measure of caution adopted, it is not possible to reconstruct any straightforward unilinear development of the Jacob story. Overall, however, two contrasting impressions have emerged: that of several distinctive episodes and that of a coherent narrative. As well as the above mentioned Bethel and Peniel episodes, other passages with older traditions behind the present form would probably include aspects of the opening scenes (25:19-34), the birth of Jacob's sons, the final treaty with

---

1   See above, p. 2.

Laban, the short note on Mahanaim, chapter 34, as well as several short notes. In addition to this are several points within passages revealing traditio-historical tensions or redactional expansions. In particular, certain passages seem to be written or included to make a comment on an episode or to bring a different perspective: for instance, the verses placed around the story of Jacob's deception of Isaac (26:34-5 and 27:46-28:9) offer a different perspective on Jacob's flight, 31:1-43 stands in contrast to 30:25ff, the meeting of the two brothers (ch. 32-33) relates to chapter 27, chapter 35 (both vv. 1-7 and 9-15) relates to the first Bethel incident. Again, these tend to add to the complexity of theological issues.

Despite these marks of distinctiveness, there is an underlying unity which certainly goes further than any particular narrative strata or theme, and which goes much deeper than the explicit references. For instance, the story of Jacob's deception of Isaac is a well constructed unit, understandable in itself, but it also presupposes certain relationships and propels the reader into the long episode in Haran. Likewise the Jacob-Laban episode, which we have had reason to liken to a Novelle, involves a long self-contained plot with its own opening and closing scenes, but certain ironies, family connections, as well as depiction of character, are only fully appreciated in a wider context. Whilst there is certainly no textual evidence of any underlying written or oral cycle for the whole Jacob story as argued by de Pury,[2] there is nevertheless the impression that these episodes have exercised some mutual influence and grown together. How much can be ascribed directly to the free creation of a later writer is difficult to judge, but such a judgement needs to account for the above mentioned distinctiveness of texts.

In terms of wider views about Pentateuchal criticism, this gives support to the idea that before considering the relation of the Jacob story to any wider context, it needs to be understood in its own right. Thus, for instance, we have seen little evidence of continuous sources running parallel through the story as we have it. The models of Rendtorff and Blum, seeking to do justice to the organic growth of units as they now stand, seem better suited.[3] However, by comparison with Blum, our own observations have shown caution in tracing out the development of texts, and there is a greater underlying unity to the story than his approach often allows.

---

2   de Pury, *Promesse Divine*.
3   Such models, as indeed my own approach, might be said to draw on some of the ideas behind supplementary and fragmentary hypotheses, largely eclipsed by the Documentary hypothesis. It would seem at the moment, that no one model or hypothesis can offer a comprehensive solution.

Furthermore, it does not seem possible to speculate too much about the historical context of any stage of development. Recently, arguments have been put forward for seeing the setting of the Jacob story in an oral, semi nomadic context,[4] during the reign of Jeroboam in the Northern kingdom,[5] or during the exile or early post-exilic era.[6] We have already remarked on the lack of evidence for any oral cycle underlying the present literary form and on the distinctive nature of many of the parts of the Jacob story. In response to Blum and especially Van Seters, I have also argued against looking for meaning and setting in supposed historical situations before giving emphasis to literary function and context.

Thus, it is recognized that behind the present unity of the Jacob story there is evidence of earlier traditions and a growing together of material. In addition, other material has been supplemented to provide new perspectives. This includes chapter 31 and the way in which chapters 32 and 33 treat the theme of blessing; it also includes the texts identified as Priestly. We have also argued at several points in the thesis that some awareness of historical development has sharpened our awareness of theological complexity and literary ambiguity in the text, showing that a historical-critical appreciation and a close reading of the present text need not be seen as mutually exclusive tasks.

The Theme of the Presence and Absence of God

This work has attempted to demonstrate that the theme of the presence and absence of God offers a valuable way of reading the Jacob story. It may seem self-evident that this theme - and especially that of the contrast of the divine and human - should be so central to a part of Biblical narrative. However, in the Jacob story it takes on a particular complexity and intensity.

In particular, the idea of divine presence and absence cannot be reduced to one individual stratum in the text nor is it represented in any one uniform way. Instead the paradox is worked out in different episodes in different ways. Thus no claim can be made regarding authorship or the intention of any particular writer or redactor. Instead the complexity seems to be rooted in the very figure of Jacob himself and the events surrounding him. Images such as Jacob struggling - whether with Esau, Laban or some supernatural

---

4   de Pury, *Promesse Divine*.
5   Blum, *Komposition der Vätergeschichte*.
6   Van Seters, *Prologue to History*. Or later still: Davies, P. R., *In Search of 'Ancient Israel'*, Sheffield: JSOT Supp 148 1999.

being or God himself - lend themselves to this paradox, as does the cunning of Jacob, the reliance on his own methods and trickery. In addition, because of the close connection made between Jacob and Israel, the figure of Jacob lends itself to a reflection on the nature of faith for Israel and its own struggles and fortunes.

At this stage, a little more precision is needed in our use of the word 'theme'. In his work on the Pentateuch, Clines defines the theme of a narrative work in several ways: the conceptualization of plot, the dominating idea in a work, the rationale of its content, structure and development, or an orientation to approaching the work.[7] All of these definitions could apply to the way we have traced the idea of the presence and absence of God. For clearer definition we might argue that in the story of Jacob are found the opposing extremes of the presence of God and the absence of God, that the driving force behind the events concerning Jacob are at times depicted in terms of the divine (guidance and intervention) and at times in terms of the human (physical endeavour, resourcefulness, deception). Clines goes on that 'the best statement of the theme of a work is the statement that most adequately accounts for the content, structure and development of the work.'[8] So far, no claim has been made that the idea of divine presence and absence is the only theme of the Jacob story, and it would be rash to do so, especially as it may well depend upon a wider context, which as Clines points out, includes the Pentateuch as a whole. Nevertheless some brief comparison with other proposed themes may be of help.

To start with the work of Clines, his own proposal for the Pentateuch is as follows: 'The theme of the Pentateuch is the partial fulfilment - which implies also the partial non-fulfilment - of the promise to or blessing of the patriarchs.'[9] Despite the inclusion of the idea of blessing in this definition, it should be noted that to all intents and purposes, Clines concentrates on the idea of promise, especially in its three-fold elements of descendants, relationship and land. Regarding the Jacob story, in an extensive list of formulations he is able to point to 28:13ff and 35:11 for the promise of descendants, to 28:13.15 and 35:9ff for the promise of relationship (though he also adds the promise of 'being with' and guidance - 28:15, 31:3), and to 28:13.15 and 35:12 for the promise of land. In addition are allusions to the promise (28:3.13ff, 31:5, 31:42, 32:10.13, 35:3, 35:12). In the

---

7   Clines, D. J. A., *The Theme of the Pentateuch*, Sheffield: JSOT Supp 10, 1978, ch. 2.
8   Clines, *The Theme of the Pentateuch*, 21.
9   Clines, *The Theme of the Pentateuch*, 29.

patriarchal narratives he sees the main focus on the promise of descendants, which is also implied in the motifs of the barrenness of the matriarch (e.g. Rebekah and Rachel) and of endangerment to the life of the heir of promise through fraternal rivalry.[10] In addition we might add references to Jacob dwelling and moving about in the land.

In the Jacob story, the promise clearly is a motif, but it is noticeable that explicit references are limited to the Bethel episodes (ch. 28 and 35). Clines' list makes no mention even of Peniel or the opening scene, despite their importance in the plot. More importantly, Clines' articulation of the theme does not really do justice to the depiction of events in very human terms and to the seeming absence of God, except insofar as these bring into question the fulfilment of the promise and so create a tension. However, in our own reading, we found that this was not the ultimate question raised in the stories themselves. Promise is indeed a motif which helps us to see the Jacob story in the wider patriarchal and even Pentateuchal story, but it does not do justice by itself to the Jacob story in its own right.[11]

A similar but more frequently mentioned motif is that of blessing, and so, for instance, Gross sees Jacob as depicted as a man of blessing more than a man of promise.[12] It is certainly true that this theme is more central to the plot in the Jacob story in its own right, but again the particular twist to the plot is in how the blessing itself leads to conflict, and also how divine blessing is set alongside human machinations and effort (compare ch. 30 and 31): blessing is accompanied by struggle and division.

One further suggestion, made by Coats, is that the theme should be considered to be 'family strife without reconciliation'.[13] Noting that the promise tradition is a secondary element within the Jacob tradition, Coats sees the above mentioned theme as much more rooted in the plot, both in terms of Jacob-Laban and Jacob-Esau. Certainly, this definition takes account of the plot itself, and Coats' readings have already been noted, but

---

10   Clines, *The Theme of the Pentateuch*, 45.

11   Even in terms of the divine side of the Jacob story, account has also to be made of the idea of blessing (see below) and of vow-fulfilment (Richter, 'Das Gelübde als theologische Rahmung.').

12   Gross, 'Jakob, der Mann des Segens'. Gross' work is centred on the Priestly tradition of Jacob. He argues that even P, who generally emphasizes the covenant as the focus of the divine-human relation (Gen. 17, Ex. 6), places the accent on blessing in the case of Jacob. However, in doing this, P is simply reflecting an association already found in the Jacob tradition. Likewise, Westermann, C., *Die Verheißungen an die Väter: Studien zur Vätergeschichte*, FRLANT 116, Göttingen: Vandenhoeck & Ruprecht, 1976, 89.

13   See especially, Coats, 'Strife without reconciliation: a narrative theme in the Jacob traditions.'

it was also felt that the phrase 'without reconciliation' overstates the case.[14] More importantly, although Coats acknowledges the importance of the theme of blessing, it is left out of his definition of theme.[15] Similarly the incidents at Bethel and Peniel are not really drawn in, and Coats tends to negate the theme of the divine.[16] It would seem therefore that Coats' definition gives expression to a significant part of the human side of our story, but does not consider how this interacts with the divine.[17]

The Presence and Absence of God in the Jacob Narrative

Returning to the theme offered in this thesis, the reading has tried to do justice to the full scope of the material. In terms of the three episodes considered first, these clearly serve to throw a divine perspective over the whole Jacob story. However, we noted that they also involve the human side of the paradox: in the opening episode, this is expressed in the picture of Jacob grasping at his brother's heel, and in the juxtaposing of the oracle - itself giving rise to as many questions as answers to Rebekah's enquiry - with Jacob's attempt to wrest the birthright by deception. Bethel contains a clear, unambiguous divine revelation, but the incident sharpens in significance when seen in the context of Jacob's situation and of the expectations it raises for the next episode. Furthermore the vow made by Jacob in response arguably reveals his own bargaining nature. Peniel is full of ambiguity and makes the connection between human and divine in a very explicit way, offering a commentary on the wider story and making a link to Israel.

After this, a reading of the wider story has shown how these above incidents shed light on the other events but also how the story itself raises the issue of divine presence and absence. For instance, the whole drama of chapter 27 revolves around how Jacob is to know what he should do in the

---

14   See above, pp 180, 191.
15   See for instance his concluding remarks ('Strife without reconciliation', 106).
16   See above, pp 180.
17   A similar definition to that of Coats which takes account of the divine is that of Mann, T. W. ('"All the Families of the Earth" The Theological Unity of Genesis.' *Int* 45 (1991), 341): 'Genesis is a book about dysfunctional families and the way in which God seeks to use those families as agents of divine grace to "all the families of the earth".' My own definition is close to this, except that interest is in the person of Jacob as an individual as well as in his family relations. Furthermore, it is not so much the family as a whole which is used by God but an individual within it. Mann's reading seems to suggest that if the family members all got on together, then there would be no problem. It does not account for the tricky question of how much the divine vocation contributes to the problems of the family and the individual.

absence of any divine guidance and around the very human circumstances in which divine blessing is communicated. Whilst Jacob goes on to Laban, God seems to have remained at Bethel, and the two cunning protagonists are left to out-trick each other. When Jacob finds himself on the receiving end of a deception, we are also left to wonder what sort of law may be in operation. Moreover, it is now, in the bleakest of circumstances, that Israel's descendants are born, with God evoked by both mothers in very ambivalent terms. But then, out of the blue, God speaks, recalling Bethel, and effecting the turning point: events are brought to a swift conclusion and we are even forced to reassess the previous events in a very puzzling way. Jacob's return to his homeland and to his estranged brother is a masterpiece of tension but also of balance of the human and the divine, so that when Jacob sees Esau and is spared, he can indeed say that it is like seeing God face to face. The following episode in chapter 34 may sit a little uneasily in its context but we can see a questioning of appropriate behaviour in the light of the Torah and Israel's exclusive covenant. Again we see how divine guidance and the story of promise are worked out amidst human shortcomings and difficult choices. Finally, Jacob returns to Bethel, the place of divine promise and human vow. As in the previous chapter, we see how Jacob and his family are moving into the age of later Israel, and in the final verses (vv. 9-15) God's blessing and the giving of a new name are confirmed in an unambiguous light: to repeat the observation of von Rad, *Deus absconditus* is now *Deus revelatus*.[18]

Finally, this theme of divine presence and absence does justice to the context of the story of Jacob within the Pentateuch and as Israel's story. It enables us to read the text theologically without having to resort to appending theological conclusions or homiletic reflections to the more scholarly respectable task of historical or literary exegesis. The text itself has proved to be the result of a process of profound theological reflection, and so to evoke the terms 'canonical' or 'final form' is not to somehow impose a foreign concept onto this material. In particular, we have seen how we are encouraged to make connections with the life and faith of Israel. That this should be so, is evident since it is to Jacob that the name Israel is given, and it is in the very manner of the giving of the name that Israel can see its own struggles and questions, and its own experience of divine presence and absence. Thus, we have often noted how Jacob is both a figure of promise and a type for Israel. We have also noted that for all the recognition of a difference between the religious expression of the patriarch

---

18   von Rad, *Genesis*, 388.

and that of later Israel, it is indeed YHWH, the God of Israel, that Jacob has encountered.

To conclude: the Jacob story is the story of divine presence and absence, God's prompting and guidance working through, and sometimes counter to, human striving and effort. To read the story in this light does justice to the text in its historical depth, in its final form, and in its place in the canon of Christian and Jewish scriptures.

Bibliography

Ackerman, S., 'The Deception of Isaac, Jacob's Dream at Bethel, and Incubation on an Animal Skin.' In G. A. Anderson and S. M. Olyan eds, *Priesthood and Cult in Ancient Israel*, Sheffield: JSOT Supp 125, 1991, 92-120.

Allen, C. G., 'On Me Be the Curse, My Son!' In M. J. Buss ed., *Encounter with the Text*, Philadelphia: Fortress Press, 1979, 159-172.

Alt, A., 'The God of the Fathers.' In idem *Essays on Old Testament History and Religion*, Sheffield: JSOT Press, 1989 (ET of *Der Gott der Väter*, 1929), 3-77.

– 'Die Wallfahrt von Sichem nach Bethel.' In idem *Kleine Schriften I*, München: CH. Beck'sche Verlagsbuchhandlung, 1953 (orig. 1938), 79-88.

Alter, R., *The Art of Biblical Narrative*, New York: London: George Allen & Unwin, 1981.

– *The World of Biblical Literature*, London: SPCK, 1992.

– *Genesis: translation and commentary*, New York: W.W. Norton & Co, 1996.

Anbar, M., 'La "Reprise"', *VT* 38 (1988), 385-98.

Anderson, F. I., 'Note on Genesis 30:8.', *JBL* 88 (1969), 200.

Baker, D. W., 'Diversity and unity in the literary structure of Genesis.' In Millard, A. R. and Wiseman, D. J. eds, *Essays on the Patriarchal Narratives*, Leicester: IVP, 1980, 189-205.

Bar-Efrat, S., *Narrative Art in the Bible*, Sheffield: JSOT Supp 70, 1989.

Barth, H. and Steck, O. H., *Exegese des Alten Testaments: Leitfaden der Methodik*, 12th ed., Neukirchen-Vluyn: Neukirchener Verlag, 1989.

Barthes, R., 'La lutte avec l'ange: Analyse textuelle de Genèse 32:23-33.' In R. Barthes et al., *Analyse structurale et exegèse biblique*, Neuchâtel, 1971, 27-39.

Bechtel, L. M., 'What if Dinah is not raped? (Genesis 34)', *JSOT* 62 (1994), 19-36.

Blenkinsopp, J., 'The Structure of P.' *CBQ* 38 (1976), 277-92.

– *The Pentateuch: An Introduction to the First Five Books of the Bible*, London: SCM, 1992.

Blum, E., *Die Komposition der Vätergeschichte*, WMANT 57, Neukirchen-Vluyn: Neukirchener Verlag, 1984.

– *Studien zur Komposition des Pentateuch*, BZAW 189, Berlin: de Gruyter, 1990.

Brenner, A., ed., *A Feminist Companion to Genesis*, Sheffield: Sheffield Academic Press, 1993.

Briend, J., 'Genèse 31, 43-54: Traditions et rédaction.' in M. Carrez, J. Dorré and P. Grelot eds, *De la Tôrah au Messie*, Paris: Desclée, 1981, 107-12.

Brodie, L. T., 'Jacob's Travail (Jer 30:1-13) and Jacob's Struggle (Gen 32:22-32): A Test Case for Measuring the Influence of the Book of Jeremiah on the Present Text of Genesis.' *JSOT* 19 (1981), 31-60.

Brueggemann, W., 'Of the Same Flesh and Bone (Gn 2:23a).' *CBQ* 32 (1970), 532-42.

– *Genesis: a Bible Commentary for teaching and preaching*, Atlanta: John Knox, 1982.

Brown, F. et al., *The New Brown-Driver-Briggs-Gesenius Hebrew and English Lexicon with an Appendix Containing the Biblical Aramaic*, Peabody: Massachusetts: Hendrickson Publishers, 1979.

Calvin, J., *A Commentary on Genesis*, vol. 2, London: Banner of Truth Trust, (ET of Latin, 1554) 1965.

Carmichael, C. M., *Women, Law, and the Genesis Traditions*, Edinburgh: Edinburgh University Press, 1979.

Cartledge, T. W., *Vows in the Hebrew Bible and the Ancient Near East*, Sheffield: JSOT Supp 147, 1992.

Childs, B. S., *Introduction to the Old Testament as Scripture*, London: SCM, 1979.

Clines, D. J. A., *The Theme of the Pentateuch*, Sheffield: JSOT Supp 10, 1978.

Coats, G. W., *Genesis, with an Introduction to Narrative Literature*, Grand Rapids, Michigan: Eerdmans, 1983.

– 'Strife without reconciliation: a narrative theme in the Jacob traditions.' In R. Albertz et al., *Werden und Wirken des Alten Testament*, (Festschrift für Claus Westermann zum 70. Geburtstag), Göttingen, 1980, 82-106.

Cohn, R. L., 'Narrative Structure and Canonical Perspective in Genesis.' *JSOT* 25 (1983), 3-16.

Coote, R. 'The Meaning of the Name *Israel*.' *HTR* 65 (1972), 137-42.

Couffignal, R., 'Le songe de Jacob: Approches nouvelles de Genèse 28, 10-22', *Bib* 58 (1977), 342-60.

Cross, F. M., *Canaanite Myth and Hebrew Epic: Essays in the History of the Religion of Israel*, Cambridge, Massachusetts: Harvard University Press, 1973.

Davies, P. R., *In Search of 'Ancient Israel'*, Sheffield: JSOT Supp 148, 1992.

Davison, R., *Genesis 12-50*, Cambridge: Cambridge University Press, 1979.

Delitzsch, F., *A New Commentary on Genesis*, Edinburgh: T. & T. Clark, 1889 (ET).

Diamond, J. A., 'The Deception of Jacob: A New Perspective on an Ancient Solution to the Problem.' *VT* 34 (1984), 211-3.

Dicou, B., *Edom, Israel's Brother and Antagonist: The Role of Edom in Biblical Prophecy and Story*, Sheffield: JSOT Supp. 169, 1994.

Dillmann, A., *Die Genesis*, 3rd ed., Leipzig: S. Hirzel, 1892.

Donaldson, M. E., 'Kinship Theory in the Patriarchal Narratives: The Case of the Barren Wife.' *JAAR* 49 (1981), 77-87.

Driver, S. R., *The Book of Genesis*, 8th ed., London: Methuen, 1911.

Ehrlich, A. B., *Randglossen zur Hebräischen Bibel*, vol. 1, Hildesheim: Olms, 1968 (orig. 1908).

Elliger, K., 'Der Jakobskampf am Jabbok. Gen 32:23ff als hermeneutisches Problem.' *ZTK* 48 (1951), 1-31.

– 'Sinn und Ursprung der priesterlichen Geschichtserzählung.' *ZTK* 49 (1952), 121-43.

Emerton, J. A., 'The Priestly Writer in Genesis.' *JTS* 39 (1988), 381-400.

Eslinger, L. M., 'Hos 12:5a and Gen 32:29: A Study in Inner Biblical Exegesis.' *JSOT* 18 (1980), 91-99.

– 'The Case of an Immodest Lady Wrestler in Deut 25:11-12.' *VT* 31 (1981), 269-81.

Fewell, D. N. and Gunn, D. M., 'Tipping the Balance: Sternberg's Reader and the Rape of Dinah.' *JBL* 110 (1991), 193-211.

Fischer, G., *Jahwe unser Gott: Sprache, Aufbau und Erzähltechnik in der Berufung des Mose (Ex 3-4)*, Freiburg, Schweiz, Universitätsverlag/Göttingen:Vandenhoeck & Ruprecht, 1989.

Fishbane, M., *Text and Texture: Close Readings of Selected Biblical Texts*, New York: Schocken Books, 1979.

Fohrer, G., *Exegese des Alten Testaments*, 5th ed., Heidelberg.Wiesbaden: UTB Theologie, 1989.

Fokkelman, J.P., *Narrative Art in Genesis*, Assen: van Gorcum, 1975.

Freedman, D. N., 'Dinah and Shechem, Tamar and Amnon.' in J. R. Huddleston ed., *Divine Commitment and Human Obligation: Selected Writings of David Noel Freedman*, vol. 1, Grand Rapids Michigan/Canterbury UK: Eerdmans, 1997, 485-95.

Fretheim, T. E., 'The Jacob Traditions: Theology and Hermeneutic.' *Int* 26 (1972), 419-36.

Fuchs, E., '"For I have the Way of Women": Deception, Gender, and Ideology in Biblical Narrative.' *Semeia* 42 (1988), 68-83.

Gammie, J. G., 'Theological Interpretation By Way of Literary and Traditional Analysis: Genesis 25-36.' In M. J. Buss ed., *Encounter with the Text*, Philadelphia: Fortress Press, 1979, 117-34.

Garcia -Treto, F. O., 'Genesis 31:44 and "Gilead."' *ZAW* 79 (1967), 13-17.

Gervitz, S., 'Of Patriarchs and Puns: Joseph at the Fountain, Jacob at the Ford.' *HUCA* 46 (1975), 33-54.

Gnuse, R., 'Dreams in the night - scholarly mirage or theophanic formula?: The dream report as a motif of the so-called elohist tradition.' *BZ* 39 (1995), 28-53.

Goldingay, J., 'The Patriarchs in Scripture and History', in Millard, A. R. and Wiseman, D. J., eds, *Essays on the Patriarchal Narratives*, Leicester: IVP, 1980, 11-42.

Greenberg, M., 'Another Look at Rachel's Theft of the Teraphim.' *JBL* 81 (1962), 239-48.

Griffiths, J. G., 'The Celestial Ladder and the Gate of Heaven (Genesis xxviii 12 and 17).' *ExpTim* 76 (1964/5), 229-30.

Gross, W., 'Jakob, der Mann des Segens. Zu Traditionsgeschichte und Theologie der priesterlichen Jakobsüberlieferungen.' *Bib* 49 (1968), 321-44.

Gunkel, H., *Genesis,* Macon, Georgia: Mercer University Press, 1997 (ET of *Genesis*, 9th ed., 1977 -orig. 1910).

– *The Folktale in the OT*, Sheffield: Almond Press, 1987 (ET of *Das Märchen im Alten Testament*, 1917).

– 'Fundamental Problems of Hebrew Literary History.' in *idem What Remains of the Old Testament and Other Essays*, London: George Allen & Unwin Ltd, 1928 (ET of 'Die Grundprobleme der israelitischen Literaturgeschichte', 1906), 57-68.

– 'Jacob' in *What Remains of the Old Testament and Other Essays*, London: George Allen & Unwin Ltd, 1928 (ET of 'Jakob', 1919), 150-186.

Hamilton, V. P., *The Book of Genesis: Chapters 18-50*, Grand Rapids: Eerdmans, 1995.

Haran, L., 'Behind the scenes of history: determining the date of the priestly source.' *JBL* 100 (1981), 321-33.

Hauge, M. R., 'The Struggles of the Blessed in Estrangement.' *ST* 29 (1975), 1-30.

Hendel, R. S., *The Epic of the Patriarch: The Jacob Cycle and the Narrative Traditions of Canaan and Israel*, HSM 42, Atlanta: Scholars Press, 1987.

Herbert, A. S., *Genesis 12-50*, London: SCM, 1962.

Hermisson, H.-J., 'Jakobs Kampf am Jabbok (Gen 32:23-33).' *ZTK* 71 (1974), 239-61.

Hertz, J. H., *The Pentateuch and Haftorahs: Genesis*, London: Oxford University Press, 1929.

Hillers, D. R., 'PAHAD YISHAQ', *JBL* 91 (1972), 90-92.

Holgren, F. C., 'Holding Your Own against God. Gen 32:22-32 (In the Context of Gen 32-33).' *Int* 44 (1990), 5-17.

Horn Prouser, O., 'The truth about women and lying.' *JSOT* 61 (1994), 15-28.

Houtman, C., 'What Did Jacob See in His Dream at Bethel? Some Remarks on Genesis xxviii 10-22.' *VT* 27 (1977), 337-51.

'Jacob at Mahanaim. Some Remarks on Genesis xxxii 2-3.' *VT* 28 (1978), 37-44.

Husser, J.-M., 'Les métamorphoses d'un songe. Critique littéraire de Genèse 28, 10-22.' *RB* 98 (1991), 321-42.

Jacob, B. *Das erste Buch der Tora*, New York: Ktav Publishing House (orig. 1934).

Janowski, B., *Sühne als Heilsgeschehen: Studien zur Sühnetheologie der Priesterschrift und zur Wurzel KPR im Alten Orient und im Alten Testament*, WMANT 55 (1982), Neukirchen-Vluyn: Neukirchener Verlag.

Jay, N., 'Sacrifice, descent and the patriarchs', *VT* 38 (1988), 52-70.

Keel, O., 'Das Vergraben der 'fremden' Götter in Gen 35:4b', *VT* 23 (1973), 305-6.

Keil, C. F. and Delitzsch, F., *The Pentateuch: Volume 1*, (Biblical Commentary on the Old Testament), Edinburgh: T & T Clark, 1864 (ET).

Keller, C. A., 'Über einige alttestamentliche Heiligtumslegenden,' *ZAW* 67 (1955), 141-68; and *ZAW* 68 (1956), 85-97.

Kevers, P., 'Étude Littéraire de Genèse xxxiv', *RB* 87 (1980), 38-86.

Kidner, F. D., *Genesis*, London: Tyndale Press, 1967.

Kirkpatrick, P. G., *The Old Testament and Folklore Study* Sheffield: JSOT Supp 62, 1988.

Koch, K., 'Pahad jishaq -eine Gottesbezeichnung?' In Albertz, R. et al., *Werden und Wirken des Alten Testament*, (Festschrift für Claus Westermann zum 70. Geburtstag), Göttingen, 1980, 106-115.

– 'P -Kein Redaktor! Erinnerung an zwei Eckdaten der Quellenscheidung.' *VT* 37 (1987), 446-67.

– *Was ist Formgeschichte? Methoden der Bibelexegese*, 5th ed., Neukirchen: Neukirchener Verlag, 1989.

Köckert, M., *Vätergott und Väterverheißungen*, FRLANT 142, Göttingen:Vandenhoeck & Ruprecht, 1988.

Kunin, S. D., *The Logic of Incest: A Structuralist Analysis of Hebrew Mythology*, Sheffield: JSOT Supp 185, 1995.

Lehming, S., 'Zur Erzählung von der Geburt der Jakobsöhne.' *VT* 13 (1963), 74-81.

Leibowitz, N., *Studies in Bereshit (Genesis)*, 3rd ed., Jerusalem: World Zionist Organization, 1976.

Levenson, J. D., *The Death and Resurrection of the Beloved Son*, New Haven and London: Yale University Press, 1993.

Levin, C., *Der Jahwist*, FRLANT 157, Göttingen: Vandenhoeck & Ruprecht, 1993.

Long, B. O., 'The Effect of Divination upon Israelite Literature.' *JBL* 92 (1973), 489-97.

– 'Recent Field Studies in Oral Literature and the question of Sitz im Leben.' *Semeia 5: Oral Tradition and Old Testament Studies*, Missoula, Montana: Scholar's Press, 1976, 35-49.

Lord, A. B., *The Singer of Tales*, Cambridge, Massachusetts: Harvard University Press, 1960.

Maag, V., 'Jakob -Esau -Edom.' *TZ* 13 (1957), 418-29.

Maas, F., 'כפר to atone', in Jenni, E. and Westermann, C. eds, *Theological Lexicon of the Old Testament* vol. 2 , Peabody, Massachusetts: Hendrickson, 1977 (ET of *Theologisches Handwörterbuch des Alten Testaments*), 624-35.

Mabee, C., 'Jacob and Laban: The Structure of Judicial Proceedings (Genesis xxxi 25-42).' *VT* 30 (1980), 192-207.

Maher, M., 'The Transfer of a Birthright: Justifying the Ancestors.' *PIBA* 8 (1984), 1-24.

Malul, M., 'More on pahad yishaq (Genesis xxxi 42.53) and the Oath by the Thigh.' *VT* 35 (1985), 192-200.

Mann, T. W., *The Book of the Torah: The Narrative Integrity of the Pentateuch*, Atlanta: John Knox Press, 1988.

– '"All the Families of the Earth" The Theological Unity of Genesis.' *Int* 45 (1991), 341-53.

Martin-Achard, R., 'Un exégète devant Genèse 32:23-37.' In Barthes, R. et al. *Analyse structurale et exégèse biblique*, Neuchâtel, 1971, 27-39.

McAlpine, T. M., *Sleep, Divine and Human, in the Old Testament*, Sheffield: JSOT Supp 38, 1987.

McCarthy, D.J., 'Three Covenants in Genesis.' *CBQ* 26 (1964), 179-89.

McEvenue, S., 'A Return to Sources in Genesis 28:10-22?' *ZAW* 106 (1994), 375-89.

McKane, W., *Studies in the Patriarchal Narratives*, Edinburgh: Handsel Press, 1979.

McKay, H. A., 'Jacob Makes It across the Jabbok: An Attempt to Solve the Success/Failure Ambivalence in Israel's Self-Consciousness.' *JSOT* 38 (1987), 3-13.

McKenzie, J. L., 'Jacob at Peniel: Gen 34:24-32.' *CBQ* 25 (1963), 71-76.

Millard, A. R., 'The Celestial Ladder and the Gate of Heaven (Gen 28:12, 17).' *ExpTim* 78 (1966/67), 86-87.

Moberly, R.W.L., *Genesis 12-50*, Sheffield: JSOT Press, 1992.

– *The Old Testament of the Old Testament*, Philadelphia: Augsburg-Fortress, 1992.

Morrison, M. A., 'The Jacob and Laban Narrative in the Light of Near Eastern Sources.' *BA* 46 (1983), 155-64.

Nichol, G. G., 'Gen 29:32 and 35:22a: Reuben's Reversal.' *JTS* 31 (1980), 536-39.

Otto, E., 'Jakob in Bethel. Ein Beitrag zur Geschichte der Jakobsüberlieferung.' *ZAW* 88 (1976), 165-90.

Otto, R., *The Idea of the Holy: an Inquiry into the Non-Rational Factor in the Idea of the Divine and its Relation to the Rational*, London: Oxford University Press, 1924 (ET of *Das Heilige*, 9th ed.).

Ottoson, M., 'חלם'. In Botterweck, G. and Ringgren, H. eds, *Theological Dictionary of the Old Testament*, vol. 4, Grand Rapids: Eerdmans, 1977-1990 (ET of *Theologisches Wörterbuch zum Alten Testament*, Stuttgart, 1970ff.), 421-32.

Plaut, W. G. ed., *The Torah: A Modern Commentary*, New York: Union of American Hebrew Congregations, 1981.

Procksch, O., *Die Genesis*, 2/3rd ed., Leipzig: Deicherische Verlagsbuchhandlung, 1924.

Puech, E., 'La Crainte d'Isaac en Genèse xxxi 42.' *VT* 34 (1984), 356-61.

Pury, A. de, *Promesse Divine et Légende Cultuelle dans le Cycle de Jacob: Genèse 28 et les traditions patriarcales*, vols 1 and 2, Paris: J. Gabalda & Cie, 1975.

– 'Jakob am Jabbok, Gen 32:32-33, im Licht einer alt-irischen Erzählung.' *TZ* 35 (1979), 18-34.

– 'La Tradition Patriarchale en Genèse 12-35.' 259-270 of A. de Pury ed., *Le Pentateuque en Question: Les origines et la composition des cinq premiers livres de la Bible à la lumière des recherches récentes*, 2nd ed., Genève: Éditions Labor et Fides, 1989.

Rad, G. von, 'The Form-Critical Problem of the Hextateuch' in *The Problem of the Hextateuch and Other Essays*, London: SCM, 1984 (ET of 'Das Formgeschichtliche Problem des Hextateuch', 1938), 1-78.

– *Genesis*, London: SCM, 1972 (ET of *Das erste Buch Mose: Genesis*, 9th ed. 1972).

Rendsburg, G. A., 'Notes on Genesis xxxv.' *VT* 34 (1984), 361-6.

– *The Redaction of Genesis*, Indiana: Eisenbrauns, 1986.

Rendtorff, R., 'Yahwist as Theologian?', *JSOT* (1977), 2-10.

– *The Problem of the Process of Transmission in the Pentateuch*, Sheffield: JSOT Supp 89, 1990 (ET of *Das Überlieferungsgeschichtliche Problem des Pentateuch*, BZAW 147, Berlin: de Gruyter, 1977.

– 'Jakob in Bethel: Beobachtungen zum Aufbau und zur Quellenfrage in Gen 28:10-22.', *ZAW* 94 (1982), 511-23.

– *The Old Testament: an Introduction, London: SCM, 1985* (ET of *Das Alte Testament: Eine Einführung*, 1983).

– *Kanon und Theologie*, Neukirchen-Vluyn: Neukirchener Verlag, 1991.

Richter, H.-F., '"Auf den Knien eines andern gebären"? (Zur Deutung von Gen 30:3 und 50:23).' *ZAW* 91 (1979), 436-7.

Richter, W., 'Das Gelübde als theologische Rahmung der Jakobsüberlieferungen.' *BZ* 11 (1967), 21-52.

Rosenbaum, M. and Silbermann, A.M. eds, *Pentateuch with Targum Onkelos, Haphtorah and Rashi's Commentary*, New York: Hebrew Publishing Company.

Roth, W. M. W., 'The Text Is the Medium: An Interpretation of the Jacob Stories in Genesis.' In Buss, M. J. ed., *Encounter with the Text*, Philadelphia: Fortress Press, 1979, 103-115.

Ryle, H. E., *The Book of Genesis*, Cambridge: University Press, 1914.

Sanders, J. A., *Canon and Community: A Guide to Canonical Criticism*, Philadelphia: Fortress Press, 1984.

Sarna, N. M., *Bereishith/Genesis*, JPS Torah Commentary, Philadelphia: Jewish Publication Society, 1989.

Schenker, A., 'Koper et expiation', *Bib* 63 (1982), 32-46.

Scherman, N. and Zlotowitz, M., *Bereishis/Genesis: A New Translation with a Commentary anthologized from Talmudic, Midrashic and Rabbinic Sources*, Artscroll Tanach Series, vols 3 (2nd ed.) and 4, New York: Mesorah, 1980.

Schmid, H. H., *Der sogenannte Jahwist: Beobachtungen und Fragen zur Pentateuchforschung*, Zürich: Theologischer Verlag, 1976.

Schmidt, L, 'Jakob erschleicht sich den väterlichen Segen: Literaturkritik und Redaktion von Genesis 27, 1-45.' *ZAW* 100 (1988), 159-183.

Schmidt, W. H., *Introduction to the Old Testament*, London: SCM, 1984 (ET of *Einführung in das Alte Testament*, 2nd ed., 1982).

Schreiner, J., 'Das Gebet Jakobs (Gen 32, 10-14)', in Görg, M. ed., *Die Väter Israels: Beiträge zur Theologie der Patriarchenüberlieferungen im Alten Testament*, Stuttgart: Verlags Katholisches Bibelwerk, 1989, 287-303.

Schwartz, J., 'Jubilees, Bethel and the Temple of Jacob.' *HUCA* 56 (1985), 63-85.

Seebass, H., *Der Erzvater Israel und die Einführung der Jahweverehrung in Kanaan*, BZAW 98, Töpelmann: Berlin, 1966.

Segal, N., 'Review of *The Poetics of Biblical Narrative*, by M. Sternberg.' *VT* 38 (1988), 243-49.

Seitz, C. R., *Word Without End: The Old Testament as Abiding Theological Witness*, Grand Rapids, Michigan: William B. Eerdmans, 1998.

Seters, J. Van, 'The Problem of Childlessness in Near Eastern Law and the Patriarchs of Israel.' *JBL* 87 (1968), 401-8.

– 'Confessional Reformulation in the Exilic Period.' *VT* 22 (1972), 448-59.

– *Prologue to History: The Yahwist as Historian in Genesis*, Westminster, 1992.

Sherwood, S. K., *'Had God Not Been on My Side': An Examination of the Narrative Technique of the Story of Jacob and Laban, Genesis 29 29,1-32,2.*, Frankfurt: Lang, 1990.

Ska, J. L., 'Sommaires proleptiques en Gen 27 et dans l'histoire de Joseph.' *Bib* 73 (1992), 518-527.

Skinner, J., *A Critical and Exegetical Commentary on Genesis*, Edinburgh: T. & T. Clark, 1910.

Smith, S. H., '"Heel" and "Thigh": The Concept of Sexuality in the Jacob-Esau Narratives.' *VT* 40 (1990), 464-73.

Smitten, W. H. in der, 'Genesis 34 -Ausdruck der Volksmeinung?' *BO* 30 (1973), 7-9.

Soggin, J. A., 'Zwei umstrittene Stellen aus dem Überlieferungskreis um Shechem,' *ZAW* 73 (1961), 78-87.

Spanier, K., 'Rachel's Theft of the Teraphim: Her Struggle for Family Primacy.' *VT* 42 (1992), 404-12.

Speiser, E. A., 'I know not the day of my death.' *JBL* 74 (1955), 252-6.

– *Genesis*, Garden City, New York: Doubleday & Company, Inc., 1964.

Spurrell, G. J., *Notes on the Hebrew text of the Book of Genesis*, Oxford: Clarendon, 1887.

Sternberg, M., *The Poetics of Biblical Narrative: Ideological Literature and the Drama of Reading*, Bloomington: Indiana University Press, 1985.

– 'Biblical Poetics and Sexual Politics: From Reading to Counter-Reading.' *JBL* 111(1992), 463-88.

Sternberg, N., 'Alliance or Descent? The Function of Marriage in Genesis.' *JSOT* 51 (1991), 45-55.

Strickman, N. and Silver M. eds, *Ibn Ezra's Commentary on the Pentateuch: Genesis*, New York: Menorah Publishing Company, 1988.

Syrén, R., *The Forsaken First-Born: A Study of a Recurrent Motif in the Patriarchal Narratives*, Sheffield: JSOT Supp 133, 1993.

Terrien, S., *The Elusive Presence: Towards a New Biblical Theology*, San Francisco: Harper & Row, 1978.

Teugels, L., '"A Strong Woman, Who Can Find?" A Study of Characterization in Genesis 24, with some Perspectives on the General Presentation of Isaac and Rebekah in the Genesis Narratives.' *JSOT* 63 (1994), 89-104.

Thompson, T. L., 'Conflict themes in the Jacob Narrative.' *Semeia* 15 (1979), 5-23.

Toorn, K. van der, 'The Nature of the Biblical Teraphim in the Light of the Cuneiform Evidence.' *CBQ* 52 (1990), 203-33.

Tsevat, M., 'בכור'. In Botterweck, G. and Ringgren, H. eds, *Theological Dictionary of the Old Testament*, vol. 2, Grand Rapids: Eerdmans, 1977-1990 (ET of *Theologisches Wörterbuch zum Alten Testament*, Stuttgart, 1970ff.), 121-27.

Tugwell, OP, S., *Prayer: Living with God*, Dublin: Veritas Publications, 1975.

Turner, L. A., *Announcements of Plot in Genesis*, Sheffield: JSOT Supp 96, 1990.

Vawter, B., *On Genesis: A New Reading*, London: Geoffrey Chapman, 1977.

Wagner, S., 'דרש'. In Botterweck, G. and Ringgren, H. eds, *Theological Dictionary of the Old Testament*, vol. 3, Grand Rapids: Eerdmans, 1977-1990 (ET of *Theologisches Wörterbuch zum Alten Testament*, Stuttgart, 1970ff.), 293-307.

Wahl, H. M., *Die Jakobserzählungen: Studien zu iherer mündlichen Überlieferung, Verschriftung und Historizität*, BZAW 258, Berlin: de Gruyter, 1997.

Waltke, B. K. and O' Connor, M., *An Introduction to Biblical Hebrew Syntax*, Winona Lake, Indiana: Eisenbrauns, 1990.

Weimar, P., 'Aufbau und Struktur der priesterlichen Jakobsgeschichte,' *ZAW* 86 (1974), 174-203.

Weisman, Z., 'The Interrelationship between J and E in Jacob's Narrative.' *ZAW* 104 (1992), 177-97.

Wellhausen, J., *Prolegomena zur Geschichte Israels*, 6th ed., Berlin-Leipzig, 1927 (orig. 1878).

Wenham, G. J., 'The Religion of the Patriarchs.' In Millard, A. R., and Wiseman, D. J. eds, *Essays on the Patriarchal Narratives*, Leicester: IVP, 1980, 157-88.

– *Genesis 16-50*, Word Biblical Commentary, Dallas, Texas: Word Books, 1994.

Westermann, C., *Die Verheißungen an die Väter: Studien zur Vätergeschichte*, FRLANT 116, Göttingen: Vandenhoeck & Ruprecht, 1976.

– *Genesis 12-36*, London: SPCK, 1986 (ET of 1981).

– *Genesis 37-50*, London: SPCK, 1987 (ET of 1982).

White, H. C., 'French Structuralism and OT Narrative Analysis: Roland Barthes.' in
    Culley, R. C. ed., *Semeia 3: Classical Hebrew Narrative*, Missoula, Montana: Scholars'
    Press, 1975, 99-127.
Whybray, R. N., *The Making of the Pentateuch*, Sheffield: JSOT Supp 53, 1987.
Willi-Plein, I., 'Gen 27 als Rebekkageschichte: Zu einem historiographischen Kunstgriff
    der biblischen Vätergeschichten.' *TZ* 45 (1989), 315-34.
Wolff, H.W., 'The Elohistic Fragments in the Pentateuch', in Brueggemann, W. and
    Wolff, H. W., *Vitality of Old Testament Traditions*, John Knox Press, 1975, 41-66.
Würthwein, E., *Der Text des Alten Testaments*, 5th ed., Stuttgart: Deutsche
    Bibelgesellschaft, 5th ed., 1988.
Wyatt, N., 'Where did Jacob dream his dream?' *SJOT* 2 (1990), 44-57.
Wynn-Williams, D. J., *The State of the Pentateuch: a comparison of the approaches of M.
    Noth and E. Blum*; BZAW 249; Berlin: de Gruyter, 1997.
Zakovitch, Y., 'Through the Looking Glass: Reflections/Inversions of Genesis Stories in
    the Bible.' *BI* 1 (1993), 139-52.
Zobel, H.-J., 'יקוב/יעקב'. In Botterweck, G. and Ringgren, H. eds, *Theological Dictionary
    of the Old Testament*, vol. 6, Grand Rapids: Eerdmans, 1977-1990 (ET of *Theologisches
    Wörterbuch zum Alten Testament*, Stuttgart, 1970ff.), 185-208.
–   'ישראל'. In. Botterweck, G. and Ringgren, H. eds, *Theological Dictionary of the Old
    Testament*, vol. 6, Grand Rapids: Eerdmans, 1977-1990 (ET of *Theologisches
    Wörterbuch zum Alten Testament*, Stuttgart, 1970ff.), 397-420.

Author Index

Biblical Index

Paternoster Biblical and Theological Monographs

An established series of doctoral theses of high
academic standard
(All titles paperback, 229 x 152mm)

Joseph Abraham
Eve: Accused or Acquitted?
*A Reconsideration of Feminist Readings of the Creation Narrative Texts in
Genesis 1–3*

Two contrary views dominate contemporary feminist biblical scholarship. One finds in the Bible an unequivocal equality between the
sexes from the very creation of humanity, whilst the other sees the
biblical text as irredeemably patriarchal and androcentric. Dr. Abraham enters into dialogue with both camps as well as introducing his
own method of approach. An invaluable tool for any one who is
interested in this contemporary debate.

2003/ 0-85364-971-5 / xxiv + 272pp

Emil Bartos
Deification in Eastern Orthodox Theology
An Evaluation and Critique of the Theology of Dumitru Staniloae

Bartos studies a fundamental yet neglected aspect of Orthodox theology: deification. By examining the doctrines of anthropology, christology, soteriology and ecclesiology as they relate to deification, he
provides an important contribution to contemporary dialogue
between Eastern and Western theologians.

1999 / 0-85364-956-1 / xi + 370pp

Jonathan F. Bayes
The Weakness of the Law
God's Law and the Christian in New Testament Perspective

A study of the four New Testament books which refer to the law as
weak (Acts, Romans, Galatians, Hebrews) leads to a defence of the
third use in the Reformed debate about the law in the life of the
believer.

2000 / 0-85364-957-X / xi + 244pp

Mark Bonnington
The Antioch Episode of Galatians 2:11-14 in Historical and Cultural Context
The Galatians 2 'incident' in Antioch over table-fellowship suggests significant disagreement between the leading apostles. This book analyses the background to the disagreement by locating the incident within the dynamics of social interaction between Jews and Gentiles. It proposes a new way of understanding the relationship between the individuals and issues involved.
2004 / 1-84227-050-8 /

Mark Bredin
Jesus, Revolutionary of Peace
A Non-violent Christology in the Book of Revelation
This book aims to demonstrate that the figure of Jesus in the Book of Revelation can best be understood as an active non-violent revolutionary.
2003 / 1-84227-153-9 / xviii + 262pp

Colin J. Bulley
The Priesthood of Some Believers
Developments in the Christian Literature of the First Three Centuries
The first in-depth treatment of early Christian texts on the priesthood of all believers shows that the developing priesthood of the ordained related closely to the division between laity and clergy and had deleterious effects on the practice of the general priesthood.
2000 / 1-84227-034-6 / xii + 336pp

Daniel J-S Chae
Paul as Apostle to the Gentiles
His Apostolic Self-awareness and its Influence on the Soteriological Argument in Romans
Opposing 'the post-Holocaust interpretation of Romans', Daniel Chae competently demonstrates that Paul argues for the equality of Jew and Gentile in Romans. Chae's fresh exegetical interpretation is academically outstanding and spiritually encouraging.
1997 / 0-85364-829-8 / xiv + 378pp

Luke L. Cheung
The Genre, Composition and Hermeneutics of the Epistle of James

The present work examines the employment of the wisdom genre with a certain compositional structure and the interpretation of the law through the Jesus' tradition of the double love command by the author of the Epistle of James to serve his purpose in promoting perfection and warning against doubleness among the eschatologically renewed people of God in the Diaspora.

2003 / 1-84227-062-1 / xvi + 372pp

Andrew C. Clark
Parallel Lives
The Relation of Paul to the Apostles in the Lucan Perspective

This study of the Peter-Paul parallels in Acts argues that their purpose was to emphasize the themes of continuity in salvation history and the unity of the Jewish and Gentile missions. New light is shed on Luke's literary techniques, partly through a comparison with Plutarch.

2001 / 1-84227-035-4 / xviii + 384pp

Sylvia I Collinson
Making Disciples
The Significance of Jesus' Educational Strategy for Today's Church

This study examines the biblical practice of discipling, formulates a definition, and makes comparisons with modern models of education. A recommendation is made for greater attention to its practice today.

2004 / 1-84227-116-4 /

Stephen M. Dunning
The Crisis and the Quest
A Kierkegaardian Reading of Charles Williams

Employing Kierkegaardian categories and analysis, this study investigates both the central crisis in Charles Williams's authorship between hermetism and Christianity (Kierkegaard's Religions A and B), and the quest to resolve this crisis, a quest that ultimately presses the bounds of orthodoxy.

2000 / 0-85364-985-5 / xxiv + 254pp

Keith Ferdinando
The Triumph of Christ in African Perspective
A Study of Demonology and Redemption in the African Context
The book explores the implications of the gospel for traditional African fears of occult aggression. It analyses such traditional approaches to suffering and biblical responses to fears of demonic evil, concluding with an evaluation of African beliefs from the perspective of the gospel.

1999 / 0-85364-830-1 / xvii + 450pp

Andrew Goddard
Living the Word, Resisting the World
The Life and Thought of Jacques Ellul
This work offers a definitive study of both the life and thought of the French Reformed thinker Jacques Ellul (1912-1994). It will prove an indispensable resource for those interested in this influential theologian and sociologist and for Christian ethics and political thought generally.

2002 / 1-84227-053-2 / xxiv + 378pp

Scott J. Hafemann
Suffering and Ministry in the Spirit
Paul's Defence of His Ministry in 2 Corinthians 2:14–3:3
Shedding new light on the way Paul defended his apostleship, the author offers a careful, detailed study of 2 Corinthians 2:14–3:3 linked with other key passages throughout 1 and 2 Corinthians. Demonstrating the unity and coherence of Paul's argument in this passage, the author shows that Paul's suffering served as the vehicle for revealing God's power and glory through the Spirit.

2000 / 0-85364-967-7 / xiv + 262pp

John G. Kelly
One God, One People
The Differentiated Unity of the People of God in the Theology of Jürgen Moltmann
The author expounds and critiques Moltmann's doctrine of God and highlights the systematic connections between it and Moltmann's influential discussion of Israel. He then proposes a fresh approach to Jewish-Christian relations building on Moltmann's work using insights from Habermas and Rawls.

2004 / 0-85346-969-3 /

Mark Lovatt
Confronting the Will-to-Power
A Reconsideration of the Theology of Reinhold Neibuhr
Confronting the Will-to-Power is an analysis of the theology of Reinhold Niebuhr, arguing that his work is an attempt to identify, and provide a practical theological answer to, the existence and nature of human evil.

2001 / 1-84227-054-0 / xvii + 218pp

Neil B. MacDonald
Karl Barth and the Strange New World within the Bible
Barth, Wittgenstein, and the Metadilemmas of the Enlightenment
Barth's discovery of the strange new world within the Bible is examined in the context of Kant, Hume, Overbeck, and, most importantly, Wittgenstein. MacDonald covers some fundamental issues in theology today: epistemology, the final form of the text and biblical truth-claims.

2000 / 0-85364-970-7 / xxvi + 374pp

Gillian McCulloch
The Deconstruction of Dualism in Theology
With Reference to Eco-feminist Theology and New Age Spirituality
This book challenges eco-theological anti-dualism in Christian theology, arguing that dualism has a twofold function in Christian religious discourse. Firstly, it enables us to express the discontinuities and divisions that are part of the process of reality. Secondly, dualistic language allows us to express the mysteries of divine transcendence/immanence and the survival of the soul without collapsing into monism and materialism, both of which are problematic for Christian epistemology.

2002 / 1-84227-044-3 / xii + 282pp

Leslie McCurdy
Attributes and Atonement
The Holy Love of God in the Theology of P.T. Forsyth
Attributes and Atonement is an intriguing full-length study of P.T. Forsyth's doctrine of the cross as it relates particularly to God's holy love. It includes an unparalleled bibliography of both primary and secondary material relating to Forsyth.

1999 / 0-85364-833-6 / xii + 328pp

Nozomu Miyahira
Towards a Theology of the Concord of God
A Japanese Perspective on the Trinity
This book introduces a new Japanese theology and a unique Trinitarian formula based on the Japanese intellectual climate: three betweennesses and one concord. It also presents a new interpretation of the Trinity, a co-subordinationism, which is in line with orthodox Trinitarianism; each single person of the Trinity is eternally and equally subordinate (or serviceable) to the other persons, so that they retain the mutual dynamic equality.
2000 / 0-85364-863-8 / xiv + 256pp

Stephen Motyer
Your Father the Devil?
A New Approach to John and 'The Jews'
Who are 'the Jews' in John's Gospel? Defending John against the charge of antisemitism, Motyer argues that, far from demonising the Jews, the Gospel seeks to present Jesus as 'Good News for Jews' in a late first century setting.
1997 / 0-85364-832-8 / xiii + 260pp

Eddy José Muskus
The Origins and Early Development of Liberation Theology in Latin America
With Particular Reference to Gustavo Gutiérrez
This work challenges the fundamental premise of Liberation Theology, 'opting for the poor', and its claim that Christ is found in them. It also argues that Liberation Theology emerged as a direct result of the failure of the Roman Catholic Church in Latin America.
2002 / 0-85364-974-X / xiv + 296pp

Esther Ng
Reconstructing Christian Origins?
The Feminist Theology of Elizabeth Schüssler Fiorenza: An Evaluation
In a detailed evaluation, the author challenges Elizabeth Schüssler Fiorenza's reconstruction of early Christian origins and her underlying presuppositions. The author also presents her own views on women's roles both then and now.
2002 / 1-84227-055-9 / xxiv + 468pp

Ian Paul
Power to See the World Anew
The Value of Paul Ricoeur's Hermeneutic of Metaphor in Interpreting the Symbolism of Revelation 12 and 13

This book is a study of the hermeneutics of metaphor of Paul Ricoeur, one of the most important writers on hermeneutics and metaphor of the last century. It sets out the key points of his theory, important criticisms of his work, and how his approach, modified in the light of these criticisms, offers a methodological framework for reading apocalyptic texts.

2004 / 1-84227-056-7 /

David Powys
'Hell': A Hard Look at a Hard Question
The Fate of the Unrighteous in New Testament Thought

This comprehensive treatment seeks to unlock the original meaning of terms and phrases long thought to support the traditional doctrine of hell. It concludes that there is an alternative – one which is more biblical, and which can positively revive the rationale for Christian mission.

1999 / 0-85364-831-X / xxii + 478pp

Ed Rybarczyk
Beyond Salvation
Eastern Orthodoxy and Classical Pentecostalism on becoming like Christ

Despite their historical and cultural differences, Eastern Orthodox Christians and Classical Pentecostals share some surprising similarities. This study locates both Traditions within their cultural and philosophical meta-contexts and suggests avenues of mutual understanding.

2003 / 1-84227-144-X / xii + 426pp approx

Signe Sandsmark
Is World View Neutral Education Possible and Desirable?
A Christian Response to Liberal Arguments
(Published jointly with
The Stapleford Centre)

This thesis discusses reasons for belief in world view neutrality, and argues that 'neutral' education will have a hidden, but strong world view influence. It discusses the place for Christian education in the common school.

2000 / 0-85364-973-1 / xiv + 182pp

Andrew Sloane
On being a Christian in the Academy
Nicholas Wolterstorff and the Practice of Christian Scholarship
An exposition and critical appraisal of Nicholas Wolterstorff's epistemology in the light of the philosophy of science, and an application of his thought to the practice of Christian scholarship.
2003 / 1-84227-058-3 / xvi + 274pp

Daniel Strange
The Possibility of Salvation Among the Unevangelised
An Analysis of Inclusivism in Recent Evangelical Theology
For evangelical theologians the 'fate of the unevangelised' impinges upon fundamental tenets of evangelical identity. The position known as 'inclusivism', defined by the belief that the unevangelised can be ontologically saved by Christ whilst being epistemologically unaware of him, has been defended most vigorously by the Canadian evangelical Clark H. Pinnock. Through a detailed analysis and critique of Pinnock's work, this book examines a cluster of issues surrounding the unevangelised and its implication for christology, soteriology and the doctrine of revelation.
2002 / 1-84227-047-8 / xviii + 362pp

G.Michael Thomas
The Extent of the Atonement
A Dilemma for Reformed Theology from Calvin to the Consensus
A study of the way Reformed theology addressed the question, 'Did Christ die for all, or for the elect only?', commencing with John Calvin, and including debates with Lutheranism, the Synod of Dort and the teaching of Moïse Amyraut.
1997 / 0-85364-828-X / ix + 275pp

Mark Thompson
A Sure Ground on which to Stand
The Relation of Authority and Interpretative Method of Luther's Approach to Scripture
This study attempts a fresh examination of the most significant of Luther's comments on the nature and use of Scripture, locating each in its literary and historical context. It explores a series of connections in Luther's thought, analysing his scattered statements in terms of four categories reflected in his own terminology: inspiration, unity, clarity and sufficiency. In particular, it seeks to identify those elements which enable Luther to move with confidence between his statements about the authority of Scripture and his interpretative method.
2003 / 1-84227-145-8 / xvi + 322pp

Graham Tomlin
The Power of the Cross
Theology and the Death of Christ in Paul, Luther and Pascal
This book explores the theology of the cross in St Paul, Luther and Pascal. It offers new perspectives on the theology of each, and some implications for the nature of power, apologetics, theology and church life in a postmodern context.

1999 / 0-85364-984-7 / xiv + 344pp

Kevin Walton
Thou Traveller Unknown
The Presence and Absence of God in the Jacob Narrative
The author offers a fresh reading of the story of Jacob in the book of Genesis through the paradox of divine presence and absence. The work also seeks to make a contribution to Pentateuchal studies by bringing together a close reading of the final text with historical critical insights, doing justice to the text's historical depth, final form and canonical status.

2003 / 1-84227-059-1 / xvi + 238pp

Graham J. Watts
Revelation and the Spirit
A Comparative Study of the Relationship between the Doctrine of Revelation and Pneumatology in the Theology of Eberhard Jüngel and of Wolfhart Pannenberg
The relationship between Revelation and pneumatology is relatively unexplored. This approach offers a fresh angle on two important twentieth century theologians and raises pneumatological questions which are theologically crucial and relevant to mission in a post modern culture.

2003 / 1-84227-104-0 / xxii + 232pp

Alistair Wilson
When Will These Things Happen?
A Study of Jesus as Judge in Matthew 21–25
This study seeks to allow Matthew's carefully constructed presentation of Jesus to be given full weight in the modern evaluation of Jesus' eschatology. Careful analysis of the text of Matthew 21–25 reveals Jesus to be standing firmly in the Jewish prophetic and wisdom traditions as he proclaims and enacts imminent judgement on the Jewish authorities then boldly claims the central role in the final and universal judgement.

2004 / 1-84227-146-6 / approx xvi + 292pp

Nigel G. Wright
Disavowing Constantine
Mission, Church and the Social Order in the Theologies of John Howard Yoder and Jürgen Moltmann
This book is a timely restatement of a radical theology of church and state in the Anabaptist and Baptist tradition. Dr. Wright constructs his argument in dialogue and debate with Yoder and Moltmann, major contributors to a free church perspective.
2000 / 0-85364-978-2 / xv + 252pp

Stephen Wright
The Voice of Jesus
Studies in the Interpretation of Six Gospel Parables
This literary study considers how the 'voice' of Jesus has been heard in different periods of parable interpretation, and how the categories of figure and trope may help us towards a sensitive reading of the parables today.
2000 / 0-85364-975-8 / xiv + 280pp

PATERNOSTER PRESS

The Paternoster Press,
PO Box 300, Carlisle, Cumbria CA3 0QS, United Kingdom
Web: www.paternoster-publishing.com